EXPLORING COLOR

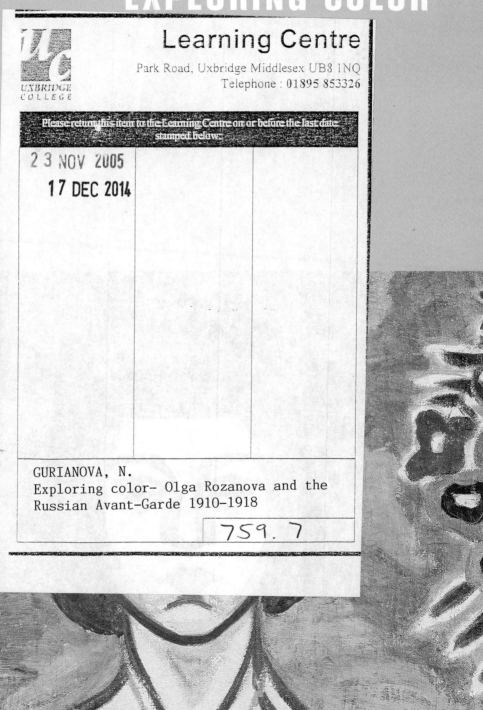

ITEM 019 372 041

D0304045

Learning Centre

UXBRIDGE
COLLEGE

Park Road, Uxbridge Middlesex UB8 1NQ
Telephone : 01895 853326

Please return this item to the Learning Centre on or before the last date
stamped below:

2 3 NOV 2005
17 DEC 2014

GURIANOVA, N.
Exploring color- Olga Rozanova and the
Russian Avant-Garde 1910-1918

759. 7

EXPLORING COLOR

OLGA ROZANOVA AND THE EARLY RUSSIAN AVANT-GARDE, 1910–1918

NINA GURIANOVA

TRANSLATED FROM RUSSIAN BY
CHARLES ROUGLE

G+B
ARTS
INTERNATIONAL

Australia · Canada · France · Germany · India · Japan · Luxembourg
Malaysia · The Netherlands · Russia · Singapore · Switzerland

Copyright © 2000 OPA
(Overseas Publishers Association) N.V.
Published by license under the G+B Arts International imprint,
part of The Gordon and Breach Publishing Group.

All rights reserved.

No part of this book may be reproduced or utilized in any form
or by any means, electronic or mechanical,
including photocopying and recording,
or by any information storage or retrieval system,
without permission in writing from the publisher.
Printed in Singapore.

Designed by POLLEN, NEW YORK

Amsteldijk 166
1st Floor
1079 LH Amsterdam
The Netherlands

British Library Cataloguing in Publication Data
Gurianova, Nina
Exploring color: Olga Rozanova and the early Russian avant-garde,
1910–1918
1. Rozanova, Olga 2. Women artists - Russia - Biography
3. Artists - Russia - Biography 4. Avant-Garde (Aesthetics) -
Russia
I. Title
709.2

ISBN 90-5701-202-2

contents

UXBRIDGE COLLEGE
LEARNING CENTRE

II

CHRONOLOGY OF THE LIFE AND WORK OF OLGA ROZANOVA

III

ARTICLES BY OLGA ROZANOVA

SELECT BIBLIOGRAPHY

INDEX

ABBREVIATIONS

acknowledgement

The life and works of the Russian avant-garde artist Olga Rozanova (1886–1918) have been for a long time yet another "blank spot" in the history of twentieth-century Russian art. Although Rozanova has thus far not attracted the sustained attention of art historians, she is usually devoted a page or two in practically all major studies on the history of the early avant-garde.

Most of the very few publications dealing directly with Rozanova are journal articles or newspaper reviews, published mostly in Russia. Particularly important among them are two essays on her posthumous exhibition in 1913–1919 written by her contemporaries: a review by constructivist Varvara Stepanova in the journal *Iskusstvo* (no. 4, 1919), and the introduction to her exhibition catalogue written by suprematist Ivan Kliun. These brief remarks directly reflect the reception of Rozanova's art by her fellow artists in the leftist artistic circle. Another critical work on Rozanova by Russian art historian Abram Efros was first published in the journal *Moskva* (no. 3, 1919) and later included in his collection *Profiles* (Moscow, 1930). His article remained the only scholarly work dedicated to Rozanova for more than forty years.

In the late 1970s the appearance of Rozanova's works at exhibitions of Russian avant-garde art in Europe and the United States was well received, inspiring essays on Rozanova by Hubertus Gassner and Wassili Rakitin published in the catalog *Russian Women-Artists of the Avant-Garde 1910–1930* (Cologne: Galerie Gmurzynka, 1979, in English and German). These articles, unfortunately not free from factual errors that were difficult to escape at a time when Russian archives were closed to researchers, provide a substantive general survey of her art. Several of Rozanova's articles were translated into English by John Bowlt at the same time. This new wave of scholarly interest revealed the importance and complexity of the role Rozanova played in the history of the Russian avant-garde in the 1910s.

However, this rise of interest in Rozanova's work was followed by another considerable hiatus lasting until 1989–1990 and the publication of several articles in the Russian press and a book by Miuda Yablonsky, *Women Artists of Russia's New Age*, 1900–1935 (London: Abrams, 1990), with a chapter on Rozanova. In 1991 a modest exhibition of Rozanova's works was opened in Moscow (the next year the show traveled to St. Petersburg and Helsinki): *Olga Rozanova 1886–1918*, ed. E. Chepik et al. (Helsinki, 1992).

Because the brief biographical entries on the artist in dictionaries and exhibition catalogs are still full of all sorts of factual errors, and because Rozanova's oeuvre has essentially not yet been studied in its entirety, some of the necessary tasks of the present book have been to reconstruct an accurate chronology of Rozanova's art and life, as well as to search out, systematize, and date painterly works by Rozanova (the artist herself almost never put a date on her paintings) scattered among private collections and provincial museums in Russia. No further research had been done until now, which presented a real problem: often the same work appeared in different publications, under different titles, and with different dates.

Many of the unpublished materials from archives constituting the necessary documentary context of the research make up a separate chronological section of this first monograph on the artist.

I would like to thank Ms. Evgeniia N. Petrova, Deputy Director of the Russian Museum, St. Petersburg as well as Ms. Elena Basner, Ms. Nataliia Kozyreva and Ms. Olga Schikhareva, curators at the same museum; Mr. Rodionov, director of the Tretiakov Gallery, Moscow, and Ms. Nataliia Avtonomova, curator at the same museum; Ms. Nataliia Volkova, director of the Russian State Archive of Literature and Art, and Ms. Elena Gasparova, curator of the same archive; Ms. Elena Pogorelskaia, curator of the State Mayakovsky Museum, Moscow; Mr. Geurt Imanse, Chief Curator for research and Documentation, the Stedelijk Museum, Amsterdam, and Mr. De Router, Director of the Foundation Cultural Centre Khardzhiev-Chaga, Amsterdam; the Thyssen-Bornemisza Collection, Madrid; Ms. K. Gmurzynska of Gallerie Gmurzynska, Cologne; Mr. Aleksandr Lavrentev, Moscow; Mr. Aleksandr Fedorovsky, Berlin; Mr. Alexsandr Parnis, Moscow; Ms. Irina N. Punina, St. Petersburg; Mr. Vladimir Goriainov of Galart Publishers, Moscow; Mr. Harvey Shipley Miller of the

Judith Rothschild Foundation, New York, and Ms. Magdalene Dabrowski of the Museum of Modern Art, New York, for their invaluable and gracious help in obtaining all these materials and providing me with the slides.

I am deeply grateful to Professor Dmitrii V. Sarabianov, whose advice and assistance made an enormous contribution to the dissertation defended in 1992, out of which the present book grew. To Professors Robert Belknap, John Bowlt, Charlotte Douglas, and Boris Gasparov, who took upon themselves the labor of reading the manuscript, I am indebted for many valuable comments. Fred van der Marck and Liza Rudneva, with great forbearance, have seen this book through the press. Charles Rougle made an excellent translation of this book, working in close collaboration with the author; and Brian Bendlin's editorial guidance decisively shaped the text. I am grateful to Skúta Helgason and Stewart Cauley of Pollen Design for their inventive, yet tactful design. My work would not have been possible without the friendly support and help of Ekaterina Bobrinskaia, Gerald Janacek, Henryk Baran, Karen Myers, the late Mr. Timushi-san, and of my mother, Alevtina Shekhter, to each of whom I would like to express my sincere gratitude.

—Nina Gurianova

foreword

This book is devoted to the life and work of Olga Rozanova, one of the most colorful figures in early-twentieth-century Russian visual art, who is finally winning the recognition she deserves. The painting of the Russian avant-garde has sometimes been presented as equivalent to the work of its "most important" representatives—Kazimir Malevich, Wassily Kandinsky, Vladimir Tatlin, Mikhail Larionov, Pavel Filonov, and March Chagall. These names alone attest to the amazing variety that is perhaps a unique feature of Russian avant-garde art, but this diversity is multiplied even more as soon as artists previously relegated to the status of "secondary" or the implementers of ideas discovered by the "leaders" are moved from the "second echelon" into the first. Nina Gurianova's book vividly illustrates that considerable progress has been made lately in this redistribution of "ranks."

The author beautifully integrates new material from archives, private collections, and early-twentieth-century periodicals into her subtle and penetrating analyses and intelligent discussion of Russian art as a whole during this period. This universalism I consider to be her principal merit. Using new archival materials, she not only presents Rozanova's complete biography and artistic legacy, but also sketches the human face of the artist in a way that allows us to sense the organic nature of her life and work. We think of Russian avant-garde art as the product of "Supermen" such as Malevidh or Filonov, who performed feats beyond the reach of others, spoke their own special language, and created incredible intellectual constructions. Rozanova, by contrast, lived an ordinary life, constantly working, experiencing the most common everyday difficulties, "ailing" from ordinary love, seeing dreams that to her appeared prophetic. Yet at the same time she created extraordinary works that penetrated a mysterious world and radically transformed reality. It is this combination of ordinary and extraordinary that makes her achievement particularly attractive.

The artist has served the scholar as a model. As she collects, describes, and revises Rozanova's artistic routine, Gurianova penetrates the very essence of the phenomenon of art with remarks that are keen yet unostentatious, and are presented as the result of a calm observation of a natural artistic process. An example of such an approach is what the author says about the romantic variant of avant-garde art. This notion can be developed and extrapolated onto the work of certain other masters, or it may even be seen to underlie more general observations on the Russian avant-garde.

Another example deserving particular attention is Gurianova's account of Rozanova's path to "nonobjectness." From Gurianova's analysis emerges an important conclusion: in her collages, Rozanova arrives on her own at forms of abstract art that may parallel Malevich's suprematism. Worth taking into account in this connection is the process by which different variants of abstract art were established in the work of Russian artists in this century's second decade. Kandinsky was followed by Larionov's rayism. The baton was then seized by Natalia Goncharova, who in works such as *Empty Space* (1913–1914) advanced her own special variety of abstract painting. The early death of Elena Guro—another of Gurianova's heroines—prevented her from doing the same. In 1914, Tatlin exhibited his counter-reliefs, which, although they cannot serve as examples of abstract painting, do introduce us to the abstract paradigm. Then came Malevich, and then together with him Rozanova. The question arises whether she was not followed by someone other than the familiar artists, such as Mikhail Matiushin.

The author, of course, has not neglected to touch upon the interrelationship of painting and poetry. She was encouraged to do so by various factors, including Rozanova's own poetic works, her long collaboration with Aleksei Kruchenykh, and her successes in the genre of the lithographed book. Although this theme has been fairly completely illuminated in the literature, Gurianova has discovered certain new and interesting aspects. Some of the most intriguing passages of the book are to be found in her interpretation of Rozanova's and Kruchenykh's album *War* and her analysis of *Game in Hell*.

There is no need to list all the merits of a book that is available to readers capable of discovering them for themselves. My task here has been to point out some of the qualities that make this first monograph on Olga Rozanova a valuable contribution to the study of the art of the Russian avant-garde.

—Dmitrii V. Sarabianov

translator's note

The transliteration of Russian names into English presents special difficulties, as several systems are currently in use. As this is a scholarly text, it follows the more accurate and formal Library of Congress system. Some Russians in the arts, on the other hand, are better known by the Westernized spellings, or certain self-chosen spellings, of their names. In these cases, the more popular spelling has been used; for example, Wassily Kandinsky, Aleksandr Scriabin, Leo Tolstoy.

A further difficulty has to do with the fact that a number of artists in Russia became known in the West under their original, non-Russian names. In these cases the non-Russian variant is used, with the Russian transliteration indicated parenthetically at first usage; for example, Pougny (Puni), Benois (Benua).

In some instances, a Russian term or title may be open to interpretability in its translation to English—that is, it may bear more than one possible translation. When this is the case, the original Russian will parenthetically follow the term, or title's English translation.

The Russian transition to the Gregorian calendar, which has been widely used in Europe since the 1500s, did not occur until after the Bolshevik Revolution in 1917. As such, there are a few places in this volume where dates are given according to the Julian calendar (and so noted), or according to both the Julian and the Gregorian calendars, with the latter date parenthetically following the former.

—Charles Rougle

PART I

QUEEN OF SPADES. FROM THE SERIES *PLAYING CARDS*, C. 1915.
OIL ON CANVAS. 77.5 x 61.5 CM. COURTESY OF MUSEUM OF FINE ARTS, SIMBIRSK.

CONTEXT
olga rozanova and the early russian avant-garde

Olga Rozanova belonged to that new race of twentieth-century artists who "came from afar, from the outside, when the rebellion was already under way; no one knew their faces or names, these junior officers and privates. But come they did, pure as a glacial lake and hard as the granite cliffs surrounding it, and threw the rebels into confusion. That is why Futurism found itself at an impasse and became overheated, as it were."[1] In the categorical statement of Kazimir Malevich, these artists came "to purge the personality of academic clutter, burn out the mold of the past in the brain and establish time, space, tempos and rhythm, movement—the foundations of the present day."[2]

 Rozanova's independent concept of art and her development as an artist were as intimately connected with her stimulating environment as they were shaped by her extraordinary personality and her exceptional talent as a painter. Links of friendship and collaboration bound her to Mikhail Matiushin and Elena Guro, Nikolai Kulbin and Aleksei Kruchenykh, Pavel Filonov and Velimir Khlebnikov, Kazimir Malevich,

1.
I. Zdanevich, *Okrest iskusstva* (1917). OR GRM, f. 177. 37.

2.
K. Malevich, "Nashi zadachi," *Izobrazitel'noe iskusstvo* 1 (1919), 28.

Ivan Pougny (Puni), and Aleksander Rodchenko. A continual search for a new expressiveness and consistent innovation were natural and regular processes in her art, and this may be why it immediately defies all attempts to enclose it within the bounds of any single tendency or group. Rozanova cannot be "assigned" only to the Union of Youth or, say, to Malevich's group, for her art is so whole and unique that it breaks all such boundaries. Her career reflects in miniature the fate of the early Russian avant-garde, which was driven by an inexorable and constant striving for renewal and a denial of previous achievements. She perceived the meaning of art in the necessity of this movement, remarking in one of her essays that "There is nothing more awful in the World than an artist's immutable Face . . . only those who have a presentiment of themselves as new can create."[3] Paraphrasing Nikolai Berdiaev's remark about Aleksander Scriabin one might say that her development as an artist was "an amazing manifestation of the creative evolution of an individual. This creative evolution sweeps aside art in the old sense of the word, which seemed eternal."[4]

As a kind of contrast with Rozanova's rich inner evolution and the striking intensity with which her talent developed (her entire mature artistic life spanned less than nine years, between 1910 and 1918), her biography seems ordinary and not very eventful. Only a page or two are devoted to her in the entry compiled for a never-published encyclopedia of the visual arts by her contemporary, the artist Varvara Stepanova:

Rozanova, Olga Vladimirovna.

Innovative painter, one of abstractionist members of the Union of Youth, Jack of Diamonds, Supremus, Left Federation of the Professional Union of Artist-Painters.

Received her training as an artist in private schools in St. Petersburg and Moscow.

All her life Rozanova championed radical new ideas in art, for which her works are especially valuable. Her highest achievements were in abstract painting (suprematism and *tsvetopis'* [literally, "color painting"; see chapter 4 of this volume—*N. G.*]), which afforded her an ample scope to ambitious use of color. Color was enormously important in her art and constitutes the foundation of her painting. Besides painting, Rozanova wrote essays on art for the journals *Supremus* and *The Union of Youth* and the newspaper *Anarchy* and composed futurist and abstract poetry. She collaborated with the poet Kruchenykh on a number of interesting books to which she contributed drawings; some of these books were printed by hand and had wood and linoleum engravings. She worked a great deal in decorative art, in which area she also demonstrated considerable accomplishment.

3.
O. Rozanova, "The Bases of the New Creation and the Reasons Why It Is Misunderstood," in this volume, 193.

4.
N. Berdiaev, *Krizis iskusstva* (Moscow, 1990; reprint of 1918 edition), 6.

At the height of her creative powers, Rozanova died in 1918 from diphtheria following a cold she had contracted while working at an airport on preparations for the first anniversary of the October Revolution.[5]

The sudden death of the thirty-two-year-old artist came as a shock to her fellow leftist artists, underlining even more forcibly the uniqueness, authenticity, and value of everything she created. Her few extant letters convey the sincerity, charm, and gentle irony of her person—the same features that account for the immediate fascination with her work.

A daring and brilliant artist, Olga Rozanova was incredibly helpless in practical, everyday matters, and she was constantly forced to steal time from her painting to do boring office work to support herself. "I have a job," she bitterly mocked herself, "which to me amounts to firewood and a bowl of porridge." There were times when she literally did not have money for paint and canvas, when "all my doubts grow into a tangle of immense proportions. . . ."[6] But all this in some sense belonged to another life that she refused to take seriously ("Don't complain of anything; complaining is a return to the past, while the future is bright," as the self-named "futurians" believed).[7] In the "furious struggle" of theories and tendencies, amid everyday cares and all those things usually referred to as "the tribulations of war and the first years of the Revolution," she managed to preserve her inner freedom and a romantic outlook on life that was alien to sentimental rapture or obtuse bitterness. For her, truth and reality consisted of everything she understood by the notion of art, by which she meant the source of joy and the will to live: "The world is a piece of raw material—for the unreceptive soul it is the back of a mirror, but for reflective souls it is a mirror of images appearing continually."[8] This is also evidenced in her correspondence: "I would like to paint big pictures, but I am waiting to get the time, for there is no point in painting in fits and starts. I only like doing things if I enjoy them! And unexpected, accidental interruptions in my work torment me and disrupt the integrity of my ideas. Speaking generally, I want to be an artist first and only then all the rest . . . I want as soon as possible to paint pictures and write articles, and I am absolutely convinced that this is what I must do!"[9]

Because her personal archive is scattered and very little of it has survived, there are almost no factual records of Rozanova's early "apprenticeship" period as an artist. For this reason, newly discovered family documents and visual materials from her brother's collection (now in the private collection of Aleksander Fedorovsky, Berlin) are

5.
V. Stepanova, "Biograficheskaia zametka o Rozanovoi" (1919). A. Rodchenko and V. Stepanova archive, Moscow.

6.
Letter of O. Rozanova to A. Kruchenykh (1913). RGALI, f. 134. 1. 190.

7.
A. Kruchenykh, V. Khlebnikov, E. Guro, *Troe* (St. Petersburg, 1913), 40.

8.
Rozanova, "Bases," in this volume, 187.

9.
Letter of O. Rozanova to A. Shemshurin, July 1917. OR GBL, f. 339. 5. 14. II. 34, 37.

especially valuable. Of particular note are her early sketch pads of drawings in pencil and ink from her Vladimir period and her time at Anatolii Bolshakov's school and with Konstantin Iuon in Moscow (1906–1907). There are also albums with pencil and watercolor drafts done in 1913 and watercolor Suprematist sketches for the *Verbovka* exhibition of decorative art in 1916 and 1917.[10] In 1904, at the age of eighteen, she graduated from school in Vladimir, where she had grown up, and went to Moscow to study painting. She began in Bolshakov's art school, where she worked under Nikolai Ulianov and the sculptor Andrei Matveev, and in the private studio of then popular landscape artist Iuon, who worked in an impressionist mode. The nude studies and landscape sketches in her early notebooks date from that period. It is only her unusual approach to the model that distinguishes her pencil drawings of nudes from many such works by other students. In contrast to the usual distance between artist and model, which causes the human body to be treated as a thing or artistic object, she injects into each drawing an individual, personal element of portraiture and indicates on every page not only the exact date, but also the name of the model, often in a friendly, diminutive nickname such as "Shura," "Sania," and so on (figure 1). Bolshakov's and Iuon's studios, where the atmosphere was fairly democratic and free from ossified dogmas, became the first serious school for many young artists who had come from the provinces to take the entrance examinations for the art colleges. As Iuon recalled later of his classes, "What did I mainly teach? I believed least of all in study that amounted to a review of current work and instructions to the students as to what should be added and deleted, precisely what had to be changed, made redder, more yellow, and so on. I always thought that above all students needed to be taught the ability to see and study the laws of the visual world."[11]

By 1907–10 the group studying drawing and painting included Rozanova's future comrades in the Supremus group, Liubov Popova, Nadezhda Udaltsova, Aleksei Kruchenykh and Serge Charchoune, and between 1911 and 1915, Varvara Stepanova. Rozanova also audited classes at the Imperial Stroganov Institute, but this was merely a brief episode in her artistic biography.

The years 1907 to 1910 may be viewed as a distinct "first Moscow" period in Rozanova's career; they were significant years in the formation of her individuality as an artist and in the laying of the foundations of her future concepts of art. It was then that she developed an

10.
Besides two notebooks with sketches of models (1906-1907) and early drawings of flowers collected in a separate album (1904–1906), Fedorovsky's collection includes two early albums with views of Melenki (pencil, ink) in the neoprimitivist style, and two notebooks with sketches done in 1913 and 1917. The main part of these consists of colored suprematist sketches in gouache and watercolors for the Verbovka exhibition of embroideries and appliqué. The collection also contains scattered sheets with suprematist sketches (1916–1917), early journal graphics in pencil and ink (circa 1907–1909), and also several futurist compositions dated 1913 to 1914. Of special note in the later sheets is a sketch of a self-portrait in red chalk (1917), evidently a preparatory composition for a self-portrait (private archive, Moscow, [figure 39]).

11.
K. F. Iuon, *Ob iskusstve*, vol. 2 (Moscow, 1959), 211–12.

1. STUDIES OF A NUDE AND A WOMAN IN A RUSSIAN FOLK DRESS, 1906.
   PENCIL. 14.3 x 20.5 CM. INSCRIBED IN PENCIL: *ZINA/7 JANUARY*.
   VERSO: NUDE WITH A VIOLIN.
   COURTESY OF ALEKSANDR FEDOROVSKY, BERLIN.

affinity for genres such as the urban landscape, the portrait, and the still life. All of these genres are dominated by a vivid still life vision, a heightened sense of the object close to the "orthodox" style of the Jack of Diamonds (who as a group held their first exhibition in Moscow in late 1910). The first profound influence on Rozanova was the Moscow school of painting, in which an emphasis on color and a tendency toward decorativeness were transformed in accordance with the national reception of impressionism and the work of Paul Cézanne.[12] Her connection to the Moscow school marks some of her 1906 to 1909 studies, mostly nudes and landscapes now in the Tretyakov Gallery in Moscow and the Russian Museum in St. Petersburg. Evidently the earliest of these is the sketch *A Nun* (c. 1907. Oil on canvas, 75.5 x 53 cm), now in the Tretyakov Gallery. The motif has no analogues in Rozanova's mature work. The fashionable turn-of-the-century theme of old Russia is treated descriptively, even naively: a girl dressed in a Russian *sarafan* sitting on a trunk holding a candle. Her forehead is nearly covered by her black shawl so that her facial features are barely visible. The entire effect lies in the reflection of the orange flame of the candle on the white sleeves of her dress. The technique is sparse and timid, and the entire composition is within the tradition of Viktor Vasnetsov, or Mikhail Nesterov, an artist working in the art

12.
Gleb Pospelov has the following interesting and detailed remark on the difference between the Moscow and St. Petersburg schools and the dominant role of Moscow in the artistic life of this period:
In the early twentieth century Moscow was already very clearly distinguished from St. Petersburg by its vigorous tradition in painting. It was there that the most important artists—Surikov and Serov, Korovin and Vrubel—were working at the turn of the century. Also connected with Moscow was the work of Borisov-Musatov, which in the first decade became a banner of the young artists.... To the "graphicness" of the "World of Art" group and later even to the "incorporeal spirituality" of Matiushin and Filonov, the Moscow masters contrasted their energetic, straightforward tsvetopis' and their gravitation toward painterly freedom. In this first decade, as well, Moscow boasted an elevated, more "sensitive" picturesqueness, a dedication to the body of things and color. [G. G. Pospelov, *Bubnovyi valet* [Moscow, 1990], 4–5.

2. GRAPHIC DESIGN FOR A MAGAZINE, C. 1907–1908.
BLACK INK, PENCIL, BRONZE PAINT. 21.3 × 13.5 CM.
COURTESY OF ALEKSANDR FEDOROVSKY. BERLIN.

nouveau style who had a very successful exhibition in Moscow in 1907. In her studies of nudes there is a certain stiffness and lack of academic precision. Some of the sketches in the Fedorovsky collection (Berlin) also fall into this category. The soft chiaroscuro modeling serves less to convey volume than to create a decorative painterly surface. The wash of lilac pink, lemon, and light blue hues creates the impression of a smooth, light-bearing texture. In the early study *House Corner and Bullfinches in Tree. Winter* (c. 1906–1908. Oil on cardboard, 63 × 50 cm, Tretyakov Gallery) the impasto is denser, and one senses Iuon's characteristic postimpressionist treatment of light and space, particularly his favorite "effect" of snow in colored reflections of sunlight. Here, with the possible exception of the color scale based on a dominance of bright and warm tones, are none of the qualities of the later Rozanova. In another early landscape study in the Fedorovsky collection, pure saturated light acquires a certain significance together with bright, contrasting shades subordinated to an alternation of colors.

All of Rozanova's early works show a sensitive reverence for, and active interest in nature. Common to all of her still lifes is the painterly theme, which consists in an attempt to reflect the typical and inherently valuable, inimitable quality of each object, and to designate each thing by combining its physical nature and its overall inner essence. Objects in these still lifes crowd out space, and impasto imparts to them an almost physical tangibility, earthliness, and body. The poetics of her early works bears comparison with the "organic" works of Guro and Matiushin, especially the latter's ideas about organic art.

Rozanova's early impressionist period determined a great deal in the evolution of her painting. As recent discoveries demonstrate, however, symbolism and art nouveau were equally important sources of her early poetics. Yet numerous unpublished sketches in pen, pencil, and watercolor from her 1906 and 1907 notebooks provide evidence of her interest in asymmetrical decorative motifs and a tendency toward stylization in her drawings, particularly in her early ink sketches to be used as journal graphics (figure 2). In the Fedorovsky collection are some 1907 to 1909 single-page studies of head-pieces and tail-pieces with figurative motifs inscribed in an oval or circle, ornamental motifs almost copied from the works of Aubrey Beardsley. They are certainly in the art nouveau style and follow the practice of book design as established by the World of Art group, Konstantin Somov, Mstislav Dobuzhinskii, and others. Stylistically related to these sketches is another group of ink drawings of flowers and leaves (Rozanova attended the so called flower class at the Bolshakov school), each drawing executed in an almost continuous line, producing a maximally stylized image transformed into an ornament.

In other albums with watercolors of flowers probably done earlier, in 1906, there is a different quality. Here we find the veneration of nature that characterizes all of Rozanova's early works, and constitutes the mechanism by which she perceived the visual world. Based on a rejection of abstract analytical cognition, this perception focuses instead on contemplative intuition and emotion: "The fascination of the visible, the charm of the spectacle, arrests the eye, and the artist's primary aspiration to create arises from this confrontation with nature. The desire to penetrate the World and, in reflecting it, to reflect oneself is an intuitive impulse that selects the Subject—this word being understood in its purely painterly meaning."[13] Even in her final, "abstract" period, Rozanova remained loyal to the momentary visual impression, that "charm of the visible" that provided the necessary impulse in the development of her extraordinary lyrical gift. At the same time, together with the suprematists she also painted what she called "real" pictures from life.

13.
Rozanova, "Bases,"
in this volume, 188.

The foundations of Rozanova's concept of art, the logical conclusion of which was her discovery of *tsvetopis'*, were undoubtedly laid in her earliest period. Already then she was capable of firmly renouncing her own achievements (that is, "old ground" that risked becoming "devices" or clichés) in favor of the novel and experimental. She immediately reacted to all the latest accomplishments and new ideas, but never lapsed into sterile borrowing and imitation. On the contrary, it was her assimilation of the experience of others that provided the impulse for the development of her own individual and characteristic approach. Mikhail Larionov's and Natalia Goncharova's Russian neoprimitivism, the French fauvism of (especially) Henri Matisse, and the Italian futurism of Umberto Boccioni, Gino Severini, and Giacomo Balla were all seminal influences that coincided with her own artistic aspirations.

This "everythingness" (*'vsechestvo'*) was in essence nothing other than a free choice of traditions: "We acknowledge all styles as suitable for the expression of our art, styles existing both yesterday and today."[14] The concept of everythingness, that is, the notion of feeling and encompassing everything, was introduced by Ilya Zdanevich, the theoretician of Larionov's group. Acknowledged by the neoprimitivists, it was typical of the new Russian art as a whole. The creative reception and often unexpected interpretation of foreign influences is among the distinguishing national features of Russian art, but it has rarely spilled over into direct stylization or the external imitation of form. As the neoprimitivist artist Aleksandr Grishchenko put it, "when the Russians took Western forms they introduced into them their own distinctive national spirit."[15]

The end of this century's first decade in Moscow witnessed the formation of numerous currents and groupings in the new art. It is difficult to overestimate the role played by the exhibitions of the time in converting many young artists to the new artistic faith. The Moscow Association of Artists began showing the work of Larionov, Goncharova, Malevich and Wassily Kandinsky. At the beginning of 1907, the *Blue Rose* exhibition was held in Moscow, and in December of that same year came *Stephanos-Wreath*, which included Larianov, David and Nikolai Burliuks, Aristarch Lentulov, and others. In April, 1908, the first *Golden Fleece Salon* opened with a French section exhibiting works by Matisse, Georges Braque, Paul Gauguin, Jean Metzinger, and Georges Rouault. Finally, Sergei Shchukin organized a unique collection of Western painting on which the young

14.
From the manifesto "Rayonists and Futurists," signed by Larionov, Goncharova, and other members of this group. [*Russian Art of the Avant Garde Theory and Critcism*, revised and enlarged edition, ed. and trans. by John E. Bowlt (New York, 1988) 90. Cf. the collection *Oslinyi khvost i mishen'* (Moscow, 1913), 12.

15.
A. Grishchenko, *O sviazakh russkoi zhivopisi s Vizantiei i Zapadom XIII–XX vekov* (Moscow, 1913), 12.

3. *MELENKI, HOUSE AND TWO PIGS*, C. 1904—1905.
   PENCIL, 13 x 25.6 CM.
   COURTESY OF ALEKSANDR FEDOROVSKY, BERLIN.

artists were "raised." The journal *The Golden Fleece* (no. 6, 1909) pub-lished Matisse's manifesto "Notes of a Painter" (1908), in which he set forth the position of the innovative artist: "It is not possible for me to copy nature in a servile way. I am forced to interpret and submit it to the spirit of the picture. . . . My choice of colors does not rest on any scientific theory, it is based on observation, on feeling, on the expe-rience of my sensibility."[16] Many tenets of this essay clearly exerted an influence on the Russian avant-garde and specifically on Rozanova, who may in certain respects have been objecting to, and polemicizing with, them in her 1913 manifesto for the Union of Youth.

The years 1911 to 1914 (from the time she joined the Union until it broke up) were perhaps the four most intense and fruitful years in Rozanova's life. This new, mature period of her work earned her a place in the history of Russian cubo-futurism, the style of the genera-tion born in the late 1870s and 1880s that burst into art on the crest of the new century. The ambition and romanticism of its representatives and their confidence in their foreordained destiny can easily be read between the lines of Aleksei Kruchenykh's reminiscence, *Our Arrival*:

> We can often easily observe resemblances in the lives of the members of
> such groups, even among persons who grew up far away from one another,
> knew nothing of their future friends, and were not even aware that they
> were the founders of a particular movement.
>
> When the evolution of one cycle of art concludes, the time comes for
> another to emerge. It is as if a drum is beating. . . . Gauguins seem to wake

16.
Matisse on art, ed. and trans.
Jack Flam (Berkeley, 1995),
40—41.

4. DRAWING BASED ON PLAYING-CARD MOTIFS AND STUDY OF A CRIMEAN LANDSCAPE.
1913. (A SHEET FROM THE ALBUM ORIGINALLY BELONGING TO LEVKII ZHEV-
ERZHEEV.) BLACK INK, PENCIL, WATERCOLOR. 23 x 31 CM.
COURTESY OF THE OSTROVSKY MUSEUM OF THEATER AND MUSIC, ST. PETERSBURG.

up, abandon their philistine office desks, forget their families, and set off
for Tahiti. New forms appear, there is the sound of laughter and jeering
from the old believers, and so on and so forth. The path of the innovator
is well known. Details vary in each case, but it is basically the same for all.
No matter that Gauguin didn't cut off his ear like van Gogh, or that
Cézanne didn't go to Tahiti, but lived instead as a bourgeois in Arles; their
biographies nevertheless sharply diverged from the stereotypical. . . . I
think that my own angularities are in keeping with the peculiarities of my
comrades, but all of us have mightily reinforced the positions of futurism.
. . . when the philistines bait and taunt us they do not understand that the
futurist cannot avoid doing things that upset them. The futurist is struggling to generate new forms. . . .

Much later, when I became acquainted with the biographies of my
futurist comrades, the "consonance" of our pasts stood out quite clearly.
All of us had the same recklessness, similar interests, an affinity for the
vivid and colorful. . . .

I by no means wish to say that there would have been no futurism without that group of "savages." It would have emerged, of course, whether we
existed or not. People would have turned up. But, probably, the lives they
lived would also have been appropriate for the destroyers of the old official
academic art . . .[17]

17.
*Iz literaturnogo naslediia
Kruchenykh: Pamiat' teper'
Mnogoe razvorachivaet,*
ed. N. Gurianova (Berkeley, 1999),
31, 35, 39.

The first generation of the Russian avant-garde was distinguished by more elements than similar personal histories. It also possessed a shared inborn sense of indestructible inner freedom, a receptivity toward renewal, and a peculiar cultural "asceticism." Theirs was a consciousness of young "nomads" whose lives and works continually violated the confining limitations of life in both its everyday and its spiritual dimensions.

Futurism took root in Russia and acquired its inimitable uniqueness as a polyglot mixture of ideas streaming into this "New Babylon" from every corner of the globe: "Moscow-Peking: here is the triumph of the continent, the spirit of the Middle Kingdom; here the heavy tracks of railway lines have been spliced into a tight knot; here the Eurasian continent celebrates its eternal name day."[18]

In the history of Russian cubo-futurism, which included both poetry and painting, we can retrospectively distinguish two dates: 1910 and 1913. The first is generally considered the movement's date of birth, while the second marks its maturity. The year 1910 may in fact be regarded as having two parts. In April of that year the first collection of the new poetry, *A Trap for Judges*, was published in St. Petersburg, joining together for the first time the future Hylaeans Guro, Khlebnikov, the Burliuks, and Wassily Kamenskii. Even earlier, on February 16, was the official registration of the Union of Youth, which became one of the main innovative groups of the artistic avant-garde.

At the source of this fundamentally new association of artists intimately connected with Rozanova's career were Elena Guro and Mikhail Matiushin. Their ideas in certain respects preceded those of Nikolai Kulbin, the organizer of the St. Petersburg exhibitions *Contemporary Currents in Art* (1908) and *The Impressionists* (1909). Although these exhibitions included the works of young artists, they can hardly be called avant-garde, as they merely foreshadowed the future flowering of the new art. Kulbin was a typical "character" of the period, as Matiushin writes, he was "above all a decadent of the nineties, later a dilettante impressionist, and that was as far as he and his group went. But he undoubtedly deserves the honor of arranging the first appearance in St. Petersburg of young artists, for whom he paved the way. Kulbin was very responsive and fought for innovation as best he could. In his attempt to define the role of various tendencies he tirelessly lectured and showed the increasingly significant accomplishments of art in the West and in Russia."[19] His paintings were of rather less significance

18.
O. Mandelstam, "Literary Moscow," in *The Collected Critical Prose and Letters*, ed. Jane Gary Harris, trans. Jane Gary Harris and Constance Link (London, 1991), 145.

19.
M. Matiushin, "Russkie kubo-futuristy," in N. Khardzhiev, K. Malevich, and M. Matiushin, *K istorii russkogo avangarda* (Stockholm, 1976), 140.

than his theoretical and critical works. Naïveté and dilettantism—he did not even attempt to appear "professional"—were in fact perhaps the most appealing qualities of his work, but he knew how to create a special atmosphere in the cultural environment that generated ideas. His organizational activity and his articles on free art and the new cycle of the word played a significant role in the evolution of avant-garde theory. In 1910, after the *Impressionists* exhibition, Kulbin edited a collection entitled *Studiia impressionistov. Kniga I-aia* (St. Petersburg: [1910]) which carried contributions by David and Nikolai Burliuk and Velimir Khlebnikov. After *A Trap for Judges*, which was published the same year, this was the first collection to deal with the new art. It included Kulbin's programmatic essay "Free Art as the Basis of Life" ("Svobodnoe iskusstvo kak osnova zhizni"), which emphasized the significance of the theory of art. The philologist and scholar of Old Russian miniatures, Andrei Shemsurin, noted of Kulbin: "He was important and valuable in the history of Russian art because he was one of only a few educated people. Kulbin was especially valuable in public presentations: educated, witty, resourceful, he was a threat to the opponents of futurism."[20]

Besides Kulbin's group (Avgust Ballier, Eduard Spandikov, Iosif Shkolnik, and Evgenii Sagaidachnyi, all of whom who later joined the Union of Youth), Guro and Matiushin participated in the *Impressionists* exhibition. However, as Matiushin reminisces, as early as the end of 1909 "a process of differentiation separated the most active participants from Kulbin's group. . . . We attempted to organize a circle to set up exhibitions. We held a general meeting on Litseiskaya Street that resolved to found the Union of Youth artists' society."[21]

Poet and artist Guro and artist and musician Matiushin wanted to create not merely an association for organizing exhibitions, but also a strong union of like-minded artists supporting experimentation, united not so much by their age as by their sense of modernity and receptivity toward novelty. From the outset, the association was based on the notion of the unity and synthetism of the new culture. It was no coincidence that Guro was among the initiators of the first two associations (in poetry and painting), for her ideas and personality greatly influenced the members of the Union of Youth and had an almost magnetic impact on Khlebnikov and Kruchenykh.

At the very beginning of 1910, even before the first Union of Youth exhibition opened in February, Guro and Matiushin for no immediately apparent reason suddenly withdrew from the association.

20.
A. A. Shemshurin, "Biograficheskie zameki o moikh correspondentakh. 1920—e gody." OR GBL, f. 339. 6.. On Kulbin see also Boris Kalaushin's recently published *Kulbin*, vol. 1, books 1–2 (St. Petersburg, 1995).

21.
Matiushin, "Russkie kubo-futuristy," 141.

The crux of the matter was that in 1910 their dream could not yet be realized, for the Union had scarcely been founded before it rapidly became a rather eclectic and bloated organization with its own chairperson, and executive board whose only justifiable function was social rather than artistic. As Matiushin explained the move, "A studio was found on Karpovskaia Street and things seemed to be well in hand, but when we began examining the material coming in we realized that it was extremely weak. Some of the members shared our concepts and convictions in letter but not in spirit. . . . Guro and I submitted a written resignation and turned the entire matter over to L[evkii] Zheverzheev, a patron of the arts invited by Shkolnik and [Ilia] Shleifer who wanted to help those who remained."[22]

Soon, however, a "hard core" or "left" wing (to which Rozanova belonged) coalesced, and it was this wing that produced the printed collections and arranged debates and lectures. These activities were headed by the young and brilliantly trained Vladimir Markov (the pseudonym of Voldemar Matvei), and a fertile influence was also exerted by the Moscow artists—particularly Larionov's group—whom he invited to participate in exhibitions.[23]

Nineteen thirteen was the final year of the Union of Youth and also its most intense. In March of that year the Union merged with the Hylaean poets, which resulted in joint participation in debates, the third issue of the Union's journal, and the staging of the first two futurist plays in Russia. This collaboration of artistic and literary groups realized the initial idea of its founders and represented the apogee of the Union.

Later, in 1916 and 1917, Rozanova wrote of the positive significance of her futurist period that

> In force and acuity Futurism provided art with a unique expression—the fusion of two worlds—the subjective and the objective. Maybe this event is destined never to be repeated.
>
> Futurism expressed the character of our contemporaneity, and it did so with complete acumen.
>
> The unreality of the Cubo—Futurists was a product of their selfdestructive desire to convey the total reality of the object via the prism of pure subjectivity. This was so remarkable that this "non-existence", created by the artist's will, acquired the value of a new reality, of a kind of abstract absolute which killed any interest in what was actually being observed. The Cubists and Futurists were unable to free themselves from the object, but we can admire their anguish and their presentiment of new horizons.[24]

22.
Matiushin, "Russkie kubo-futuristy," 141.

23.
The first two issues of the collection of the journal *Union of Youth* were done on Markov's initiative. They included his own important article "Principles of the New Art" ("Printsipy novogo iskusstva"), which exerted a strong influence on his comrades.
In the summer of 1912, Markov visited France and Germany on behalf of the Union of Youth to organize a museum and library for the group and to arrange joint exhibitions with European artists. See Irena Buzhinska, editor. *Chteniia Matveia. Sbornik doklador i materialov. V 2–kh chastiakh* (Riga, 1991).

24.
O. Rozanova, "Cubism, Futurism, Suprematism," in this volume, 195, 198.

25.
N. Berdiaev, *Krizis iskusstva*, 26.

26.
N. Khardzhiev, "Poeziia i zhivopis'," in N. Khardziev, K. Malevich, and M. Matiushin, *K istorii russkogo avangarda*, 36. It must also be taken into consideration, however, that the Union of Youth exhibition association played a unique role by bringing together at its exhibitions all the leaders of the Moscow and St. Petersburg avant-gardes. On the Union of Youth, see also Jeremy Howard's fundamental study *The Union of Youth: An Artists' Society of the Russian Avant-Garde* (Manchester, 1992).

27.
See D. V. Sarabianov, "K svoeobraziiu zhivopisi russkogo avangarda nachala XX veka. in: D. V. Sarabianov, *Russkai zhivopis'. Probuzhdenie pamiati* (Moscow, 1998), 276–91. On the same topic see the collection of essays *Creating Life: The Aesthetic Utopia of Russian Modernism*, ed. Irina Paperno and Joan Delancy Grossman. (Stanford, Calif., 1994).

28.
Very typical in this regard is a letter of Elena Guro, the "ideologue" of the Union of Youth, in which she expresses her views on the role of contemporary art:
… I'm reading Tolstoy, and in places it is downright unpleasant; he is so prejudiced that in places he even allows himself outright sorties [*vykhodki*] against art, calling it, for example, [illegible], the art of "the masters." Here he means Segantini, Mille, who incontestably belong to the new school—these singers of religious sensibility, singers of labor in the very highest sense! And Levitan, and Edelfeldt, and Beethoven, and Wagner with his Lohengrin, then, are also devoid of religious feeling, that is, of a higher aspiration to the ideal? … And all of this

Futurism gave the "tired" art of the preceding centuries that vitally necessary injection of novelty and "regenerative barbarism without which the world would have irretrievably perished." In the eyes of the Russian intelligentsia this was the chief virtue of the movement. As Nikolai Berdiaev, one of the most perceptive twentieth-century Russian philosophers, wrote, "Barbarism of spirit and barbarism of flesh and blood drawing its strength from the dark and deepest sources of being . . . out of the unilluminated bottomless deep not yet transformed by culture must sweep over human culture in a mighty wave as it grows weary and begins to decline. . . . Futurism is this new barbarism at the pinnacle of culture. It has barbaric crudity, barbaric wholeness, and barbaric ignorance."[25] Describing the Union of Youth as one of the three major innovative organizations, Nikolai Khardzhiev nevertheless notes that "(with the exception of Filonov and Rozanova, who joined in 1911) most of the representatives of this group failed to advance beyond either eclecticism or aesthetic modernism."[26]

In early 1913, Rozanova was elected to the executive board of the Union together with Zheverzheev, Matiushin (who rejoined at the beginning of January), Spandikov, and Matvei. She was seriously involved with the theory of the new art and worked on a translation of Albert Gleizes's and Jean Metzinger's well-known book on cubism. The result was her essay "The Foundations of the New Art and Why It is Not Understood," which served as the basis of the manifesto of the Union published as a separate leaflet on 23 March 1913. Acknowledging the dominant role of art in life and the uniqueness of the historical period, Rozanova's philosophy was based on the necessity of creative freedom and an assertion of the intuitive nature and special spirituality of art. Primary in her view was the idea of the life-giving beauty of the real, a beauty that is regarded not only as an aesthetic, but also an ethical, category. In no small measure due to the overall ideologization of Russian art that occurred in the nineteenth century, the cubo-futurists based their definition of the goal and essence of art on the notions of life building and the "sacralization" of the creative process,[27] objecting both to the then widespread "art for art's sake" theories and to the utilitarian principle advocated by the followers of Leo Tolstoy.[28]

The opposition of early-twentieth-century avant-garde artists to the mediocre majority in society and to officially recognized art inevitably developed into a resistance to inertia and decay in life and art. This did not mean, however, that artists isolated themselves from

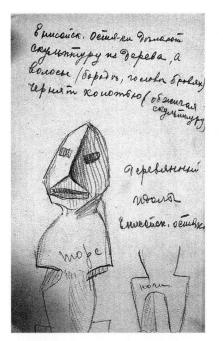

5. STUDY OF A WOODEN IDOL FROM THE ENISEI RIVER, 1913.
PENCIL. 16.7 × 10.5 CM. VERSO: SKETCHES OF TURKISH SHAMANS STATUES.
COURTESY OF ALEKSANDR FEDOROVSKY, BERLIN.

society; on the contrary, proclaiming the principle of "art for life and life for art," they actively attempted to introduce art into life.

With the sensitivity characteristic of a poetic—that is, an intuitive, suprasensual—attitude toward life, Rozanova's manifesto reflected the basic ideas of her fellow-thinkers, who called for the demolition of clichés, dogmas, and hierarchically structured consciousness. In this sense it is close to the declarations of the Hylaeans and the pronouncements of the Italian futurists, in which art is no longer assigned the role of an easy chair in which the spectator can relax from physical fatigue; art becomes struggle, action, the creation of a new life.[29]

Almost all the manifestos of the new art and poetry themselves read very much like works of art and poetry. Written to express more fully the program of the movement, they have nothing in common with the dry factuality of "program" documents, but convey the very melody of the movement—that is, the mentality, purity, and power of perception that distinguish avant-garde poetics.

Rozanova's manifesto can be analyzed as an entirely autonomous work of art possessing its own rhythm, metaphors, and so on. Art had moved beyond painting. As is evident from the flowing metaphorical prose of Kandinsky, and the ecstatic style of Malevich, in their articles

because these works are not accessible to our poor underdeveloped people? ... I do not agree with his definition of beauty, for I think it is too narrow, and again causes confusion.... Yet another thought comes to mind: is it so that "the people do not yet understand our art"? It seems to me they understand a great deal, at least in painting and dramaturgy, and perhaps even in music.... You can only agree with him on his one true idea, which is that art should not only be for enjoyment but should also have a deeper content [E. Guro, letter to M. Matiushin, 1909. RGALI, f. 134. 1. 44. l. 38].

29.
As Khardzhiev notes, "... echoing the manifesto 'A Slap in the Face of Public Taste,' the sharply polemical tenor of this declaration corresponded far more to the creative aspirations of the author than to the moderate innovation of the other members of the Union of Youth." (N. Khardzhiev, "Poeziia i zhivopis'," 41.)

the leaders of the avant-garde were attempting not to replace the critics, but merely to continue the search for new forms in a different
area. These works are a kind of "hint" to their contemporary critics,
who simply had not been able to catch this profound hermetic tone in
discussions about art. Artists were searching for a new language with
which to comprehend the very notion of art,[30] and the theoretical
works of the early avant-garde were a necessary and integral part of
their artistic production:

> "We declare war on all the jailers of the Free Art of Painting who have fet-
> tered it in the chains of the everyday:politics, literature, and the night-
> mare of psychological effects. . . .
> We declare that to limit creativity is to poison art. . . . Our slogan:
> The Future of Art is in uninterrupted renewal!"[31]

30.
Werner Hofmann devotes considerable attention to this problem.
He notes:
Heidegger's remarks on the
bridge and the dam shed light on
this new mindset. Reflection is
not merely a bridge spanning the
work of art; in its own uniquely
accessible way it attempts to
possess it. It reprocesses the
work of art and leads it into its
channels of thought. The original
raw material of this process is
the work of art, a ready-made
product—its interpretation, which
also becomes a work—the result
of intellectual labor.
The work of art does not exist
today outside its interpretation
and presentation to the viewer. . . .
Its creator cannot dismiss this
reflective world, but must be prepared to enter into a discussion
of it. Art created under such circumstances paves new roads for
itself. For this reason its historical face is completely distinct
from the art of earlier periods. . . .
Hofmann, Werner, *Die Grundlagen
der Modernen Kunst. Eine
Einfuhrung in ihre Symbolischen
Formen.* Stuttgart: Alfred Kröner,
1966, 41-42.

31.
"Manifest obshchestva khudozh-
nikov 'Soiuz molodezhi'" (1913).
Leaflet.

32.
O. Rozanova, "Cubism, ...," in this
volume, 194, 196.

The manifesto of the Union of Youth was the first in a series
of famous 1913 declarations that included Larionov's "Rayism,"
Kruchenykh's "The Word as Such," and Aleksander Shevchenko's
"Neo-Primitivism," and "The Manifesto of the Rayists and Futurists."
All of these documents marked a completely new period in the evolution of the avant-garde as it turned to abstract art. Four years later, in
a 1917 article for the journal Supremus, Rozanova once again asserted
her artistic credo: "We propose to liberate painting from its subservience to the ready-made forms of reality and to make it first and
foremost a creative, not a reproductive, art. . . . The aesthetic value of
the non-objective painting lies completely in its painterly content."[32]

In 1912 and 1913, Rozanova definitively moved into futurism and in
numerous landscapes and in the paintings *The Port* (1913. Oil on canvas,
100.4 x 79.2 cm. Private collection), *Circus* (1913, Oil on canvas, 93.5 x
102.5 cm. Location unknown), and *Fire in the City* (plate 10) created the
purest variant of Russian futurist painting. She never traveled outside
Russia, which was rather exceptional among artists of the time—witness
the biographies of other avant-gardists such as David Burliuk, Liubov
Popova, Nadezhda Udaltsova, Alexandra Exter and Aleksander
Shevchenko. There was practically no cubist period at all in Rosanova's
work, and her path to futurism lay exclusively through neoprimitivism, in
which style her mature work organically combined the achievements of
the Moscow and St. Petersburg traditions. The laconic, expressive, and
vivid childlike manner of her early works (1910–1911) are fully within
the neoprimitivist styles that were a variant of the expressionist current in

European art. Paintings such as *The Smithy* and *Urban Landscape* of 1910 (both now in the Russian Museum), and *On the Boulevard* (plate 3), must have looked rather surprising at Union of Youth exhibitions among the eclectic postimpressionism and symbolism of Sagaidachnyi, Spandikov, Shkolnik, Avgust Ballier, and Zelmanova, for they were much more in tune with the works of Muscovite participants such as Larionov, Goncharova, Aleksei Morgunov, and others. In the cheerful, good-natured irony and popular-print style of *The Smithy* and *On the Boulevard*—scenes reminiscent of Rozanova's native Melenki (figures 3, 45)—can be sensed the same spirit that exists in Morgunov's *Butcher's Shop* (1911), Malevich's *Province* (1911–12), or the characteristic figures of Larionov's well-known "provincial" series. Rozanova, a younger contemporary of Larionov and Goncharova, was as organically linked as they to the Russian provinces, and like them she kept alive the memory of the aesthetic and creative elements in both folk art and Old Russian art. When she was in Vladimir she frequently sketched in her albums icons and decorative frescoes from the cathedral, which was decorated by Andrei Rublev. Later, like many European and Russian avant-gardists who rejected Eurocentrism in search of new directions in art and aesthetics, she was interested in the primitive and the traditional art of various historical periods and cultures. Among the drawings she hastily executed from the works in art and ethnographical museums of Moscow and St. Petersburg there are sketches of statuettes of Scythian stone images (Goncharova also created an entire group of canvases with this motif), Tungusian shamans, wooden Enisei (figure 5) and North American idols, fragments of Buddhist icons, and Egyptian motifs, all provided with meticulous explanatory notes indicating materials, techniques, and colors. Worth mentioning in this context is a recently discovered gouache sketch of a sitting angel (now in the Fedorovsky collection in Berlin). Probably done in 1914, the undated work, *Angel*, was shown at the posthumous exhibition of Rozanova's works in late 1918. Its present whereabouts are unknown. The aforementioned gouache (50.7 x 68.5) also has a badly damaged colored sketch of a figure from Rozanova's playing card series. In the figure of the angel she uses the same formative devices as in the primitive sculpture she once copied. Its expressive laconism, and the angularity of lines and forms that seem to be hewed from wood, are atypical of her other works but extremely close to the neoprimitivist style of this period as a whole. The same device of "primitivist grotesque" underlies *Self-portrait* (figure 6) and *Portrait of Anna V. Rozanova* (Olga's sister) (plate 4), in which the model seems to be parodying a femme fatale as, in compliance with the laws of the genre, she casually lounges on a couch like a new *Madame Recamier*, or Edouard Manet's *Olympia*. This mischievous dramatization involuntarily recalls Petr Konchalovskii's early Jack of Diamonds *Portrait of Georgii Yakulov* (1910), or Ilya Mashkov's *Self-Portrait* (1911).[33]

As the urban theme became firmly established in Rozanova's painting and graphic work, in a number of pieces from these years it took on a social coloring in the theme of the monstrous and vulgar everyday humdrum viewed "from within." The painting *The Cafe* (plate2) (reproduced in Kruchenykh's book *Let's Grumble!* as *The Haven*) was shown at the second Union of Youth exhibition in 1911, where Rozanova made her debut as an artist. The motif, which was a favorite among French impressionists such as Gauguin, Henri de Toulouse-Lautrec, and Edgar Degas, and which appeared in endless variations in twentieth-century European art, found an original expression in Rozanova's urban poetics. The mood of hopeless loneliness in this picture is in keeping with the old St. Petersburg tale of the man "with nowhere left to go," a theme found in the works of Nikolai Gogol, Fyodor Dostoevsky, Andrei Bely and the early Vladimir Mayakovsky. The color structure of the entire composition is centered on a skillful simulation of cold electric light dully reflected on empty, dazzlingly white tablecloths. The uncongenial anonymity of the scene is underscored by the gray pictures, which seem to hover against the background of garish lemon-yellow walls, raspberry upholstery, and green curtains. This emotionally intense palette and the physically palpable, glaring color clash convey a sense of restlessness and anguished hopelessness. Rozanova admitted in a letter that there were moments in her life in St. Petersburg at the time when "despair literally suffocates me and I am prepared to run I don't know where, to look at the very same things in a motion picture theater, just to avoid being alone. . . ."[34]

Another scene—*In the Cafe* (plate1)—contains an entire set of vulgar attributes of the "luxurious" life of the courtesan: dark blue plush blinds with pompons, a bowl of fruit, a strange woman in a feathered hat tightly clutching a glass. All of this is painted deliberately crudely and straightforwardly, as though the artist is roughly parodying the situation in Aleksander Blok's poem "The Stranger" ("Neznakomka") by exaggerating it to the point of the grotesque.[35]

33.
Pospelov describes these Jack of Diamonds portraits as conceived in "the devices of the primitivist grotesque," and considers them "a tribute to Larionov's interest in the immediate 'theatricalization of the plot'" (Pospelov, *Bubnovyi valet*, 106).

34.
Kruchenykh, Khlebnikov, and Guro, *Troe*, 40.

35.
As also occurs in the poetry of Khlebnikov and Kruchenykh, who on several occasions parodied the subjects and style of symbolists such as Blok and Balmont.

With the possible exception of the subjects, there is nothing futuristic in the urban landscapes of these years. As a rule these are heartwarming, lyrical scenes alien to the spirit of urbanism—harmoniously balanced compositions that invariably contain an almost impressionistically precise sense of space and atmosphere, the sky that Rozanova loved so well "sparkling and naive in a provincial kind of way."[36] She tried in such works to get away from the neoprimitivist tendency toward literariness— that discernible quality of "plot" or narrative that figured so significantly in the works of Goncharova and the painters of Larionov's circle and determined the representational distinctiveness of their works in the years 1908 through 1911. From 1912 to 1913, Rozanova tried to develop her own formula for the purely painterly incarnation of the hidden "inner" plot, similar to the inner symbolism of Kandinsky and the artists of Der Blaue Reiter. This formula is brilliantly realized in the portrait of her mother *Lady in Green Dress* (plate 5), which she painted around 1912, and in the portrait of her older brother Anatolii Rozanov (c. 1912. Oil on canvas, 60 x 44.5 cm. Fedorovsky collection, Berlin), probably painted at the same time. In this latter portrait, there is no dramatization, play, or striking detail as in the picture of her sister, and the model is no longer "posing," but merely confronts the viewer face to face, openly and directly. Both portraits are both sensitively developed, yet free from superfluous details, and the full-face pose of the model resembles a black-and-white photograph. With respect to color, by contrast, the portrait is quite complex and expressive. Of fundamental significance here are the fluid, vibrating gradations in the cold, dark-blue hue of the eyes, and in the precisely identical background, in which the young man's black hair and black jacket seem to dissolve, so that the basic contrastive color chord is in his face and his dazzlingly white shirt. The entire figure of this smart young man with the intelligent and resolute gaze is marked by a kind of cold, energetic purposefulness.

By contrast, the strict and even somewhat "elevated" solemn simplicity of the compositional structure, palette, and general tonality of *Lady in Green Dress* (plate 5) is similar in spirit to the frank manner of early secular Russian portraits of the seventeenth century, or the provincial works of the early nineteenth. Rozanova set the painting in the family home in Vladimir. It was here in this house, in fact, that she did many of her paintings, for she spent every summer and fall in Vladimir, where she could work and rest from the daily concerns and bustle of St. Petersburg life. Her mother, Elizaveta Vasilevna, was the

36.
Letter of O. Rozanova to A. Shemshurin, 4 April, 1917. OR GRB, f. 339. 5. 14, l. 37.

daughter of a priest and a deeply religious and well-educated woman. Widowed rather early, she was obliged to provide for her four children on her own. The deliberately impassive, almost ascetic facial expression of this prematurely aged woman reflects her serene authority, her intelligence and inner dignity, and the effects of her harsh solitude.

These two portraits owe their extraordinary expressiveness not so much to the "psychological" characteristics of the model ("psychologism," in the traditional understanding of the term as it applies to painting, is entirely absent here) as to its precision of coloring, to the essence of Kandinsky's remark "the superficial impression of color may develop into an experience."[37] The character and mood of the model are conveyed exclusively by means of color and its psychological and emotional resonance. It is no coincidence that the painting later acquired the second title *Lady in Green Dress*, because it was precisely this cold, deep-green tone verging on blue that was the dominant color, and high point, in the work.

"Color is the keyboard, the eyes are the hammers, the soul is the piano with many strings," wrote Kandinsky.[38] According to him, blue-green expresses depth, seriousness, thoughtfulness. His symbolic theory of color echoed the notions of Rudolph Steiner, whose works were well known in Russian artistic and literary circles. To all appearances, Rozanova was acquainted both with Steiner's writings and Kandinsky's book *On the Spiritual in Art*, which influenced the creative aspirations of many avant-gardists.[39]

In Rozanova's portrait of her mother, which is laconic in its means of expression and almost devoid of details, there is a singular monumentalism, as it were, that is utterly uncharacteristic of her art of these years and would not appear again until her suprematist works. She has recourse to the rather unusual device of modeling the head and arms in the same tone of ocher, as is done in preparatory studies in which color is not yet indicated. In some respect this is reminiscent of a monochrome sketch of a sculpture, and in the finished portrait the contrast with the colored background produces a shocking, defamiliarizing effect underscored by the bared artificiality of the device.

Rozanova perfected her gifted use of color and allowed it increasing latitude in her still lifes, which she never failed to display at the exhibitions in which she participated. Her original impulse to create derived, as before, from her love of earthly nature and the natural beauty of all that exists, be it a product of human hands, such as a simple decorated

37.
Wassily Kandinsky, *Concerning the Spiritual in Art, and Painting in Particular*, a version of the Sadleir translation, with considerable retranslation by Francis Golffing, Michael Harrison, and Ferdinand Ostertag (New York, 1947), 43.

38.
Kandinsky, *Concerning the Spiritual*, 45.

39.
Kandinsky's paper "On the Spiritual in Art," which he later reworked into the book-length essay, was first delivered in late December 1911 at the All-Russian Congress of Artists in St. Petersburg. Kulbin read it in Kandinsky's absence.

6. *SELF-PORTRAIT*, 1912.
   OIL ON CANVAS. 52 × 62 CM.
   COURTESY OF MUSEUM OF FINE ARTS, IVANOVO-VOZNESENSK.

clay pitcher, or a living flower born of nature itself. Her paintings of models are memorable for the generosity of this beauty, which is expressed in a joyful and sincere lavishness of color. In 1912 and 1913 Rozanova painted a series of flower still lifes using an extremely refined color scheme. Her watercolor drawings for the "flower class" at the Bolshakov school may have served as the starting point for such a project. In the painting *Blue Vase with Flowers* (figure 7), in the Russian Museum, for example, she combines into a single pictorial bouquet the living flowers in a vase, their reflection in the mirror, and a simply sketched blossom on the vase. In another variation of the same motif (plate 6), the never-ending instability of these reflections is emphasized by a futurist displacement of form that disrupts the outlines of the objects. Color in this still life is diluted and very soft, and despite the rather thick impasto the paint seems as shiny and transparent as a watercolor. Rozanova seems to draw with the brush, marking with lines of color the contours of objects bereft of volume and weight, and incorporeal as colored shadows.

The subtlety of the palette and the inimitable resonance of each color allows comparison of her still lifes with Matisse's virtuoso compositions (which Rozanova may have seen in Sergei Shchukin's Moscow collection). Her still life with a vase and yellow cushions on a red background (1912. Oil on canvas, 99 x 81 cm. Astrakhan State Picture Gallery), particularly, has much in common with these. Inspired by oriental motifs refracted through early-twentieth-century European painting, this canvas "reads" like an open quotation or improvisation on a set theme. Its free, blazing colors—red on red, yellow, green and blue—are a theme in themselves. For another still life, by contrast—of a white pitcher and pears (plate 7)—she chose a cold, deep spectrum of light blue, emerald green, black, and gray speckled with yellow and red. In this work, which is among her most delicate and perfect color compositions, the color scale "sounds" like a musical étude. The black serves as a kind of tuning fork that tunes the other colors. As Kandinsky noted, "Shades of color . . . are of a much finer texture and awaken in the soul emotions too fine to be expressed in prose. . . . there will always be something left over, which the word fails to express and which yet is not supererogatory but the very kernel of its existence."[40]

Rozanova uses the symbolic, nonmaterial nature of color in contrast with the ordinariness of the depicted objects to underscore the unusual setting, in which the pitcher and pears are lying on a drape that seems to form in the center of the picture a hovering, black, horizontal line, frozen unsupported in space.

During this period, however, the still life was secondary in importance to the urban landscape, for it was in this genre that Rozanova perceived the passage to the new abstract art and the possibility of penetrating the painterly laws governing the relationships among color, texture, and rhythm. By 1913 she was working with an entirely new type of landscape dominated by the new "supplemental element" of futurist dynamism, rhythmical "displacement," and dissonance. Here may also be included such works as *The Factory and the Bridge* (plate 8), *The Port*, *Fire in the City* (plate 10), *Building Site* (plate 9), and *Man on Street* (1913, The Thyssen-Boznemisza Foundation). In *Embankment* (plate 11), now in the Thyssen-Bornemisza Collection, the depicted subject can only be guessed at from details that seem to be randomly and chaotically torn loose by the eye of the artist. The palette is reserved, consisting of

40.
Kandinsky, *Concerning the Spiritual*, 63.

grays, browns, and lilacs, and the colors are for the most part applied in layers of glaze followed by lined, dotted, or impasto strokes to create the impression of a shimmering, quivering texture that takes on an autonomous painterly value of its own.

It is interesting to note the titles of the works Rozanova showed at the last Union of Youth exhibition in November 1913: *Landscape-Inertness*, *Dissonance*, and *Trajectoglyphs of Movements of the Soul* (*Puti-pis'mena dushevnykh dvizhenii*). The last title calls to mind Boccioni's series *Stati d'animo* (1911), and in fact all of these stylistically disparate works share a dynamism and an aspiration to convey not externally visible, but inner, spiritual, movement. Rozanova's intuitive, sincere, and pure perception of reality links her painting with the works of the Italian futurists, who in one manifesto declared themselves "primitivists with a renewed sensitivity."

Rozanova not only shared many of the Italians' theoretical propositions published in their "Manifesto dei pittori Futuristi," but even used them as the basis for her article and manifesto, "The Union of Youth." It is this shared ideology that permits us to speak of her text as the only manifesto of Russian painters directly connected with the documents of Italian futurism. The Italians' declared "universal dynamism" corresponds to what she says about the "impetuous rush of time" and continuous renewal. The futurist call to "free the eye of the scales of atavism and culture" is reflected in her summons to "view the world opened wide." But her main and all-encompassing idea posited the freedom of creativity as the principal condition for originality, the purging of the language of "creative emotions in painting," and the spontaneous rendition of "spiritual states."

When he visited St. Petersburg and Moscow in 1914, the leader of Italian futurism, Filippo Tommaso Marinetti, could not fail to note not only the originality of Russian painting, but also the fact that the similarity between the inner aspirations of Russian cubo-futurism and Italian futurism in painting was far greater than in literature. The ideas and manifestos of Boccioni, Severini, Balla, Carlo Carra, and Luigi Russolo (known in Russia primarily from the 1911 French edition *Le Futurisme*) fell on fertile soil. Interest on the part of the Union of Youth is evident from its publication, in the journal of the same name (issue 2, 1912) of a Russian translation of "Gli espositori al publico."

In Russia, Marinetti became acquainted with the painting of Larionov's Moscow group and visited the *Jack of Diamonds* exhibition; in

7. *BLUE VASE WITH FLOWERS*, 1912–1913.
   OIL ON CANVAS. 66 × 52.5 CM.
   COURTESY OF THE STATE RUSSIAN MUSEUM, ST. PETERSBURG.

St. Petersburg, his artist-guide was Kulbin. We can judge his reaction from the enthusiasm and energy with which he immediately conceived two parallel exhibitions: one of Italian art in Moscow, the other of Russian painting in Italy.[41] He suggested to Kulbin that he organize a "Russian section" to exhibit Russian art at the futurists' gallery in Rome; Kulbin recruited for the task not only his erstwhile comrades in the Union of Youth, which by early 1914 had already disintegrated, but his Moscow colleagues as well. This is evident from a letter of February, 1914, to Lentulov, one of the leaders of the Jack of Diamonds: "A permanent gallery in Rome . . . according to Marinetti

41.
See part 2 of this book,
"Chronology of the Life and Work
of Olga Rozanova."

is the citadel of futurism. Marinetti wants the Russian section "to be large and of enormous importance to Italy." Marinetti visited Russia on my invitation. Before he met with me I warned him of the basic differences between the views of the Russian and Italian schools and of the possibilities of unpleasant complications . . . he is willing to accommodate all of our wishes and proposes "parallel presentations" in which the complete freedom and independence of the Russian artists will be preserved."[42]

Unfortunately, this alluring idea never materialized, evidently because of the disorganization of the Russian artists, who did not manage to send their works in time, and also because these shipments would have been at their own expense; many of them could not afford the cost. Nevertheless, a small Russian section was opened in 1914 at the Sprovieri Gallery in Rome, although not as a permanent exhibition but as part of *Prima Esposizione Libera Futurista Internazionale*, which also featured English, Belgian, and North American sculptors and painters. Besides Kulbin, participating Russians included Exter, Rozanova, and Aleksander Archipenko. Archipenko and Exter were by this time already fairly well known in Europe, while the paintings of Rozanova, who never left Russia, were shown now for the first time abroad. Why was she, a practically unknown artist there, one of the four participants at the exhibition? Thus far no documents have been found that might explain this circumstance or suggest she personally met Marinetti during his trip to Russia. There is only a photograph from the reception for him at the St. Petersburg Kalashnikov Exchange, at which Rozanova was also present (figure 47).

During this period in the development of Russian art, Rozanova's painting was the most futurist in spirit. In his essay on her written after her death, the well-known critic Abram Efros noted in his characteristically striking and sometimes paradoxical manner that "Rozanova was born a Futurist. If the movement had not moved in her direction already formed and complete, she would have been obliged to invent something of the sort very close in form and entirely identical in essence."[43]

A review in the newspaper *Lacerba* of 1 June 1914 mentions Rozanova's works as among those deserving to be described as "avant-garde and exhibiting futurist daring."

In *The Factory and the Bridge* (plate 8), one of the paintings Rozanova showed at this exhibition, the forms arbitrarily expand and the composition is subordinated to a dynamic rhythm that becomes the

42.
N. Kulbin, cited in E. Murina and S. Dzhafarova, *Aristarkh Lentulov* (Moscow, 1990), 209.

43.
A. Efros, *Profili* (Moscow, 1930), 229.

UXBRIDGE COLLEGE
LEARNING CENTRE

"nerve" of the entire work. The key theme of the city is realized through the idea of a kind of rhythmical unity in which disparate elements, objects, and forms are transformed into an autonomous organism.[44] Unlike the Italian futurists, Rozanova's attitude toward the city and machine is cautious, but she poeticizes it as endowed with an unintelligible, dangerous allure. In her futurist urban landscapes of 1913, the "actors" or "characters" are buildings, lampposts, factory chimneys. Humans seem either to dissolve in such an environment or, more often, are simply absent.

In *Building Site* (plate 9), which was shown at the 1914 Union of Youth exhibition, the composition is structured on a rhythm of the balanced and repetitive movements of faceless workers who suddenly begin to seem parts of some sort of mechanism, while the opposite is true of the building site, which appears as an organic living structure.

Futurist painting destroyed dogmatic nineteenth-century conceptions of time and space (much as this destruction occurred in science). For Russian artists, futurism became a school of world cognition and above all a lesson in the transcendence of linear time; this took place on the levels of both form and subject. It is no coincidence that clocks appeared so frequently in paintings of this century's second decade, for the clock is an image of time, or a "symbol of faith." The futurists dismantled and anatomized its mechanism; the object was "animated" and individualized. (In this respect these avant-gardists are rather like savages who know how to invoke, worship, and play with objects. For them to draw something means to possess and control it and create it anew.)

The clock mechanism in Rozanova's *Metronome* (figure 8) is a kind of prototype of a combination of the eternal and the momentary—the perpetuum mobile of historical time, and a symbol of its infinity.

Achronic consciousness was a typical feature of early-twentieth-century aesthetic and philosophical theories. Here belong Nikolai Fedorov's penetration of essences and "resurrection" of deceased generations, Petr Ouspensky's supratemporal reality, Velimir Khlebnikov's study of the metaphysical laws of time, and so on. The neoprimitivists and futurists—the "futurians"—continued this line, which led to a heightened relevance of cultural memory; retrospectivism, in the broadest sense; an archaization of language; and the free choice of tradition.

This represented the breaking of "taboos" in all areas of life, from the everyday, to art, to thought and language. In Russian cubo-

44.
An interesting comparison between this painting and Maiakovsky's early poetry is discussed by J. Stapanian in her *Mayakovsky's Cubo-Futurist Vision* (Houston, 1986), 56–57.

8. *METRONOME*, 1914.
    OIL ON CANVAS, 46 x 33 CM.
    COURTESY OF THE STATE TRETYAKOV GALLERY, MOSCOW.

futurism there was a complete switch of reference points: "The most amazing, the most modern doctrine of futurism can be transferred to Assyria or Babylon, while Assyria . . . can be brought to what is called our age. . . . The futurist movement can only be regarded as an extratemporal phenomenon."[45]

    Interest in ancient cultures brought about a rediscovery of the art of Egypt, Assyria, and China. Larionov's close collaborator, Mikhail

45.
M. Larionov, *Luchizm* (Moscow, 1913).

Le Dantu analyzed the laws of composition with the help of drawings of ancient Egyptian reliefs. Larionov organized a sensational exhibition of old popular prints that included not only Russian, but also Persian, Indian, Chinese, and other works. Vladimir Markov, a leader of the Union of Youth, became fascinated by Chinese painting and calligraphy and was very nearly the first in Russia to publish a serious collection of Chinese poetry (*The Chinese Pipes*). In her best graphic illuminations in futurist books, Rozanova achieved the calligraphic precision and universal expressiveness of ancient hieroglyphics.

Olga Rozanova was equally gifted as a painter and a graphic artist. Typically in her work she remains faithful to some motif or theme for which she then plays out all possible variations. Her experiments in printed graphics, particularly her design of Khlebnikov's and Kruchenykh's books, won her special acclaim.

INVENTION
futurist shift

During the first quarter of the twentieth century, the visual arts were greatly concerned with apprehending their own language and the language of contiguous spheres, such as literature and music. This was expressed not so much in the synesthesia typical of fin-de-siecle symbolism as in the "linguistic" consciousness of modernism and the early avant-garde, which manifested itself in a tendency to expand the domains of the poetic and visual languages and in the gravitation of painters toward poetic forms and of poets toward visual categories. In 1919, Malevich published his essay "On Poetry," the principal concepts of which are based on the thesis that there is a generic similarity between certain abstract categories in painting, poetry and music: "There is poetry in which there remains pure rhythm and tempo, like movement and time; here rhythm and tempo are based on letters, as signs containing one or another sound . . . the same as in painting and music."[1]

It is noteworthy that in 1910 one exhibition, organized by Kulbin, featured the painting of the Burliuks, Exter, Matiushin, and

1.
K. Malevich, "O poezii,"
Izobrazitel'noe iskusstvo
1 (1919), 32.

Kamenskii displayed for the first time alongside the drawings and autographs of Russian writers—Blok, Bely, Khlebnikov, Vengerov, Maksimilian Voloshin, Sergei Gorodetskii, Evreinov, and Aleksei Remizov. In the catalog Kulbin noted, "We arranged their exhibition not only to illuminate questions of art, but also to enjoy painting as works of art. . . . The writer who creates a picture out of words experiences impressions similar to those experienced by the painter. He merely expresses his experience in words rather than colors. . . . A revelation? Unconscious creation? Immediacy? Sometimes the other way around? How do epics, lyric poetry, and so on affect pictures?"[2]

The problem of synthesis and universality was a recurrent topic in the essays and programmatic documents of the avant-garde leaders of this century's first decade—documents such as the theoretical works of Kandinsky, and David Burliuk (who at a Union of Youth debate in 1913 read a paper entitled "The Visual Elements of Russian Phonetics"); and Kulbin's "New Cycle of the Word." Those who attempted to resolve it in their art included Larionov and Goncharova, Guro and Matiushin, and Rodchenko and Stepanova. Occupying a special position in this series is the collaboration between Rozanova and Kruchenykh, which contemporaries regarded as incarnating the union of abstract art and "transrational" poetry; the poet and the painter were quite literally each other's *alter egos*.

Aleksei Kruchenykh began his career as an artist. In 1909 he participated in the well-known *Impressionists* and *Wreath* exhibitions. In 1912 he was a member of the futurist group of poets that included Guro, Khlebnikov, Burliuk, Mayakovsky, and Benedikt Livshits. From then on, his name was associated with the most daring experiments in verbal art and the search for new forms not only in poetry but also in painting, theater, and book design and production. The first representative and theoretician of transrational language, in 1913 Kruchenykh published a broadsheet with his manifesto "Declaration of the Word as Such," which established "a new verbal form," "a language lacking definite meaning—a transrational language."

It was Kruchenykh who inspired and created the first lithographic futurist books in Russia. What Malevich described as his "sharp, uncompromisingly daring, extraordinary intellectual creative talent"generated the idea of a new, and in some sense paradoxical, interpretation of Russian illuminated medieval manuscripts and the visual qualities of handwritten documents, as well as the widespread

2.
N. Kulbin, "Pervaia vystavka risunkov i avtografov russkikh pisatelei," in *Katalog vystavki Treugol'nik-Venok* (St. Petersburg, 1910), 23.

distribution of the *lubok* book (a folkish, woodcut-illustrated book geared toward the less literate lower classes) beginning in the eighteenth century. The futurist book as such existed as an unrepeatable artistic and aesthetic fact.³ Undoubtedly possessing the rare gift of artistic prescience, Kruchenykh returned artists to the book by placing them on the same footing as authors and making them not intermediaries but literally coauthors. Each page of the futurist books was accorded the status of an original, unique work of art.

The manuscript form itself promises the singularity, enigma, and immediacy of a letter addressed to a single reader. Nikolai Burliuk wrote of the existence of a "living organism" of the word, and the same may be said of the lithographic books. Kruchenykh enlisted the cooperation of the leading artists of the Russian avant-garde: Larionov, Goncharova, Malevich, Rozanova, Kulbin, Kirill Zdanevich, and others. These unique editions of the years 1912 to 1917 belonged not only to the creative laboratory of the poet himself (in which, as David Burliuk noted in 1920, "are made entire models of the new style"),⁴ but also to the laboratory of the new art as a whole.

The first book in this series Kruchenykh entitled *Game in Hell* (*Igra v adu*), a narrative poem he coauthored with Khlebnikov. (Mentioned together with it in the August 1912 *Chronicle of Books* [*Knizhnaia letopis'*] was another of Kruchenykh's poems, "Old-Fashioned Love" ["Starinnaia liubov'"], whose cover bore the note "embellished" insted of "illustrated" by Larionov.)

In the memoirs Kruchenykh wrote in the 1930s, he related the following about his first book: "in Khlebnikov's room, untidy and bare as that of a student, I pulled out of my calico notebook two sheets, some 40–50 lines of a draft of my first poem, *Game in Hell*. I humbly showed it to him. Suddenly, to my surprise, Velimir sat down and began adding his own lines above, below, and around my text. That was typical of him—he was ignited by the tiniest spark. He showed me the pages filled with his minute handwriting. Together we read them, argued, revised. That was how we unexpectedly and involuntarily became coauthors."⁵ Khlebnikov recalled this work in turn in his 1920 poem "To Alesha Kruchenykh," which began with the line: "The game in hell and work in paradise . . . "⁶

This poem, the first line of which has retrospectively acquired new symbolic meaning, first presented to the world the proverbial "futurist devil," the direct descendant of Nikolai Gogol's and Aleksander Pushkin's denizens of the underworld. Poets "performed" the traditional lubok

3.
The role of the Old Russian tradition in the culture of the Russian poetical avant-garde and the evolution of the "genre" of the futurist book demands separate treatment. The well-known expert on Old Russian literature, Dmitri Likhachev, points out a parallel between the "depicted" word in ancient manuscripts and "in all types of twentieth-century art," particularly cubism and futurism. (D. S. Likhachev, *Poetika drevnerusskoi literatury* [Moscow, 1979], 27–28.) On the futurist book see also E. F. Kovtun, *Russkaia Futuristicheskaia kniga* [Moscow, 1989]; Gerald Janecek, *The Look of Russian Literature* [Princeton, N.J., 1984], and Susan Compton, *The World Backwards: Russian Futurist Books, 1912–1916.* [London, 1978].

4.
Cited in the collection *Zhiv Kruchenykh!*. Sbornik Statei. [Moscow, 1925], 18.

5.
Kruchenykh, *Iz literaturnogo naslediia Kruchenykh*, 56.

6.
Игра в аду и труд в раю—
Хорощсуки первые уроки
Помнишь, мы вместе
Грызли, как мыши,
Непрозрачное время?
Сим победиши!

subject of the devil playing with a sinner who has bet his soul on a card. . . . The Russian futurists, or "futurians," as they called themselves, consciously used the "low" tradition of the urban primitive, in which cards were associated above all with a spirit of adventurism, gambling, tricks, and the devilry of the fairground puppet booth, or *balagan*. Moreover, for the futurists, cards were transformed into yet another means of shocking and challenging the accepted norms of "good tone"; they were yet another "slap in the face of public taste." The card-sharping in hell is not coincidental. The futurists chose as their subjects rural, provincial games that were vulgar from the viewpoint of the card-game "table of ranks" of the nineteenth century. One need only recall, for example, the card game "three sheets" in the section "As a Boy" in Mayakovsky's "I Love":

I was gifted in measure with love.
Since childhood,
people
have been drilled to labor.
But I
fled to the banks of the Rion
and knocked about there,
doing absolutely nothing.
Mama chided me angrily:
"Good for nothing!"
Papa threatened to belt me.
But I,
laying my hands on a false three-ruble note,
Played at "three sheets" with soldiers under the fence.[7]

This game "with soldiers under the fence," which brings to mind Larionov's images, was the poet's symbolic challenge and served as a metaphor for his freedom and provocative lack of similarity to "people drilled to labor." The "play principle," which is based on a mixture of imagined and real, contains an active element of irony that in early Russian futurism is not so much a total theatricalization of life, "theater as such," as a model of the free and spontaneous "game as such." The play principle penetrates the stylistics of the early Russian avant-garde and becomes an instrument of self-cognizance and the author's self-identification as a "player." The space of its "game" became all of the new art, whose principal condition of existence was to integrate as intimately as

7.
Я в меру любовью был
 одаренный
Но с детства
людьё
трудами муштровано.
А я—
убёг на берег Риона
и шлялся,
ни чёрта не делая ровно.
Сердилась мама:
<<Мальчишка
 паршивый!>>
Грозился папаша поясом
 выстегать.
А я,
разживясь трехрублевкой
 фальшивой,
играл с солдатьём под
 забором в
<<три листика>>

V. Maiakovsky, "I Love," in *The Bedbug and Selected Poetry*, transl. Max Hayward and George Reavey, ed. and with an introduction by Patricia Blake (Bloomington, Ind., 1960), 151–53.

9. ILLUSTRATION FOR *LET'S GRUMBLE* (*VOZROPSHCHEM*) BY A. KRUCHENYKH, ST.
PETERSBURG, 1913. LITHOGRAPH, 12 × 10 CM.
COURTESY OF THE JUDITH ROTHSCHILD FOUNDATION.

possible creative action and the free delight of play, with its love of improvisation, its vital energy, and candid childlike spontaneity. An irrepressible game began that was unconstrained by the framework of the "hell" of the everyday, and its rules not only underlay the new "scriptures" of art but also became the principle of life and art for the players.

"Game in hell" and "work in paradise" were the first creative lessons for all the Russian "futurians," poets and painters alike, who learned to ignore derision, despise "everything dead," refrain from sinking into the quotidian and the topical to avoid becoming part of it, and, although they were in hell, not to belong to it. As Kruchenykh wrote, "Despite its 'meaninglessness,' the world of the artist is more rational and real than the world of the philistine even in the philistine sense."[8] It is the process of the game (and, by analogy in this particular situation, the creative process), its rhythm, or the rhythm of time existing outside the goal and purpose, "without why," according to its own laws—unpredictable, unrepeatable, and momentary—that guides the actions and emotions of the author-player.[9] At a certain level the game grows into a dynamic and unpredictable model of esoteric being, of a way of life.

In the very history of how these books came about (Kruchenykh remarked that he was as proud of publishing them as he was of writing them) there is an element of unpredictable chance, that Russian "you-never-know" attitude, a game with fate in which self-directed irony and seriousness are always fused:

8.
Kruchenykh, *Vozropshchem*
(Moscow, 1913) 9.

9.
Hans-Georg Gadamer argues that the general principle of the experience of play is similar to the experience of art: "The subject of the experience of art, that which remains and endures, is not the subjectivity of the person who experiences it, but the work itself. . . . For play has its own essence, independent of the consciousness of those who play. . . . Inasmuch as nature is without purpose and intention, just as it is without exertion, it is a constantly self-renewing play, and can therefore appear as a model for art." (H.-G. Gadamer, *Truth and Method* [New York, 1988], 102, 105.

10. FUTURIST LANDSCAPE. 1913.
      BLACK INK, 24.1 x 17.7 CM.
   COURTESY OF THE JUDITH ROTHSCHILD FOUNDATION.

So much work went into those first appearances in print! Needless to say, they were done on our own resources, which were anything but ample. To put it more simply, we didn't have a kopeck. Both *Game in Hell* and my other (also irreverent) little book *Old-Fashioned Love* I copied myself in lithographic pencil. . . . Natalia Goncharova's and Mikhail Larionov's drawings, of course, were a friendly gratis favor. We were forced to scour Moscow for the three-ruble down payment to the printer. Fortunately he regarded me as an old customer (he remembered the caricatures and postcards he had done for me) and was generous with credit and paper. But paying for the edition did not go entirely smoothly. Finally realizing that he couldn't get anything more out of me and frightened by my desperate behavior, wild appearance, and contents of the book, my benefactor (imprudent little proprietor that he was) declared:

"Sign a receipt stating that you have no claims on us. Pay another three rubles and pick up your things as soon as possible!"

Again I had to run around half of Moscow to scare up the money. I was in a hurry, fearing that the printer would change his mind and the whole business would collapse . . .

It cost me nearly the same effort to publish my subsequent "EUY" [EUY was the name of Kruchenykh's press] works (1912–1914). The books published by "Hylaea" were done on David Burliuk's modest means. The burden of *A Trap for Judges I* and *II* was shouldered by Elena Guro and Mikhail Matiushin.[10]

The year 1913, when the Hylaean futurist poets joined with the Union of Youth, marks the beginning of Rozanova and Kruchenykh's

10.
*Iz literaturnogo naslediia
Kzuchenykh*, 57.

collaboration. In that year, Kruchenykh dedicated his book *Let's Grumble!* to "Olga Rozanova, the best artist in Petrograd." There, preceding and on opposite pages from the poetical texts (in typographically printed letters of varying sizes), were two lithographs by Malevich and one by Rozanova (figure 9). It is an abstract composition tuned to a disharmony of broad black lines, spots, and the unclear, barely discernible reflection of a human face (figure 9). It is played like a little musical piece imbued with a single mood and sounds like a confession hidden in Kruchenykh's alogical prose:

again in love inadvertently inappropriately he said
I only wanted to fall concentrate busy myself with
my extraordinary discoveries about aerial
united by the lake when an interesting woman appears and takes a
    liking
everyone thinks I'm from the northwest when I don't say anything
    and
don't want to name why are men and women created
when there could be only men (why create anything superfluous)
    and
as soon as I want I can become an immortality for anyone . . .
O. thought I was the most complete person although I
never talked with anything in particular with her she only
asked the whole time don't talk please don't talk
that amused me and I ate black bread with salt
"everyone thinks you're a genius only snivelers accuse you
don't notice your brilliance nakedly
she wanted to take off her dress but I ordered her she
fell on her hands sat down on the floor and began leafing through
    my notebooks[11]

The dialogue between poet and painter continued right up until Rozanova's death in their correspondence, their articles, and the art of their handmade books.

June 1913 witnessed the publication of *Forestly Rapid* (*Bukh lesinnyi*) and the first edition of *Explodity* (*Vzorval'*), in which Rozanova's lithographs figured together with the works of Kulbin, Malevich, and Goncharova. The second edition appeared at the end of the year, along with *Duck's Nest of Bad Words* (*Utinoe gnezdyshko durnykh slov*), and in 1914 came *Te li le* and the second edition of *Game in Hell*. At that time

11.
Kruchenykh, *Vozropshchem*, 8. In this poem Kruchenykh indicates the name "Olga" with the single initial "O."

Rozanova finished working on a series of lithographs on playing-card themes that were later included as illustrations in Kruchenykh and Aliagrov's (the pseudonym of Roman Jakobson) *Transrational Boog* (*Zaumnaia gniga*). In addition, she participated in the design of Kruchenykh and Khlebnikov's famous *The Word as Such* (1913), and in two small books of Kruchenykh's criticism, *The Devil and the Wordmakers* (*Chert i rechetvortsy*, 1913) and *The Poetry of Mayakovsky* (*Poeziia Maiakovskogo*, 1914). For the first of these she designed the cover, which shows a devil—a futurist bard (*baiach–budetlianin*) devouring effeminate word-makers—who in some elusive yet unambiguous way resembles the author of the brochure (figure 12).

Rozanova's first experiment in book graphics was the design of Khlebnikov and Kruchenykh's *Forestly Rapid*, for which she created the lithographed text, the cover, two laconic little compositions at the beginning and end of the book, and a gentle, ironic drawing parodying a "pastoral scene" with a pair of lovers (also done with a lithographic technique).

The head-pieces and tail-pieces in the book are by Kruchenykh, who is here both poet and artist. An eclectic stylizer as an artist, Kruchenykh borrowed the most vivid and recognizable cubo-futurist devices from earlier works by Larionov and Goncharova, but this did not prevent him from "orchestrating" the book to achieve an impression of unity. The third participant was Kulbin, who provided a lithographed portrait of Kruchenykh at the beginning of the work.

In this edition, Rozanova was a follower of Natalia Goncharova, the "discoverer" of the genre. Goncharova's illustrations by no means presupposed an illustrative approach. For her (as for Larionov), the important thing was the search for a concordant text, adequate plastic image, and visual metaphor.[12] The principal "law of the genre" that she discovered was an organic synthesis of design and text in which one flowed out of the other and the "pictorial" nature of the letter and handwritten text is continued, and is inseparably connected with the reader's perception of the drawing done in lithographic pencil.

12.
Goncharova disdained the word "illustration" and tried to avoid it. She considered that traditional illustrations fulfilled a merely supplemental function to the text of the book and are put there for "unenlightened" readers. Marina Tsvetaeva mentions this in her sketch "Natalia Goncharova. Zhizn' i tvorchestvo" in *Prometei, kniga 7* (Moscow, 1969), 152.

Olga Rozanova and Natalia Goncharova are often mentioned together. Even their contemporaries compared their talents in various ways. Aleksander Benois (Benua), although his attitude toward the new artists was prejudiced, never missed a futurist exhibition, and in the margins of the catalog he sometimes sketched works that had made an impression on him. Things he especially liked he marked "buy," and in

11. FUTURIST CITYSCAPE. SKETCH FOR THE UNION OF YOUTH (SOIUZ MOLODEZHI), NO. 3,
1913. LITHOGRAPH, 18 × 27 CM.
COURTESY OF THE JUDITH ROTHSCHILD FOUNDATION.

this honor roll included works by Larionov, the Burliuks, Malevich,
Tatlin, and Rozanova. Opposite one of her works he wrote: "What's
Goncharova in comparison!" Here he was referring to Rozanova's
independent talent as it emerged in 1912 and 1913, which forced him
to regard her not as a follower, but as a rival of her recognized contemporary, Goncharova.[13]

One very strong individual quality that to some extent immediately
established the independence of Rozanova's talent was her lyrical gift—
what Efros called "the programmatic emotionality of her works"—her
ability to improvise.[14] Over Goncharova's favorite narrative scenes,
Rozanova preferred abstract compositions executed at a stroke, as it
were, in a single spirit and mood (figures 10, 11). It is these that impart
a special resonance and acuity to the design of *Forestly Rapid*. The second
edition of this book, in which Kruchenykh put it and *Old-Fashioned Love*
(designed by Larionov) together in one volume, came out in 1914 and
proved unsuccessful.[15] Instead of lithographed text it used various type
faces, and the combination of Larionov's and Rozanova's drawings in
the same book was purely mechanical. Perhaps the reason for the
book's failure was that Kruchenykh's original idea could not be implemented. He wanted to enlist Elena Guro, requesting her in early 1913
to illustrate the second edition of his book *Old-Fashioned Love*. Guro was

13.
The catalogs of the exhibitions
from Benois' personal library are
in the rare book division of the
Russian Museum in St.
Petersburg. I would like to
express my gratitude to Nina
Mikhailovna Vasilieva for pointing
them out to me.

14.
Abram Efros, "Vosled ukhodi-
ashim," *Moskva* 3 (1919), 5.

15.
Khlebnikov and A. Kruchenykh,
Starinnaia liubov'. Bukh lesinnyj.
Ris. Larionova, Rozanovoi,
Kulbina I Kruchenykh.
(Moscow, 1914).

unable to do this—she died in May of that year—but she wrote a letter to Kruchenykh shortly before her death:

> I was delighted by your invitation to draw for you. But can I? Promise in any case that you will not hesitate to reject anything that is not suitable. . . . The one thing I'm afraid of is that if you need an old-fashioned stylization, I'm no expert on styles and lack that ability to resurrect them that others are born with. But then again sometimes feeling makes things possible.
>   . . . Dissatisfaction . . . with form threw me into my present rejection of form, but here I suffer from shortcomings of scheme, from an insufficiency of that laconic "presumption" that makes you decode a book and ask of it a new, partially revealed potential. Something that is so wonderful in the new tendencies. For example, ready to peer forth in the spaces between lines in your works is an essential something for which there is as yet no name in human language, the quintessence that corresponds to your new words. That which they evoke in the soul, without immediately tying to it a narrow meaning—isn't that so?[16]

It is evident from this letter how interesting Guro's contribution to the book would have been, for in it her work would have joined that of Rozanova, an artist who shared her own delicate painterly intuition and inborn poetic sensibility.

Rozanova began on the road discovered by Goncharova, but she knew how to develop ideas that in the work of the latter were only implicit or plotted but never elaborated upon later. For example, Goncharova was the first to use collage in a book *Worldbackwards* (*Mirkontsa*), but she did so only this once, whereas Rozanova discovered the rich potential of the technique in print graphics. She created a completely new variant of the futurist book through a brilliant implementation of the notion of equivalence between the line and the word, and between color and sound. She was so involved with transrational poetry that under Kruchenykh's influence she began to write it herself, and between 1915 and 1917 the two of them worked out their own variant of visual poetry. Her graphics were the most adequate to the stylistics, poetic intonation, and inner logic of Kruchenykh's poetry, and she participated as a designer in ten of his books in the years 1913 to 1915. As he wrote in his note "On the Books of the Bards," in *Three* (*Troe*): "I really don't like endless works and big books—they can't be read at a single sitting, and they do not give you any sense of wholeness. Books should be small, but contain no lies; everything is its own, belongs to that book, down to the last ink stain."[17]

16.
A. Ljunggren and N. Gurianova, eds., *Elena Guro: Selected Writings from the Archives*, (Stockholm, 1995), 92.

17.
Kruchenykh, Khlebnikov, and Guro, *Troe*, 13.

In another book, *The Word as Such*, which he wrote together with Khlebnikov, he asserted:

1. That it be written and perceived in the twinkling of an eye!
   (singing splashing dancing, scattering of clumsy constructions, oblivion, unlearning. V. Khlebnikov, A. Kruchenykh, E. Guro; in painting, V. Burliuk and O. Rozanova).
2. That it be written tightly and read tightly, more uncomfortable than blacked boots or a truck in the living room
   (plenty of knotted ties and buttonholes and patches, a splintery texture, very rough. In poetry, D. Burliuk, V. Mayakovsky, N. Burliuk, and B. Livshits; in painting, D. Burliuk, K. Malevich).
        What is more valuable: wind or stone?
        Both are invaluable![18]

These ideas were reflected in the second, revised and augmented edition of *Game in Hell*, in which Kruchenykh noted that "this time the devil was painted by K. Malevich and O. Rozanova." Malevich did three drawings and the cover, but the tone of the work was unquestionably set by Rozanova, who accounted for most of the illustrations—over twenty compositions and illuminations (figures 13–15). Differences from the first edition included not only changes in the text but also a different distribution of accents in the design of the work. Specific rhythm and tempo were dictated by the improvised nature of the marginalia. In short, the result was an entirely new book.

The "ancient archaic devil" that Goncharova mocked in her lithographs was, in the second edition, supplanted by a phantasmagorical, parodical array of odd demons—devils with bird beaks, seductive witches, and entertainingly scary werewolves, all of them joined together in a card-playing scene. These devils not only filled the margins but also unceremoniously crept in among the lines of text sprawled headlong across the page. Thus, they have nothing in common with Goncharova's static and rigid characters, who indifferently confront the viewer as a kind of parodical antipode to the saints on icons. This was the substance of Goncharova's bold mockery of dogmatic and moribund religiosity (she was in fact herself a sincere Christian). Such substitutions were rather common in popular carnival culture and the *lubok* tradition toward which Goncharova's art was directly oriented. In contrast, entirely dominated by the dynamics of "futurist displacement," Rozanova's figures seem to dash from page to page in an effort to stay ahead of the reader turning the sheets of the book.

18.
A. Kruchenykh and V. Khlebnikov, "The Word as Such," in *Russian Futurism through its Manifestoes, 1912–1928*, ed. Anna Lawton, texts trans. and ed. by Anna Lawton and Herbert Eagle (Ithaca, N.Y., 1988), 57.

An analysis of the compositional structure of Goncharova's and Rozanova's graphic page designs reveals the entire disparity between their approaches and the differences in their methods and goals. Goncharova's arrangement of images in the margins and illuminations beginning a page follow the strict canon of old manuscripts. She draws a boundary between pictures and the text (written in Kruchenykh's hand and also stylized in the ornamental *viaz'* manner of Old Slavic manuscripts), and this is emphasized by the black background marked in her drawings. Such an approach is entirely within neoprimitivist stylistics, in which manner Goncharova in fact designed *Game in Hell* (1912), and Kruchenykh's *Hermits* (*Pustynniki*). Rozanova still follows these prescriptions in a number of compositions, but in her best ones she breaks up the composition and fractures the traditional architectonics of the page (figure 13). If she uses a tradition, it is the tradition of marginalia, or more precisely, her drawings resemble those that poets sometimes "doodle" on their draft manuscripts.

Goncharova's parodical irony develops in Rozanova into a brilliant, sparkling buffoonery resembling the phantasmagorias of Pushkin, Gogol, E.-T.-A. Hoffmann, and Edgar Allen Poe. Its romantic tone is perhaps better suited to the poem itself. As Osip Mandelshtam has noted, "Russian futurism . . . is much closer to romanticism [than is symbolism]. It contains all the features of a national poetic revival, in particular, its reworking of the national treasury of language and its conscious concern over poetic heritage—both indicative of its ties to romanticism."[19]

By the beginning of the twentieth century, playing cards already had a history of their own from the Russian culture of the late eighteenth and early nineteenth centuries, when, as Mikhail Lotman has noted, cards and card-playing acquired features of a "universal model of the card game" that was projected onto life and became a center of myth creation.[20] In the poetics of the early Russian avant-garde, the card game acquired a new meaning and a new "rhythm." The avant-gardists used this romantic tradition in their own way; they were heirs to the romantic motifs of the duel and sometimes the "game with death," but their accent fell on a parodical and ironical, almost nihilist lowering of this idea. This "black" parody is especially prominent in Kruchenykh and Khlebnikov's *Game in Hell*, which was probably inspired by Gogol's "The Lost Letter" and Pushkin's unfinished "Infernal Poem" ("Adskaia poema").[21] Quite characteristically, the futurists preferred the grotesque

19.
Mandelstam, "Storm and Stress," in Harris, ed., *The Collected Critical Prose and Letters*, (London, 1991), 171.

20.
M. Iu. Lotman. "Tema kart I kartochnoi igry v russkoi literature nachala XX veka," *Uchenye zapiski Tartusskogo universiteta*, vyp. 365 (Tartu, 1975), 132.

21.
Nikolai Khardzhiev mentions this poem on numerous occasions in connection with Gogol's "Lost Letter" ("Propavshaia gramota"); see, for example, his article on Kruchenykh in the Italian newspaper *Rinascita* 30 (23 July 1966).

А. Крученых

ЧОРТ и РѢЧЕТВОРЦЫ.

12. COVER DESIGN FOR *THE DEVIL AND THE SPEECHMAKERS* (*CHORT I RECHETVORTSY*) BY A.
KRUCHENYKH, ST. PETERSBURG, 1913. LITHOGRAPH, 18 × 13 CM.
THE COURTESY OF THE JUDITH ROTHSCHILD FOUNDATION.

devil of the lubok and Gogol's cunning cossack to the tragic Herman of
"The Queen of Spades." Attention in the Futurist poem is focused not
so much on the fate of the anonymous hero as on the process of the
game itself, which differs radically from the Romantic model, where the
plot always centered on the subjective drama of the main character.

In his sophisticated textological analysis of Kruchenykh and
Khlebnikov's poem and the verbal and graphic motifs of Pushkin's
unfinished "Infernal Poem," Roman Jakobson penetratingly perceived
a connection that provides a new key to deciphering the visual design of
the second edition of *Game in Hell*. Jakobson underscores the "derisive
depiction of devils" in both works, noting that Khlebnikov and
Kruchenykh's poem has points in common with Pushkin's "infernal
drawings . . . even in motifs which have no parallels in Pushkin's fragments."[22] An analogy—paradoxical and at first glance inconceivable for
Russian futurism—arises with the drawings of Pushkin, whom the
futurists proposed to "throw overboard from the Ship of Modernity."

It seems that, like Malevich, Rozanova was not only familiar with
Pushkin's ink drawings on the draft of his unfinished "Infernal Poem,"
but also picked up from them certain recurring motifs and images.
This includes the devil who sees a woman's elegant profile in his day-
dreams, and the locks of hair his imagination weaves out of a rising

22.
R. Iakobson, "Igra v adu u
Pushkina i Khlebnikova," in
Sravnitel'noe izuchenie literatur
(Leningrad, 1976), 36. Pushkin's
drawings were reproduced in his
Sobranie sochinenii, ed. S. A.
Vengerov (St. Petersburg, 1908).

column of smoke. This motif is quoted almost exactly in one of Rozanova's lithographs depicting a devil playing cards with a half-naked woman who seems to be hovering behind him (figure 15). Others include the devils with bird beaks, absent from Goncharova but constantly present in Pushkin's drawings, and the figure of a witch on a broom that can be glimpsed in his manuscripts. Rozanova devotes a separate page to this heroine, using in her mischievous, cunning drawing the notorious futurist shift, or "displacement," to mix the bodies of the devil and the witch in order to create an ambiguous illusion that could be that of either flight or falling (figure 14).

"Olga Rozanova knows how to introduce feminine guile into all the 'horrors of Cubism,'" Kruchenykh once remarked, "And this is so startling that many are confused by it."[23] The erotic motifs discernible in this poem are full of this subtle, provocative cunning.

Pushkin's drawings are distinguished by precise movements and expressive silhouettes done in simple outline. Their principal quality is an almost lapidary simplicity, while their dynamics of action and gesture are yet another feature that allows him to be called a futurist (the unexpected analogy Jakobson draws with Picasso is by no means coincidental).[24] These sketches contain not only the dash, irony, and buoyancy of the "playful" Pushkin, but also the sagacity of Pushkin the researcher, who destroyed ossified canonical verbal and artistic forms and created new structures belonging to the future. It is no oddity that the futurists should address Pushkin, the most daring and profound Russian romantic poet of the nineteenth century and the reformer of the poetic language, for the avant-garde movement of the 1910s has deeply hidden romantic roots. This becomes especially obvious if a break with the old and discovery of the new is considered the principal criterion. As Roman Jakobson noted in his 1921 essay, "The Latest Russian Poetry," "The romantics are constantly described as the pioneers of the spiritual world, the bards of emotional experience. Yet, to contemporaries, romanticism was regarded exclusively as a renewal of form and the rout of the classical unities."[25]

If one agrees with the notion that in Russia there was no tradition of artistic discovery but that there was a tradition of "the break"[26]—of rejection what had gone before in favor of the new—then we can understand why Khlebnikov wrote what he did in Zheverzheev's guest album in 1915: "The futurist is Pushkin in the light of the World War, in the coat of the new century, teaching our age the right to laugh at the Pushkin of the nineteenth century. And in 1913 the dead Pushkin was

23.
A. Kruchenykh, "Zametki ob iskusstve," in Kruchenykh, Khlebnikov, and Guro, Troe, 40.

24.
"The impetuous, condensed, feverish phantasmagoria of Pushkin's daring graphics ... full of cunning humor and at times sarcastic, frivolous, blasphemous notes, has a close counterpart in the technique and theme of Khlebnikov's Game in Hell and at the same time unexpectedly echoes Picasso's "Bullfight." (R. Iakobson, "Igra v adu u Pushkina i Khlebnikova," 36–37.)

25.
R. Iakobson, Raboty po poetike (Moscow, 1987), 275.

26.
The notion of the "tradition of the break" is one of the central theses in Dmitri Sarab'ianov's conception of the evolution of modern Russian art (D. V. Sarab'ianov, "K svoebraziiu zhivopisi russkogo avangarda," 99–100).

13. DEMON WITH PLAYING CARDS. ILLUSTRATION FOR *GAME IN HELL* (*IGRA V ADU*) BY
A. KRUCHENYKH AND V. KHLEBNIKOV, SECOND EDITION, ST. PETERSBURG, 1914.
LITHOGRAPH, 17.5 × 10.7 CM.
COURTESY OF THE JUDITH ROTHSCHILD FOUNDATION.

defended by Dantes, who murdered Pushkin in 18XX. *Ruslan and Liudmila* was called a peasant in bast sandals who came to a gathering of the nobility. The murderer of the living Pushkin, who spilled his blood on the winter snow, hypocritically donned the mask of the defender of his glory (the glory of his corpse), to repeat an abstract shot at the rise of the new century's herd of young Pushkins."[27]

The second edition of *Game in Hell* may have been undertaken to realize this "obverse side," and, by changing the context (here, the visual appearance of the book), to give both poetry and plot a different resonance. Also of certain significance here was the futurist poets' principle of "incompleteness" or "implication," which imparted to the work ambiguity and afforded the critic or viewer the possibility of various interpretations. It is important to recall that none of the new editions of futurist books were mechanical repetitions of the first one. The very fact of republication asserts the right to continual renewal, artistic metamorphosis, and maintaining a balance on the border dividing action from finished result. For the Russian avant-garde of the early 1900s, the flowing process of creation was itself the principal goal and result. Such thinking simply could not accommodate any repetition of anything that

27.
Zheverzheev's guest album is in the State Theater Museum in St. Petersburg.

14. NAKED WITCH WITH A BROOM. ILLUSTRATION FOR *GAME IN HELL (IGRA V ADU)* BY
A. KRUCHENYKH AND V. KHLEBNIKOV, SECOND EDITION, ST. PETERSBURG, 1914.
LITHOGRAPH. 15.3 × 12.8 CM.
COURTESY OF THE JUDITH ROTHSCHILD FOUNDATION.

was old or had already been experienced. The Italian futurists' principle
of "universal dynamism" was understood and implemented by their
Russian counterparts as a creative method, the sum of their works: ". . .
the Italians relied on tendentiousness. Like Pushkin's little devil, they
sang praises to modernity and carried it on their shoulders, but instead
of preaching modernity they should have jumped on its back and sped
off; they should have delivered it as the sum of their works."[28]

The second reprinting of *Game in Hell* appeared in early February,
1914, and coincided with Italian futurist leader Marinetti's visit to
Russia. His sojourn in Moscow and St. Petersburg was accompanied by
the reading of lectures, a party in honor of the "master" in the famous
St. Petersburg artists' cabaret the Stray Dog, and a flurry of newspaper
reviews that ranged from derogatory to shocking to rapturous.

The principal goal of the "first futurist," however, was not so much
to make the acquaintance of the Russian public, for whom he was a kind
of "exotic" greeted with the thoughtlessly enthusiastic curiosity typical of
all crowds, as to meet the Russian "futurians." The encounter turned out
to be much more complicated than they had imagined, causing irritation
on both sides and mutual accusations of *passéisme*. Jakobson summoned

28.
In Lawton, ed., *Russian Futurism
through its Manifestoes*, 55–56.

Kruchenykh in a letter of February 1914: "Marinetti, incidentally, is eager to meet our futurists and wants a debate, if only through the medium of an interpreter. Knock him and his junk and cheap tricks to pieces, that's easy for you. And this will be very important."[29]

Marinetti accused the Russians of a lack of futurist aspirations and a devotion to national archaisms—of existing in the "plusquamperfect"[30]—while they charged that he was naively devoted not to the future, but to the present, to the "cheap junk" of a tendentious symbolist romanticism that could just be glimpsed through his futurist armor. Although they in no way disputed the chronological and historical priority of the Italians, the Russian futurists accused them of "betraying" their former ideals and contemptuously rejected all "fairy tales about Russian imitators."[31] Furiously defending the independence of his movement, Larionov wrote in *The Evening News* of 26 January 1914, "We will arrange a solemn meeting for him. Everyone will attend the lecture who values futurism as the principle of eternal movement forward, and we will shower this renegade with rotten eggs. . . . Let him know that Russia is not Italy—she knows how to avenge traitors."

They understood, of course, that they had a great deal in common, and the impudence of the first futurist manifestos, which became well known in Russia, inspired the movement to issue its own declarations in 1912 and 1913: "A Slap in the Face of Public Taste" by David Burliuk, Kruchenykh, Mayakovsky, and Khlebnikov, "Rayism and Futurists" by Larionov's group, Kruchenykh's "Declaration of the Word as Such," and a great many essays proclaiming a "new technological age" by the Burliuks, Kulbin, Mayakovsky and Livshits. Common to all of these were a spirit of negation and the call to "purge the old" and declare war against "common sense" and "good taste" in art and poetry; the hatred of "ossified" language and the proclamation of a new free rhythm; the "phonic characteristics" of the word; "disrupted syntax;" and the destruction of punctuation.

In the evolution of the Russian avant-garde, however, the energy, impetuosity and acceleration of the movement are concentrated to a far greater degree, and former pupils sometimes passed their teachers, achieved unexpected results, and exchanged roles with them. The substance of all of the above manifestos, therefore, is still new and original and sometimes reflects even a diametrically opposite worldview. The concept of the "innovative word" appears as early as in the "Slap in the Face of Public Taste" (1912):

29.
R. Jacobson, letter to A. Kruchenykh, 1914, in Bengt Jangfeld, *Jacobson the Futurist* (Stockholm, 1992), 74.

30.
C. de Michelis, *Il Futurismo italiano in Russia 1909–1929* (Bari, 1973), 34–35. See also Charlotte Douglas, "The New Russian Art and Italian Futurism," *Art Journal* 34, no. 3 (Spring 1975), 229–40.

31.
V. V. Maiakovskii, "Babuskham akademii," *Polnoe sobranie sochinenii*, vol. 1 (Moscow, 1955), 367. In the notes to another paper, entitled "The Achievements of Futurism" ("Dostizheniia futurizma"), in the same volume, he wrote: "Literary parallelism. The West and we . . . Marinetti. The thick novel. Sound imitation. The autonomy of Russian futurism. People of the fist and fighting; our contempt of them" (31).

We *order* that the poets' *rights* be revered:

I. To enlarge the *scope* of the poet's vocabulary with arbitrary and derivative words (the innovative word) . . . [32]

This notion of the autonomous and self-sufficient word (*samovitoe slovo*) was the foundation upon which all of Russian futurism grew, and this is what defined its "unlikeness": its national coloring, the "temporal shift" or anachronism that the futurists elevated to the methodological principle of "the world backwards." In his "Technical Manifesto of Futurist Literature" (1912), Marinetti proclaimed the dawning of a new age that must then be expressed in a new language, but despite all his innovations, novelty of theme still predominated over novelty of method. And the new language describing the new age existed mostly on the level of new content, for Marinetti did not go beyond introducing unexpected analogies and grammatical irregularities. The "flesh and blood" of his poetry remained the language of literary figurativeness and symbolism connected above all with this new content. The Russian futurists' goal was to effect a profound and well-researched renewal of language on the level of structure. Khlebnikov's and Kruchenykh's principal idea was that "the work of art is the art of the word."[33] They recognized only the self-sufficient (*samotsennyi*) word-image as the independent structural unit of poetry. "A new verbal form creates a new content, and not vice versa," Kruchenykh expressed in his "Declaration of the Word as Such" (1913) and went on in "New Ways of the Word" (1913) to declare: "Our verbal creativity is generated by *a new deepening* of the spirit, and it throws new light on everything. Its genuine novelty does not depend on new themes (objects)."[34]

Marinetti sensitively caught this uniqueness of the Russians when he accused them of a predilection for the archaic. The fact of the matter is that Russian cubo-futurism was born deep within neoprimitivism ("We all went through Larionov's school," as Mayakovsky put it),[35] and it is no coincidence that Larionov and Goncharova were the first illustrators of futurist books. To the clamorous idea of destruction and aggressiveness in art they contrasted a special and complex approach to tradition that flowed into the concept of "everythingness" introduced by Ilya Zdanevich and Goncharova.[36]

The chief, and indubitable, achievement of Italian futurism as far as the Russian poets and artists were concerned was the idea of the new "universal dynamism" and rhythm, which in Kruchenykh's articles was transformed into the "futurist shift" of temporal and spatial forms. Malevich discerned this principle as a "supplemental element" of futurism

32.
In Lawton, ed., *Russian Futurism through its Manifestoes,* 51; emphasis in the original.

33.
Ibid., 55.

34.
Ibid., 68, 77; emphasis in the original.

35.
N. Khardzhiev, "Poeziia i zhivopis'," in Khardzhiev, Malevich, and Matiushin, *K istorii russkogo avangarda,* 61.

36.
On "everythingness" ("*vsevech-estvo*") see chapter 1.

15. DEMON AND WITCH PLAYING CARDS. ILLUSTRATION FOR *GAME IN HELL* (*IGRA V ADU*)
BY A. KRUCHENYKH AND V. KHLEBNIKOV, SECOND EDITION, ST. PETERSBURG, 1914.
LITHOGRAPH. 16.8 × 11 CM.
COURTESY OF THE JUDITH ROTHSCHILD FOUNDATION.

and regarded it as the most essential contribution of the movement to progress in art. "Universal dynamism" was distinctively reflected in one of the main notions current in Russian cubo-futurism, namely in "the world backwards" (or *worldbackwards*, as the futurists wrote it), which rejected linear time. Only such a principle could serve as the foundation for an article like "Futurists in Fourteenth- Thirteenth- and Fifteenth-Century Manuscripts" by the philologist and expert on Old Russian miniatures Andrei Shemshurin, a scholarly supporter of the futurists.[37]

Many of the characteristic features of Russian futurism were most fully expressed in Kruchenykh's *Explodity* (illustrated by Kulbin, Rozanova, Malevich, and Goncharova), whose very title implies a break or abrupt shift. One of Kruchenykh's main poetic principles here—the structuring of verse on disharmonious, alliterative cacophony—is transmitted to Rozanova's graphics, which are based on splitting, shifting, even "exploding" forms in a parallel to the "wild tempo" of the poetry. As Kruchenykh recalled later, in the 1920s,

> My ideal in 1912–13 was a mad tempo, which is why the poetry and prose was structured entirely on syntactical and other shifts, the models for which are in my books *Let's Grumble!*, *Explodity*, and others.

37.
A Shemshurin, "Futuristy v rukopisiakh XIII, i XV vekov" (1917–1918), OR GRB, f. 339.

I think that there will be a return to this some time in the future—this is the source of our futurism and sharp emphasis on expression. . . .

Very significantly, in *Explodity* and *Worldbackwards* there was a tremor, an explosion, that was expressed not only in the structure of phrases and lines, but in the exploded script as well. . . . [38]

Rozanova painted watercolors over several of her lithographs, which merely served to emphasize the device (plate 14). In this "simplification of forms, the break and shift" Shemshurin perceived features "linking Rozanova's art to ancient compositions . . . of the initial."[39] The overall ornamentalism and decorativeness of the hand-colored page, where the letters of transrational poems begin to exist as a part of this ornament, is in fact structurally reminiscent of Old Russian initial miniatures.

In the visual structure of the composition there is a kind of mirror reflection of poetic devices (plate 14) the realized metaphor, deformation, shift—a play based on a noncoincidence between unit of meaning and word that parallels deliberate coloration in painting (as, for example, in the lubok, or in children's drawings) that ignores and goes beyond the outline of the depicted object. This becomes particularly emphatic in the rhythm and shape of the lines in the written poetic text itself. The Russian futurists assigned particular importance to handwriting and handcrafted "madeness" in their books, considering that only the handwriting of the poet in the original manuscript was capable of fully conveying the music, texture, and rhythm of the verse. Rozanova skillfully caught this intonation of the author's hand and organically used it as a kind of tuning fork for her lithographs.

What the Italian futurists wanted to achieve in dramatic phonic declamations of their poetry the Russians sought instead in inimitable visual images of the word:

A poem consisting entirely of vowels creates an impression of height or of a painting done only in bright colors.

Vowels are close to music . . . the one step from the sound as such to *the letter as such* is a step that before us has not been fully investigated in Russian literature. . . . I have already spoken about the significance of outline (about the letter, handwriting, and so on) of the work; now we can write not only using vowels or consonants but using a mere single sound, where variety and nuances are provided by its different outline, by different letters!

In Chinese, many letters are not pronounced (have no sound); consequently verbal art is possible without words and without sounds, and recently Khlebnikov amazed a certain society of poets by reading a poem

38.
Letter of Kruchenykh to A. Ostrovskii, n.d. (1920s). OR RNL f. 552. 90.

39.
A Shemshurin, "Futuristy v rukopisakh."

consisting only of commas, colons, and exclamation points (which also have no corresponding sounds!).

The letter is not a means but a goal in itself. Those who realize this cannot reconcile themselves with the factory letter-label (script) [Khlebnikov crossed out the word *fabrichnaia* (factory) and changed it to *torgasheskaia* (for sale)].

. . . or, to give verbal art complete freedom, we use arbitrary words to liberate ourselves from the subject and study the *color*, the *music* of the word, syllables, sounds. To get away from the definiteness of former words and notions and create words without any definite logical meaning. The difference between earlier existing words and ours is the same as that between notions and experience . . . the latter is life itself with all its irrational elements . . .[40]

Yet another generic feature of Russian futurism is the visual nature of word and letter, which allowed the word to be perceived as an "object," or painterly theme. In all of the Futurists' poetic declarations the visual image of the word is accorded considerable definitive significance, and the concept "word-image" became a kind of symbol of the synthesis of poetry and painting to which the cubo-futurists aspired. The specific essence of the notion becomes apparent when it is compared with the Italian *tavole parolibere*, which at first glance directly echoes the "auto-writing" (*samopis'mo*—Kruchenykh's term) of futurist books.[41]

The first experiments in this direction appeared in 1912, in Marinetti's "parolibere" in Italy and in Kruchenykh's first lithographed books in Russia. They were followed up next year in Marinetti's manifesto "L'imaginazione senza file e le parole in liberta" and Kruchenykh and Khlebnikov's *The Word as Such*. In parolibere, the next logical step was taken after *vers libre* (Paolo Buzzi's "verso libero"). There Marinetti declared that the Italian futurists had liberated not only meter and rhythm but also syntax, and introduced a new orthography and means of deforming words, attaining a new level of *pluralita grafica*. In "parole in liberta" he generally took the machine as his ally—"l'uomo moltiplicato della macchina"—which produced a suprapersonal, extraindividual result, a kind of deus ex machina. (Depero even introduces the concept of "libro macchina.") Underlying parolibere was the all-encompassing idea of Italian futurist poetry, namely onomatopoeia, which was to be expressed visually in "rivoluzione tipografica."

The concept of the handwritten or painted "word-image" became a kind of symbol of the synthesis of poetry and painting toward which the Russian cubo-futurists aspired. Kruchenykh entrusted "the word as such" not to the typographer but to the individuality of the artist or painter, who restores to it the uniqueness of the pictorial quality of

40.
A. Kruchenykh, "Gamma glasnykh" (1914); emphasis in the original. Collection of Aleksandr Parnis, Moscow. I would like to take this opportunity to thank Aleksandr Parnis for the materials he so generously made available to me, and for his support on this project.

41.
For the works of Italian futurism enumerated herein see, for example, the exhibition catalog *Scrittura visuale e poesia sonora futurista* (Firenze, 1977).

writing, thereby transforming the written or printed "word" into a work of art. This presence of the artist's hand is what erases the boundary between the two genres or forms of creative activity.

Even in the handwritten Italian tavole parolibere of 1914 and 1915 and later, none of the authors (Marinetti, Balla, Buzzi, Carrado Govoni, and Francesco Canguillo) permitted themselves such a bold fusion of the poetic and painterly canons. After all, the manuscript of the poet—even if he is experimenting with the potential of the graphic shape of the word—still belongs first of all to the autonomous poetical tradition rather than the painterly one. Also belonging in equal measure to this tradition are Khlebnikov's and Kruchenykh's autographs (but not the books done by Kruchenykh) and the Italians' tarole parolibere, which had ties of kinship with the culture of the poetic manuscript in France that crystallized in the works of the symbolists, Stéphane Mallarmé, and the new twentieth-century poetry that came after him.

If we compare the makeup of tavole parolibere published in the 15 February 1915 edition of *Lacerba* and Rozanova's 1914 composition dedicated to the memory of the poet Ivan Ignatev and executed to Khlebnikov's verses, their difference becomes immediately obvious. In the first case the author's drawing or compositional fragmentation of words functions like a kind of graphic "text" or mime of an actor illustrating his speech with movements and gestures. For example, in Canguillo's parolibere "Le Coriste," the pictographic human figures seem to be the mirror reflection of letters and compositionally distributed chains or lines. As also in Govoni's "Il Palombaro," and in many other works, the drawing presumes that the reader will subject it to a logical and adequate process of reading. What we seem to have to deal with here is a visual analogue of onomatopoeia in poetry.

In Rozanova and Khlebnikov's composition (which was published separately and never included in any book), there is a reverse metamorphosis in which the poetic "text" seemingly "melts" in the drawing and is subject to the laws of painting. This graphic sheet, executed using a two-tone (black and blue) hectographic printing technique, creates the impression of a painterly work.

The synthesis of two structures—color and sound, painterly and poetic—became complete in Khlebnikov and Kruchenykh's colored, autographic *Te li le*. It was in this edition that Rozanova (Kulbin was her coauthor in the illustration of Khlebnikov's verses) concentrated her art of the last period. Kruchenykh wrote of this work:

Many have already noticed that the genius of external beauty is highest of all, so that if anyone likes best of all the way, say, *Te li le* is written (from the painterly aspect) but not its meaning (toothless meaning, of which, by the way, there is none in zaum [their term for transitional poetry] and not the practical aspect (of which there is none in zaum either), then it seems that such a reader is right and not a ruffian at all.

The word (letter), of course, has undergone a great change here; perhaps it has even been replaced by painting, but what does a "drunkard of paradise" care about all this prose? And I have already met persons who bought *Te li le* without understanding anything about dyr-bul-shchyl but who admired its painting. . . .

On the matter of instantaneous writing:

1. the first impression (by correcting it 10 times we lose it and perhaps therefore lose everything).

2. by correcting, thinking over, polishing, we banish chance from art that in momentary art of course occupies an honored place; by banishing chance we deprive our works of that which is most valuable, for we leave only that which has been experienced and thoroughly acquired, and all of the life of the unconscious goes to pot![42]

The visual properties of poetry and language begin to play an important role in this book, determining its artistic structure and poetics. In *Te li te* Kruchenykh included his own and Khlebnikov's poetry from their earlier books, where they had widely exploited the potential of the "irregularities" of zaum and the rich possibilities they offer to create that laconicism of "implied meaning" that Guro claimed "forces one to decode the book and ask of it a new, partially revealed potential."[43] A priori, owing to their individual features, Rozanova's graphics are close to the internal structure of the poetical line (with its rhythmical construction, repeatability, erratic rhythm and consonance or dissonance of the parts as a whole, the "color" of sounds). She focuses particular attention on this characteristic and elaborates upon it. A real master of color, she plays on its resonance, and it is in this area that she concentrates her search, sensing the passageway to "painterly zaum" in the abstraction of the properties of the materials.

Rozanova was most likely familiar with Blaise Cendrars's and Sonia Delaunay-Terk's *Le Transsibérien,* which became the first European equivalent of the Russian futurist handmade book and chronologically coincided with her experiments in the area of what she called "*tsvetnoe samopis'mo*" (colored auto-writing). Cendrars's *La Prose du Transsibérien et de la petite Jehanne de France* was published in 1913 in Paris in an edition of 150 copies (Text by Blaise Cendrars, pochoir illumination by Sonia

42.
Letter of Kruchenykh to A. Shemsurin, 29 September 1915. OR GRB f. 339. 4. 1.
In some respects Kruchenykh's auto-writing precedes the method of automatic writing developed by the French surrealists. This question merits separate consideration.

43.
Ljunggren and Gourianova, ed., *Elena Guro,* 92.

Delaunay. Published by Éditions des "Hommes Nouveaux; Paris, 1913), and at the end of that year one of these was shown in St. Petersburg. The poem was printed on a single, large, folded sheet so that it could be viewed "simultaneously" all at once. When opened, it resembled a decorative easel *panneau*. The artist, Sonia Delaunay-Terk, created a colored background for the text, which was printed typographically in script of various sizes. One invaluable merit of this work was the very idea of coloring the poem, creating a kind of "chromopoetry" analogous to Aleksander Scriabin "chromomusic."

Acquaintance with this work may have enriched Rozanova's own color experiments and reinforced her in her choice of direction. In fact, her original research led her to a new printing technique in which color and texture began to assume very nearly the main role. The visual image is continued in the poetic theme and image, and the word becomes an inseparable part of the graphic composition. (As Kruchenykh noted, "I am increasingly convinced that the letter and the word in poetry are drawing and painting."[44]) The "hieroglyphic" quality or "visual image" of the word is intensified, and its ornamental nature eclipses the concrete, everyday meaning contained in it. At some moment the poetic word is completely transformed into image and is primarily perceived visually as an inimitable, enigmatic picture. The word is viewed rather than read, and what is comprehended above all is not its semantic meaning, but its graphic, visual sense, which is apprehended momentarily (as though its meaning were unintelligible or unknown).

> Through instantaneous writing a given feeling is expressed in its fullness.
>
> Otherwise labor rather than creation, many stones and no whole, and then it smells of [Valery] Bryusov. Khlebnikov's "Laughsters" and "Bobeobi" and many other works were written instantly and this is why they are so fresh.
>
> Dostoevsky tore up his unsuccessfully written novels and rewrote them—achieving a wholeness of form.
>
> (Instantaneousness is mastery).
>
> Writing and reading must be instantaneous![45]

Kruchenykh noted in his usual cocky and categorical way:

> I remember the following from the time of Marinetti's visit to Russia: I showed him a copy of *Te li lé* with Olga Rozanova's unusual drawings and asked him: "Do you (Italians) have anything similar to this on the surface?"
>
> "No!" he said.
>
> "Then if you don't have anything similar on the surface, you don't have anything similar in substance either!
>
> Marinetti and his Italian friends were shocked.[46]

44.
Letter of Kruchenykh to A. Shemsurin, 29 September 1915. OR GRB f. 339. 4. 1. 19.

45.
Ibid.

16. RUSSIAN FUTURIST BOOKS (1913-1916) DESIGNED BY OLGA ROZANOVA.

National peculiarities merely underscored the fact that the new art and the new poetry of the twentieth century shared generic features and were capable of "extending" national boundaries. As Mayakovsky declared in a letter to the editor of the newspaper *Virgin Soil* commenting on Marinetti's arrival in Russia: "Denying any borrowing from the Italian futurists, let us note a literary parallelism: Futurism is a social current born of the big city, which itself destroys all national distinctions. The poetry of the future is cosmopolitan."[47] Naturally, this meeting confirmed that both the Italians and the Russians were correct in choosing their own independent paths, and that the latter in no way fit into the modest niche of epigones of Italian futurism that Marinetti (before his trip to Russia) had reserved for them. The Russian futurists were in general not inclined to feel dependent or reverent toward any ideas or works, and here they made no exception for their own.

Kruchenykh and Khlebnikov exclaimed in the heat of polemics, that the ungifted and the apprentices like to labor

(Bryusov the industrious bear; Tolstoy, who rewrote and polished his novels 5 times, Gogol, [Ivan] Turgenev) the same can be said of the reader. Wordwrights should write on the cover of their books:

once you've read it—tear it up![48]

46.
Letter of Kruchenykh to A. Ostrovskii, n.d. (1920s). OR GPB, f. 552. 90.

47.
Maiakovskii, *Polnoe sobranie sochinenii*, vol. 1, 369.

One of the main principles of their aesthetic "religion" was to overcome what they considered to be this "uncreative" feeling. Reverence does not presume active knowledge and independent judgement. Experienced practitioners, the Russian futurists preferred to question the ideas of others, yet in fact they studied them carefully and seriously, taking from them what they needed for their own artistic quest. This is why the futurist Kazimir Malevich once rightly noted that "the alpha of futurism was, is, and will be Marinetti. The alpha of zaum was, is, and will be Kruchenykh."[49]

Te li le was shown together with Rozanova's paintings at the *First Free International Futurist Exhibition* in Rome in the spring of 1914. The second item selected by Marinetti for this showing was a copy of Kruchenykh's hand-watercolored book in lithograph, *Duck's Nest of Bad Words*, which was published in December 1913 (plate 12, 13). Here Rozanova created a unique model of the artistic dramaturgy of the book. Its precisely calculated alternation of illustrations and Kruchenykh's handwritten verses in lithographic pencil resembles a sequence of frozen movie frames containing a succession of various planes, unity of action and authorial intonation, climax and depiction of the lyrical hero (or rather antihero), whose portrait image begins and concludes the book.

With respect to its melody or mood this book is the most autobiographical piece written by Kruchenykh during this period. It is no coincidence that the lithographs in it (which at first appear to have little relationship to the text) contain many details from the realia of the artistic and bohemian life of the time. The café interiors in Rozanova's illustrations resemble that of the well-known St. Petersburg cabaret The Stray Dog, while in the portrait of the poet at the very beginning of the book and in the image of him with his female friend (Rozanova's self-portrait?) on the last page certain details are captured from the bearing and manner of Kruchenykh himself as recorded in photographs of him from the 1910s. (It was also at about this time that Rozanova painted his portrait, which has unfortunately been lost.)[50] The autobiographical, confessional quality of this book is of a special kind; it is a poetic autobiography in which the poet creates a myth about himself out of shards of reality, absurd dreams, allusions, and impressions. Here, perhaps, is the source of the myth of the "apache in poetry" that pursued Kruchenykh his entire life and still, in the view of many, "takes over" his image as an artist. The book opens with the poet's dedication, addressed to the reader:

48.
In Lawton, ed., *Russian Futurism through its Manifestoes*, 61; emphasis in the original.

49.
K. Malevich, "Velimir Khlebnikov," *Tvorchestvo*, 7 (1991), 4.

50.
"Portrait of the poet A. Kruchenykh" was shown at the Union of Youth exhibition in late 1913 as catalog no. 107, and at the *Exhibition of Moscow Futurist Pictures and Drawings* organized by Kruchenykh in Tbilisi in 1918 as *Mechanical portrait of A. Kruchenykh*, catalog no. 100. See *Katalog vystavki kartin obshchestva khudozhnikov "Soiuza molodezhi"* (St. Petersburg, 1913, Tbilisi, 1918).

17. *CITYSCAPE*, 1913. SKETCH FOR AN ILLUSTRATION TO *MAYAKOVSKY'S POETRY* (*STIKHI MAYAKOVSKOGO*) BY A. KRUCHENYKH, ST. PETERSBURG, 1914. BLACK INK. 17.5 x 11 CM. COURTESY OF THE RUSSIAN STATE ARCHIVE OF LITERATURE AND ART.

> A slush of foul language
> my self-styled cries
> don't need any foreword
> —I'm great as is
> even when abusive![51]

The page is designed as an abstract illumination in the spirit of the futurist poetics of dynamism, with the rhythm of sharp corners, impetuous demolition, and anguished lines. Rozanova tries in this composition to convey dissonance and an intonation of what the Futurists called *zlo-glas* ("cacophony") as would a musician patiently matching a melody to poetry. The theme is repeated in the following stanza:

> If it had made you sick
> Like it did me in the evening
> in books you would have read bile
> wearing a crown of pots on your head[52]

The lines are crowded onto the margin of the page by a portrait of the poet in a top hat and black half-mask, while the sun seems to have set on his shoulder. From behind his shoulder we see his shadow—a double or fractured reflection of him—and beyond all this yawns a city in clouds of smoke. In this lithograph Rozanova creates at once the plot of the

51.
Жижа сквернословий
мои крики
        самозваные
не надо к ним
        предисловья
—я весь хорош
даже бранный!

52.
Если б тошнило вас ...
как меня вечерами
в книгах прочли бы вы
желочь
голову увенчавши
горшками

18. *SELF-PORTRAIT*, 1913.
PENCIL, 17 × 12 CM.
PRIVATE COLLECTION, MOSCOW.

entire book, which is analogous to Kruchenykh's provocative foreword. She boldly plays upon a variation of the melody that she came upon in the preceding sheet. The next page is taken up entirely by a picture, or more precisely, a "portrait" of the city, which is not only the setting of the action but also one of the main characters in the book. Rozanova regards it as if through a lens, so that everything—buildings, trees, and so on—begins to become rounded, deformed, and indistinct.

Other pages, beginning with the poem "Ef-luch," are dedicated to the death of the city, which is inseparably tied to the poet as his evil double, his prison, his mortal enemy, his curse. The urban theme in Kruchenykh's works, like the perception of the city by many futurists, such as Mayakovsky and Guro, always carries a very negative emotional charge.[53] Elena Guro wrote in her diary: "It is distressing in the city, amidst hourly killing. Perhaps in the teeming city we fluids of the intelligentsia will be given credit for frontline duty. New people. They wear out quickly here."[54] Even in Mayakovsky, in whose early poetry the city is a central theme, there is not even a hint of the Italian futurists' "positivism." In his autobiography, Kruchenykh recalled a book on Mayakovsky he had written and published: "In 1914, the publishing house EUY (i.e. much) [in Kruchenykh's own special idiolect—*N. G.*] issued the brochure "Mayakovsky's Poems"—an investigation (inquiry) into his work. On the cover there is a portrait of Mayakovsky by David

53.
On the reception of a city by Russian futurism see Kjeld Bjornager Jensen, *Russian Futurism, Urbanism and Elena Guro* (Århus, 1977).

54.
E. Guro, "Dnevniki poslednego perioda" (1912). RGALI, f. 134. 1. 3.

Burliuk, and just before the text a sketch by Rozanova characterizing the themes of the early Mayakovsky—the outskirts of the city, a telegraph pole, passers-by . . ."[55]

In this first critical work of Kruchenykh on the poet, the text is anticipated by Rozanova's cityscape (figure 17), in which the essence of Mayakovsky's urbanism is grasped almost "verbatim":

> And the present day throbs convulsively!
> Here is Bryusov's stupidly serene miniature little city:
> reigning majestically o'er the valley,
> lights piercing the firmament

. . . it's different in Mayakovsky. Here there is not even any superficially descriptive side, but only the inner life of the city, which is not contemplated but experienced (futurism in full swing!). And so the city disappears, and what reigns instead is a kind of hell.[56]

In the menacing and yet liberating light of "Éf-luch" this "city-hell" issuing from Mayakovsky's poetry is embellished in the color of the terrible end of the Apocalypse. The increasing tempo of Kruchenykh's poetic speech is impetuous, structured on the principle of "incorrectness" he discovered, in which his abstract zaum is interjected into traditional narration. This brings to mind an oral tradition that contrasted with the written canon, namely the ritual language of the Khlyst flagellant sect.[57] In this discourse all usual coordinates of "practical speech" have been lost, and the logical intellect does not have time to grasp a word it has recognized submerged in the alogical context. This greatly intensifies the hidden potentialities of language that Kruchenykh studied in his theoretical articles. The result is that the texture, color and melody of the finished poetic phrase convey more than an "exploded" logical meaning. Concentrated in his poetical compositions is a vital, indomitable, irrational energy of creation—that very "joy of creation" that produces art. Sheets with handwritten text are interspersed with separate sheets with equally irrational lithographs in which, as in a dream, recognizable details disappear into an infinity of abstraction, and the artist has the same recourse as the poet to devices of deformation of the object and realized metaphor.

Roman Jakobson wrote to Kruchenykh in February 1914 that "until now, after all, poetry was colored glass. Like the sun to glass, its

55.
Iz literaturnogo naslediia Kruchenykhlz, 78.

56.
A. Kruchenykh, *Stikhi V. Maiakovskogo (vypyt)* (Moscow, 1914), 23.

57.
It should be noted that Kruchenykh's correspondence from this period indicates that he was reading works on sects and the Old Believers such as D. V. Konavalov's *Religious Ecstasy in Mystical Russian Sects* (*Religioznyi ekstaz v russkom misticheskom sektantstvea*) and the April 1908 issue of the *Theological Bulletin* (*Bogoslovskii vestnik*).

romantic demonism gave it picturesqueness (through glass). But then there is the victory over the sun and éf-luch (of your works). The glass has been shattered, and from the fragments, or bits of ice (this from [Hans Christian] Andersen's fairy tales) we make patterns for the sake of liberation. From demonism, from zero, we create any arbitrariness, and in its intensity and power the pledge of aristocracy in poetry (I'm saying this to spite you). And you laugh and say: beautiful dream and so on. It's not a dream, but the breathing of which Martynov speaks, the joy of creation of which you write, the ability to color noted by Marinetti."[58]

The entire book reads like a single poetic theme—inner liberation and victory over death in all its hypostases, the immortality of art and the poet, his daring spirit disdaining earthly laws and rules.

To a significant extent, Rozanova's graphics are "linguistic," corresponding to the internal structure of language. In this book, she and Kruchenykh both interweave transrational and ordinary, conceptual language, playing on unexpected associations and intuitively combining the representational and the abstract.

Roman Jakobson recalls that Kruchenykh once wrote him about transrational poetry: "Transrational poetry is a good thing, but it's like mustard—you can't get full on mustard alone."[59]

It was perhaps another book Kruchenykh prepared in 1914, *Transrational Boog* (*Zaumnaia gniga*) that is the most paradoxical and most similar in idea and language. His coauthor this time was the young Roman Jakobson, under the pseudonym Aliagrov: ". . . Kruchenykh and I published *Zaumnaia gniga* (*gniga*—he was irritated if anyone referred to it as *kniga*). Incidentally, it is not correct that it came out in 1916. Kruchenykh put that date so that it would be a book of the future. But it came out earlier. In any case, everything was sent in 1914."[60] Thus, although the cover shows 1916, the work was done in 1914 and appeared in 1915. The principal futurist "devices," beginning with the contamination of the Russian words *kniga* ("book") and *gniga* (which suggests *gnida*—"nit"), are taken to an extreme. Behind this deformation of the word for book was the destruction of the very concept of the book or book knowledge. The imperative "*I forbid you to read this in a sound mind!*" that stands as the introduction declares the supremacy of extraintellectual communication and freedom from words and signs, and through "words as such" forces the reader to turn to "life as such," to its organic, irrational essence existing outside all canons. In his

58.
Bengt Jangfeldt, *Jacobson the Futurist* (Stockholm, 1992), 73-40.

59.
Jacobson the Futurist, 19.

zaum Kruchenykh is appealing not to his readers' logic and their ability to solve verbal rebuses, not to their book knowledge, but to the facts of their personal experience beyond the boundaries of the intellect.

The object of transrational discourse here becomes the discourse itself, and there is an abstraction and sacralization of the creative process that acquires the meaning of both the object and the result of creation. This discourse is self-sufficient. Present in this extreme broadening of the space of poetry is the danger that poetry will self-destruct and "dissolve" its own structure.[61]

One of the first theoreticians of transrational language, Viktor Shklovskii, wrote of it in the 1980s:

> What do I think now, 70 years later, about transrational language? I think that we never did manage to figure it out completely. . . . Above all, it is not meaningless language. Even when it was deliberately stripped of meaning, it was a form of negating the world. In this sense it is somehow close to the "theater of the absurd."
>
> It is difficult to speak of transrational language in general. There were different poets, and each had their own mind and zaum. There was Khlebnikov, and Kamensky, and Kruchenykh. . . . And each had his own transrational language.
>
> What do I find especially interesting in zaum today? The fact that the futurist poets tried to express their sense of the world in a way that would bypass established linguistic systems. Their sense of the world is not linguistic. Transrational language is a language of pre-inspiration, the rustling chaos of poetry, prebook, preword chaos out of which everything is born and into which everything disappears.[62]

In his zaum Kruchenykh tears apart, "from within," the written canon of the book tradition. His books would seem to exist within this tradition and to issue from it, yet at the same time they successively destroy it. The orientation toward the culture of ancient manuscripts that is clearly noticeable in his first lithographed publications grows into its negation. In the "painting" of *Te li le* the structure of the text in the usual meaning of the word has already been destroyed. In the transrational language of *gniga* this destruction reaches its apogee in a passage such as the following, which is a provocative leveling of the concept of the book canon:

> *Eugene Onegin* in 2 lines
> eni voni
> te i tsia [63]

60.
Ibid., 20.

61.
On transrational poetry and its development see G. Janacek's valuable recent study *Zaum: The Transrational Poetry of Russian Futurism* (San Diego, 1996)

62.
V. Shklovskii, "O zaumnom iazyke. 70 let spustia." Russkii literaturnyi avangard. Dokumenty I issledovaniia, ed. M. Marzaduri, D. Rizzi, and M. Evzlin. (Trento, 1990), 304.

63.
Евгений Онегин в 2строчках
сни　　　вони
те　　и　　тся

In the design of *Zaumnaia gniga* as well there was a trick substitution for the traditional book form. As illustrations to the poetry, which was printed in ink with rubber stamps, Rozanova used linocuts from her "playing cards" series of 1914,[64] which was in no way connected with the verses (figure 20).

She fit the names of the cards in the margins of the linocuts, thus "framing" the folio with the captions: "Simultaneous Representation of Four Aces"; "Simultaneous Representation of Queens of Spades and Hearts"; "Simultaneous Representation of Kings of Hearts and Diamonds: "King of Spades"; "King of Clubs"; "Queen of Spades"; "Queen of Hearts," "Jack of Spaces;" "Jack of Diamonds"; "Jack of Clubs." Her use of the term "simultaneous" here may be interpreted as a verbatim translation of the French *simultané*.

After *Game in Hell*, Rozanova became so interested in the playing-card theme that it assumed a special "trump" position in her work, and during the next two years she repeatedly used cards in both her graphics and her painting (figure 4, plate 15). In 1916, she even sent one of her friends a postcard with a watercolor drawing of the queen of diamonds.[65]

In her series of linocuts mentioned above Rozanova moved away from the traditional iconographic structure of the card cliché, but with some alterations. Its easily recognized prototype were the "one-headed" face cards, very widespread in Europe and Russia in the eighteenth and nineteenth centuries, which showed the figures in full (although Rozanova depicts them from the waist up) and single rather than doubled. This experiment may have been suggested to her by Larionov's much noted lubok exhibition; she may also have been impressed with the poster announcing the first Jack of Diamonds exhibition, which was done in the style of a lubok card by Aleksei Morgunov. The lubok tradition and card design were very close and sometimes intersected; both used the same printing technique—at first xylography, and then from the middle of the nineteenth century on, lithographs painted by hand in watercolors.[66] Rozanova was undoubtedly also attracted by the opportunity to try an original method of printing by hand (she modified the linocut technique in accordance with her artistic intentions), combining her own hand printing technique with the canonical form of playing cards. In colored linocuts that she hand inked on blue, gray, and white paper, she continued experiments begun in futurist books in the area of "colored auto-writing" (*tsvetnoe samopis'mo*—her term). She was at any rate not alone in her

64. That this series of linocuts was done in 1914 rather than in 1915–1916 (as it is incorrectly dated) is evident from Rozanova's letter to Shemshurin. On the basis of the correct dating it is possible to state that the linocuts preceded the series of playing-card paintings, which was completed in 1915.

65. Rozanova sent this unique postcard, which she drew by hand, to Andrei Shemshurin. It is now in OR GRB, f. 339, 5. 14/2, l. 20.

66. The motif of the card game figured in many lubok subjects such as the popular "The Soldier and the Devil." As Pospelov notes, "the very associations with playing cards [that appeared in the work of the neoprimitivists] came from their interest in the lubok." (G. G. Pospelov, *Bubnovyi Valet*, 98. There were also playing cards in the lubok collection that Larionov showed at the lubok exhibition he and Vinogradov organized in 1913. The *lubok* was attractive because of its universally comprehensible primitive subjects. Behind the avant-gardists' interest in it was an aspiration to penetrate its artistic language.

67. In the late eighteenth century, for example, Jean Louis David was commissioned by the republican government to develop a new and politically partisan card symbolism for mass production and distribution. In Russia at the end of the nineteenth century, Bilibin Narbut and Nikolai Ulyanov, all practitioners of art nouveau, with its gravitation toward the problem of the relation between the individual and the masses, were enlisted to design cards in the "new style,"

19. POSTER FOR THE FUTURIST THEATER, 1913.
LITHOGRAPH IN THREE COLORS, 100 × 68 CM.
COURTESY OF THE STATE MUSEUM OF LITERATURE, MOSCOW.

treatment of cards: many earlier artists not only used "card motifs" in their own works, but, crossing over into applied art, tried their hand at designing packs of cards.[67]

Nevertheless, Rozanova's experiment does not entirely fit within this tradition, for both her artistic position and the goals she set herself were different.[68] Her object in using the motif was not to design a new pack as an article of applied art. Her linocuts exist now as "things as such" that are in no way meant actually to be used as a real deck. Devoid of this initial functionality and lacking any sort of practical purpose, her cards figure as pure artifacts. The same forms of card signs are used in her collage in *Zaumnaia gniga*, in the first version of the cover that was never published (1915, Mayakovsky Museum). There is another collage of colored paper (in the Russian Museum) on the same theme: on the borders of a white sheet are pasted the four suits, cut from red and white paper, and in the very center on a lilac square

and did several sketches for the card factory in St. Petersburg. A rich historical tradition of "card-painting" inspired artists to stylizations and new "variations on a theme," which resulted in cards in the "nouveau" style, the "historical" style, and so on. In 1920 in Europe, Sonia Delaunay-Terk even produced an abstract design of a pack of cards. Tarot cards gradually attracted the attention of the French surrealists. At the peak of this fascination with the magical, on the basis of playing cards and the French variant of the Tarot (*Marseilles*) they invented not only a new pack, but also a new game—*Le Jeu de Marseilles* (André Breton, Marcel Duchamp, Max Ernst, Wifredo Lam, and Tristan Tzara, *Le Jeu de Marseille* [Paris, 1983]). It is interesting to note that after his emigration even Aleksander Remizov treated Tarot cards. In his handmade "Cards of Swedenborg" (this album of sketches is in OR IRLI, f. 256. 1. 54) he invented his own series of visual symbols and explained their meanings in a special appendix to the text. Remizov's graphics, which were once enthusiastically acclaimed by André Breton, were known and appreciated in French surrealist circles.

68.
Yet she may have entertained the idea of doing sketches for a "factory" deck. This is suggested by one little-known drawing of 1914 to 1915 in the Tretyakov Gallery that shows a sketch of the queen of clubs dressed as a peasant. This sketch is executed in the tradition of patterns for the special, so-called edifying cards, which sometimes used the costumes of various regions or social classes.

blazes a scarlet heart. This heart, cut from glossy red paper, remained on the final version of the cover. It was affixed to the cover by a real button, which was also pasted on. The alogism of this collage with the button—now it seems a timid predecessor of Marcel Duchamp's "ready mades"—was an ideal visual counterpart to Kruchenykh's and Aliagrov's "shocking" transrational poetry (zaum) of 1914.

In late 1913, Rozanova tried her hand at yet another, for her completely new, type of graphics, designing the first poster for futurist theater (figure 19). The composition she used in it was close to that in the painting *The Circus*. The poster was a lithograph in three colors, the white background of the paper also being exploited as a color. Red, green, black and white spin like a whirlwind around the center, and gradually in this interweaving there appear letters, the word *fututea*, then the outlines of a face, a top hat, and a hand grasping a packet of tickets.

The futurist theater staged two plays—the tragedy *Vladimir Mayakovsky*, and Kruchenykh's *Victory Over the Sun*, which was designed by Malevich. In his sketches of the decorations, curtain and costumes, Malevich used, for the first time, purely geometrical, abstract forms, and his remark that "suprematism began in 1913" is directly related to this experiment. It exerted an enormous influence on Rozanova, indicating to her the direction in which her own version of abstract painting would develop.

Zaumnaia gniga was the last futurist book that Kruchenykh and Rozanova did together. While it is true, however, that the very beginning of 1915 saw the publication of the first *Archer* collection (edited by Aleksander Belenson), in which their works together with that of other authors appeared in the same volume. In this collection, which was published in a traditional manner on expensive, thick paper and with color reproductions, Belenson first attempted to unite the two theretofore irreconcilable literary camps of symbolists and futurists. Critics close to the futurists reacted with puzzlement: "Is this really so—is it sacrifice, or merely a new page in the life of 'would-be youthful oldsters' in the one case, and, in the other, the 'last' antic of eccentrics who have exhausted themselves? . . . What is *The Archer*—a major literary phenomenon or merely . . . a minor literary escapade?[69] The appearance of this collection, which Mikhail Matiushin (with reason) called the "funeral procession of cubo-futurism," came to symbolize the end of an entire epoch in the history of the avant-garde as an abyss yawned wide between "yesterday" and "today."

69.
V. Khovin, "Bezotvetnye voprosy," *Ocharovannyi strannik*, vyp. 7(Moscow, 1915), 10. It is interesting to note that judging by a sketch in the Fedorovsky collection, Rozanova had been commissioned to design the cover of the second *Archer* collection published in 1916. In the center of the composition, which was done in watercolors, is a ribbon in a vertical spiral in whose semicircles she intended to inscribe the names of the contributors to the collection. The sketch evidently remained unfinished, for the published variant of the cover was done by another artist.

TRANSITION
toward suprematism

The year 1915 is the milestone that marked the definitive transition to the new poetics of abstract art. It set a new and even more impetuous rhythm and tempo in the evolution of the entire avant-garde trend that "forced minds to break the boundaries of the known."[1]

The chronicle of the artistic life of 1915, summarizing the quest and premonitions of the previous two years is framed by two exhibitions in Petrograd: in March of that year the "First Futurist Exhibition Tramway V," whose "clank, clang and clamor" (as Matiushin put it) was essentially the final farewell of the exhausted aesthetics of futurism; and, opening the 1915–1916 season, the "Last Futurist Exhibition 0.10," which pointed entirely toward the future. It was at the latter, at this perhaps most famous of all avant-garde exhibitions, that Malevich and his colleagues Ivan Kliun, Mikhail Menkov, Ivan Pougny, Ksana Boguslavskaia and Olga Rozanova officially "published" their suprematism and announced their "struggle for the liberation of objects from the obligations of art."[2] Corresponding in spirit to "Tramway

1.
V. V. Maiakovskii, *Polnoe sobranie sochinenii*, ed. V. Kastanian vol. 1, 397.

2.
K. Malevich, "From Cubism and Futurism to Suprematism" in *Russian Art of the Avant Garde, 135.*

20. *SIMULTANEOUS REPRESENTATION OF KINGS OF HEARTS AND DIAMONDS*, 1914.
ILLUSTRATION FOR *TRANSRATIONAL BOOK* (*ZAUMNAIA GNIGA*) BY A. KRUCHENYKH
AND ALIAGROV, MOSCOW, 1915. LINOCUT. 21.9. x 14.9 CM.
PRIVATE COLLECTION, MOSCOW.

V,"and taking place at the same time was the Moscow "Exhibition of the
Art of 1915," which by exhibiting Tatlin's painterly reliefs and counter-
reliefs, and assemblages by David Burliuk, Mayakovsky, and Kamenskii
loudly rejected "easel art."

This one calendar year represents a complex transitional stage not
only to a qualitatively new aesthetics but also to a completely different
philosophy of art reflected in the apparently mutually exclusive theories
of Malevich and Tatlin. In short, this year was a historic cross-section
that witnessed the principal trends in the evolution of the avant-garde
from futurism to suprematism and constructivism.

Olga Rozanova's works at *0.10* represented a fusion of the fresh
shoots of suprematism (which not only forced her to search for a new
painterly style but also, as she herself put it, to subordinate it to a "new
aesthetic psychology") and the achievements of cubo-futurism. This
duality lends a special charm to the novel and unpredictable quality of
her 1915 works, which seem to balance on the barely perceptible boundary between the representational and the abstract. These same features
can be discerned in what is perhaps her most fantastic and alluring
cycle, *Playing Cards*, which has no counterpart in either Russian or
European painting, and also in the unique *War* album of linocuts illustrating Kruchenykh's poetry, which are certainly among the treasures

of twentieth-century graphic art.[3] Following Rozanova's works chrono-logically through the exhibitions of the year, one cannot help but notice a real metamorphosis in her art from the entirely orthodox cubo-futur-ist portraits of 1913 and 1914, and the dramatic *Fire in the City* (plate 10), displayed at the "Tramvay V" to the unprecedented abstract reliefs *Automobile* and *Bicyclist* at *0.10*. The futurist notions of rhythm and dynamism are now transformed into laconic suprematist shapes (semi-sphere, triangle, rectangle) that are enhanced by a spatial three-dimen-sional solidity of form.[4] Together with *Parfumery* (*Barbershop*) (1915. Oil on canvas, 71 x 53 cm. Tretyakov Gallery), *Clock and Cards* (*Gambler's Dream*) (1915. Oil on canvas, 61 x 40.5 cm. Samara Art Museum) and *Room* (plate 22), the three compositions *Cupboard with Dishes*, *Workbox*, and *Writing Desk* (figure 31) displayed at the *0.10* constitute a single whole possessing a genre and style of its own. Distinct from her earlier cubo-futurist works of 1913 and 1914 and her future mature suprematist works of 1916 and 1917, they also form a link between the two.

Against this background, her eleven-painting series *Playing Cards* (plates 16–19), which was first shown in April 1915 at the *Exhibition of Leftist Trends* at the Dobychina Art Bureau, may initially seem a purely retrospective glance at the neoprimitivism of Larionov and Goncharova. It does indeed appear to be inspired by a typically neo-primitivist motif often found in the lubok, and it is difficult to imag-ine more banal, familiar objects than cards, which were an inseparable part of everyday life and rather kitschy romanticized notions.

As was mentioned earlier, within the rich social and cultural con-text of the period, the theme of playing cards occupied a prominent place in the visual lexicon of the Russian avant-garde, having been grafted onto early avant-garde culture by the light hand of Mikhail Larionov, in whose works there is a tendency to revive genre painting. In his *Card Players*, painted in 1902 in Tiraspol, and in his later *Soldiers* (1910) from the so-called soldier series of works (1909–1911), Larionov used what was in many respects a traditional genre motif that Russian realists of the latter half of the nineteenth century inherited from baroque Italian painting and sixteenth- and seventeenth-century Dutch genre pieces.[5]

In neo-primitivism, and specifically in the aforementioned series by Larionov, where "the synthesis of free primitive play and a vivid observation of life reaches its apogee,"[6] playing cards were in many respects attractive as an obligatory attribute of contemporary urban

3.
On this album see R. M. Mason, ed., *Moderne. Postmoderne* (Geneve, 1988); N. Gurianova "Voennye graficheskie tsikly Goncharovoi I Rozanovoi," *Panorama iskusstv 12* (Moscow 1989), 63–88.

4.
These works (*Automobile* and *Bicycle*) are presumed lost. They were, however, reproduced in black and white in the magazine *Ogonek* (3 January 1916), 11. There are also pencil sketches of them in the Costakis collection, Art Co., Ltd., Athens (see Angelica Zander Rudenstine, ed. *Russian Avant-garde Art: the George Costakis Collection* (New York, 1981), 455.

5.
The conflict and drama inherent in the dynamics of the game made it a rewarding theme for the genre painter. Another "quotidian" quality, which enabled cards to figure in paintings as a genuine, typical detail of day-to-day life, was especially attractive to the nineteenth-century artists close to the Wanderers.

6.
D. V. Sarabianov, *Istoriia russkogo iskusstva kontsa 19–nachala 20 veka* (Moscow, 1993), 186. On Larionov, see also Parton, Anthony, *Michael Larionov and the Russian Avante-garde* (Princeton, N.J., 1993). Larionov soldier series is of course considered one of the classics of neoprimitivism. Noisy and boisterous, his card-playing soldiers cling to the walls of the barracks, literally filling space. This "folkloric hyperbolization," as Pospelov calls it, distinguishes them from, say, the metaphysical quality of Cézanne's gamblers, for whom the game is not an obligatory element but is merely implied—a repetitive ritual through which the everyday is transformed into eternity.

21. *SIMULTANEOUS REPRESENTATION OF FOUR ACES.* FROM THE SERIES *PLAYING CARDS*,
C. 1915. OIL ON CANVAS. 85 × 67.5 CM.
COURTESY OF THE STATE RUSSIAN MUSEUM, ST. PETERSBURG.

7.
Cards were a very widespread everyday and cultural artifact. Some twelve million packs were produced annually by 1912. Moreover, the superficially interpreted symbolism of cards was marketed ad nauseum in all sorts of books on fortune-telling and dreams, in specially published series of postage stamps; and in the design of cases and boxes, crockery, and even furniture.

8.
For example, the popular journal *Theater in Caricatures,* which had carried interviews with avant-gardists, called its issue number 12, of 1914, a satirical "theatrical fortune-telling" issue, and featured a parodical, or, as the editors dubbed it, "scholarly-fortunetelling-theatrical" lecture by Evgenii Ivanov, "On Cards and Cartomancy." In the process, the original semantics changed—"money . . . cards . . . fate . . . luck . . . evil, terrible raving." These lines in one of Aleksandr Sukhovo-Kobylin's plays are an excellent illustration of such a parodical chain of the associations.

folklore (or the lubok in the broadest sense); for this reason they were among the signs of this "universal" artistic language.

Besides the use of the traditional and folkloric semantics of cards associated in Russia with the extremely popular tradition of Gypsy cartomancy (which in many respects crowded out and supplanted the tarot until the beginning of the twentieth century), the neoprimitivists also employed and played upon the stereotypical and vulgarly interpreted symbolism developed and propagated by the mass media.[7] The same stereotypes can be found in political cartoons in the magazines and newspapers of the time, where the face cards became common metaphors.[8] Phrases from the card-playing lexicon became firmly entrenched in the conversational idiom of society. Focusing precisely on this "reverse side," Larionov brilliantly provoked an indignant reaction from the social strata identified in the popular mind as the "educated public" when he dubbed his group's first exhibition the *Jack of Diamonds*.[9]

After the series of linocuts on card motifs (figure 20), Rozanova took up cards in her paintings as well, making a truly Dadaist move in the eleven paintings of *Playing Cards*, perhaps her most fanciful creation: *Simultaneous Representation of Four Aces* (Russian Museum, St. Petersburg), *Simultaneous Representation of Queens of Spades and Hearts* (location unknown), *Simultaneous Representation of Kings of Hearts and Diamonds* (Astrakhan Art Gallery), *King of Spades* (location unknown), *King of Clubs* (Regional Museum, Slobodskoi)(plate 17), *Queen of Spades* (Simbirsk Art Museum)(plate 16), *Queen of Hearts* (location unknown), *Queen of Diamonds* (Nizhnii Novgorod Art Museum and another version in a private collection in St. Petersburg)(plate 18), *Jack of Hearts* (Regional Museum, Slobodskoi)(plate 19), *Jack of Diamonds* (location unknown), and *Jack of Clubs* (Ivanovo-Voznesensk Art Museum). In contrast to the linocut series, this series contained a new card, the *Jack of Hearts*, replacing the earlier *Queen of Clubs* and *Jack of Spades*. Here, much in the spirit of Lewis Carroll's paradoxes and Kazimir Malevich's absurdism, she created a formal "portrait gallery" of unreal characters—queens, kings, and jacks. She enters into an ironical game with the viewer, calling into question the very notion of the representational in art, parodying the portrait genre and, within it, the holiness of humanist civilization—the very conception of individuality nurtured in the portrait genres of earlier cultural traditions.

In her card figures there is a striking contrast between vivid colors and the black-gray grisaille in which are painted the faces and hands of the half-alive characters from "beyond the looking glass." There is the villainous Queen of Spades (who recalls Pushkin's story of the same name, and its epigraph taken from "a recent fortune-telling book": *The Queen of Spades signifies secret ill-will*); the Jack of Diamonds, impetuous and abrupt as a bird, with a falcon on his arm; and other figures. Although compositionally Rozanova draws from, in some detail, her own linocuts from the 1914 graphic series previously discussed in chapter 2, the style of the painted portraits is very different. The very idea of doing such a series in painting and the manner in which it is executed go beyond neoprimitivism or cubo-futurism and, however paradoxical this may sound, in some sense anticipate the aesthetics of pop art. The grotesqueness of the subject is repeatedly underscored by the

9.
John Bowlt explains this phenomenon as deriving not so much from *épatage* as from the need to destroy the old system of aesthetic values in order to create a new one in which the conventional boundaries between "high" and "low" in art would be erased:

"The primary members of the Russian Avant-garde took an active part in the desanctification of high art by superimposing scandalous images, imbuing 'unartistic' objects with an 'artistic' sense (e.g. telephones and postcards), placing a work of art within a profane environment, and applying 'absurd' or misleading titles to their art exhibitions." (John Bowlt, "A Brazen Can-Can in the Temple of Art: the Russian Avant-Garde and Popular Culture," *High & Low* [exhibition catalog] [New York, 1991], 143.) Russian researcher Gleb Pospelov provides a witty history of this name, connecting it with Ponson du Terrail's then very popular, two-volume adventure novels *Rocambole*, which was read by everyone, "from servants to artists." (The characters in the second volume were the jacks of all suits.) Pospelov notes that *Rocambole* was so popular that journalists quickly christened a trial in Moscow in the 1870s "the trial of the jacks of hearts," the jack referring to a swindler. In colloquial speech the same meaning attached to the jack of diamonds. (Pospelov, *Bubnovyi valet*, 99–100.) Also supporting Pospelov's hypothesis is the fact that Rozanova, who participated in joint exhibitions with Larionov's group, titled one of her 1913 commentaries "Rocambole Resurrected" ("Voskreshii Rokambol'"); GRM, f. 121. 82.). It is interesting to note that the second volume of the du Terrail novel was also entitled *La resurrection de Rocambole*. The commentary was an ironic response to the scandal that erupted around the vandalization of I. E. Repin's painting *Ivan the Terrible Murders his Son*, which the tabloid press had attempted to attribute to the avant-gardists. See also page 143-44 of the present study.

paintings' rough and grotesque method of execution that brings to mind a handpainted photograph or a brightly colored postcard sold at some provincial fair.

The phantasmagorical figures that stare out with the inescapable serenity of ghosts seem to draw the viewer into their absurd world even as they turn away. This aspect of their invasion into the space of the spectator contains an active element of irony and is based on a mixture of the imagined and the real, fantastic detail and everyday context. Elevated to an absolute, the card stereotype becomes not only a representation of a representation of a mass cliché, but begins to acquire the autonomous significance of a doll that has come to life or a shadow that has departed from the person casting it. In this embodiment, in the "simultaneous representations" of the kings and queens, there is the hint of the beginning of a kind of plot or conflict. Here as nowhere else in her works Rozanova introduces a sense of theater, a noticeable element of dramatization. It is no coincidence that her cards recall Malevich's theatrical sketches for *Victory Over the Sun* (1913), in which grotesque expressiveness also plays a leading role. It is interesting to note that in one variant of his sketches of the costumes of the Futurist Strong Man, Warrior, and the Turkish Warrior (all three in the Russian Museum), Malevich used card suits to describe his characters. In his Strong Men (who have the emblems of various suits instead of heads) there is the same personification of face cards found in the works of Rozanova. This dehumanization is diametrically opposite the reverse reincarnation in which real historical persons are identified with cards, as in the special historical decks produced in Europe or in Ponson du Terrail's *Rocambole. Le club des valets de court,* [10] where the characters adopt nicknames from the face cards. But the similarity to Malevich's sketches does not stop here. Rozanova's manner; her lapidary local color; her fragmentation of complex forms into simple geometrical shapes whose autonomy is emphasized by their black contours; and finally, her neutrality of the background, which is equivalent to the absence of background, have a great deal in common with Malevich's protosuprematist sketches. In the *Simultaneous Representation of Four Aces* (figure 21) there is an already only geometrized "primal element" of the card sign: diamond, circle, cross.

10.
See P. du Terrail, *Rocambole,* 2 vols. (Paris, 1992).

The year 1915 was remembered by contemporaries not only as a year of artistic discoveries, but also as the second wartime year in Russian history. World War I gave the avant-garde artist the necessary initial impulse to revise the spiritual and moral values of the human world, to rewrite world history and culture, and to scrutinize the past to discover and show the full extent of the alienation between the superficially visible and real, secret, invisible matter. Deriving the artistic consciousness from the chaos of the war, the leaders of the avant-garde created their own historical myth, revealing the sacral, mystical meaning of war in history and in their own fate—to face the "Demon of Time":

> The battlefield. The field on which history invades life. . . . The years passed, stagnating in sequence as if out of habit. Perhaps out of absent-mindedness? Who knew their face, and as for them, did they make out anyone's face?
>
> And here is one of them ending, the 1914th in succession . . . in fire and smoke the Demon of Time appeared to you and only you.[11]

Russian art during this period was engaged in an active process of self-definition and self-cognition. The war itself was variously refracted in the worldview of the artist.

One of the basic principles of Russian avant-garde poetics of this period (or any other innovative trend seeking to destroy the established canon) was the creation of an "entirely real language to express new sensations and ideas."[12] In the visual language of the new art there is a developed hierarchy of significant concepts—visual archetypes possessing hidden symbolism. In painting, this contributed to the evolution of a special iconography and new canons within the avant-garde belonging to entire trends, and individual artists.

The emergence early in the century of a mythology of war both reflected an eschatological worldview and represented the continuation of a romantic utopia in which the images and concepts of war figured as central elements in epics and in historical myth. The semantics of war in the early Russian avant-garde was complicated, more a metaphor than a subject. For the leaders of the movement, the concept was bound up with the idea of innovation and the destruction of old forms and aesthetics for the sake of the new creativity. The theme of war in avant-garde poetics had little in common with the actual war that broke out in 1914, although it was unexpectedly and profoundly refracted in the painting and graphics of the young generation of

11.
B. Pasternak, *Ob iskusstve* (Moscow, 1990), 130.

12.
I. Kliun, "Primitives of the Twentieth Century" in *Russian Art of the Avant-Garde, 137.*

22. COVER DESIGN FOR THE PORTFOLIO *WAR* (*VOINA*), POETRY BY A. KRUCHENYKH,
LINOCUTS BY O. ROZANOVA. PETROGRAD, 1916. COLLAGE, LINOCUT IN BLACK ON
TAN PAPER. 40 × 31 CM.
COURTESY OF THE JUDITH ROTHSCHILD FOUNDATION.

13.
In the final analysis this was a
question of the purpose of art, its
proper sphere of influence, and
the traditional problem of the
interrelationship of artist and
viewer. As David Burliuk put it,
"We were brought up in the school
of Russian rationalists—Pisarev,
Chernyshevsky, Dobroliubov. This
ferment in us is so powerful that
the work of those whom Andrei
Bely led in the footsteps of
Vladimir Soloviov is merely a thin
crust from under which the reminiscences of youth shine forth
rather clearly and steadily." [D.
Burliuk, *Fragmenty iz vospomi-
nanik futurista* [St. Petersburg,
1994], 144.]

Russian avant-gardists whom the conflict affected directly as it vio-
lently intruded upon their lives. Larionov, Le Dantu, Shevchenko,
Filonov, and Sergei Chekrygin, all served at the front, and all of them
in one way or another addressed the theme of war in their art. Works
by Mayakovsky, Malevich, Lentulov, Chekrygin, and Larionov for
Margarita Sabashnikova's publishing house, Contemporary Popular
Prints, (Segodniashnii lubok) were widely known.

Because it altered the usual march of time, the war afforded the
avant-garde an immediate opportunity to infuse a social content into
their modern artistic experiments, and the creation of new forms was
harnessed to the search for an expressive language in which to portray
social cataclysms.[13] The disintegrating self-awareness of twentieth-
century society, however, introduced a corrective into this program
that echoes Goncharova's bitter remark, "If I do find myself in conflict

with society, it is only because the latter does not understand the basis of art in general, and not because of my individual peculiarities, which no one is obliged to understand."[14]

The interconnection between life and art—between *war* and art—was a central concern of the leaders of the new art and poetry. The decade between the two Russian revolutions, a time swept by a "flood of premonitions," was particularly sensitive toward these problems. The prominent eschatological consciousness of this period defined the poetics of war as a turning point, a crisis, catastrophe, and subsequent catharsis.[15]

Owing to the tragedy and uniqueness of the historical situation, all these premonitions of a mystical spiritual battle coincided with the inhuman real war. For contemporaries, the shocking new technology and gigantic scale of World War I created a new image of war: total war beyond human pain and passions, in which individuality counted for nothing.[16] The modernist artists, who represented different movements reflect in their works different, sometimes even opposite, aspects of war. It was not always an obvious representation of military subject matter.

An extensive body of works inspired by the war was produced by expressionism. Here may be mentioned the series of graphics and paintings by the Germans Otto Dix, Kathe Kollwitz, and Max Pechstein, as well as individual lithographs on a theme by Ernst Barlach.[17] There is also the famous cycle *Miserere*, by the Frenchman Georges Rouault, and, finally, Natalia Goncharova's *Mystical Images of War* (1914), in the neoprimitivist style that was the Russian variant of expressionism.

Another movement was of course futurism, represented by Marinetti, Boccioni, Severini, and Carra in Italy and by vorticism, and particularly the art of Windham Lewis, in England.[18] The Italian futurists proposed not only an aesthetic but also a political program that advocated war as the path to a national rebirth. In the visual language of this trend, a considerable role was played by the dynamics, rhythm, and "mass gesture" of combat. The impetuous rush of time that so occupied the Italians is rightfully associated with the concept of battle, which can be perceived as the most powerful manifestation of the dynamism and simultaneity. In its ideology and apolitical spirit, Russian futurism was often the complete opposite of the Italian version. Expanding this purely aesthetic notion to the level of a philosophical outlook, Berdiaev noted:

14.
Vystavka kartin N. Goncharovoi. 1900–1913 (Moscow, 1913), 3.

15.
See Ben Hellman, *Poets of Hope and Despair: The Russian Symbolists in War and Revolution 1914–1918* (Helsinki, Helsinki University Press, 1995).

16.
In one of his early articles Mayakovsky (whose articles of 1914 to 1916 accurately reflect the evolution of the artistic consciousness toward the war from rapture to disgust and finally rejection) wrote, with daring candor, that "as a Russian, every effort of the soldier to wrench a piece of territory away from the enemy is sacred to me; as a man of art, however, I am obliged to think that perhaps the entire war was invented merely so that someone could write a single good poem." (Maiakovskii, *Polnoe sobranie sochinenii*, vol. 1, 304.)

17.
On the European avant-garde and the First World War see Theda Shapiro, *Painters and Politics. The European Avant-garde and Society 1900–1925* (New York, 1976).

18.
See Wyndham Lewis, ed., *Blast 1–2* (London, 1914–1915). Charlotte Douglas ("Bezpredmetnost' i dekorativnost'," *Voprosy iskusstvoznaniia* 2–3 [1993]: 103–4) even notes traits that Wyndham Lewis's 1915 compositions share with the Rozanova's nonrepresentational compositions.

We must accept futurism, understand its meaning and move toward new creation. . . .

We Russians are the least futuristic in this war. . . . We must pass beyond and overcome Futurism both in life and in art. It can be overcome by going deeper, by moving into another dimension, the dimension of depth rather than surface, through knowledge, not abstract knowledge but knowledge of life, knowledge of being.[19]

The actual war was for contemporaries not a theme but an everyday reality that touched their own lives and to one or another degree changed the usual course of time. It could not but affect the thousands of men and women who lived a nightmare of fear for the lives of their loved ones. A letter Rozanova wrote to Kruchenykh in the fall of 1914 is a striking testimony to the time:

You are not averse to preaching, but I assure you that if you were not on standby but in the ready reserve you would be sitting not in Shuvalov, but on the Austrian or German border. Your preaching would not persuade me in the least. But all right, now I've stifled my last sobs and will quiet down.

I simply don't know how to tell you about my dreams! You would hardly find them interesting, but it is above all they that have put me in the state you criticize. . . .

I saw you lying at our place in the courtyard, together with a crowd of people. You were ill and couldn't get up and go, as if you had lost consciousness. It was necessary to get you into the house, but no one but me wanted to do it. In brief, you were dying and were left there to die.

People were looking out of our windows wondering what I was doing near you and who you were. And if you were brought into the house someone was going to stop us and shoot us, but if you weren't brought in you would die, and this was the problem I had to solve. Of course I could not take you away all by myself, but no one wanted to help me and I simply held your hands and watched you die and couldn't stop anything. When later war was declared and for a long time I didn't get any letters from you this dream bothered me, and I decided that you weren't writing because you didn't want to upset me. But now today or tomorrow what I saw in my dream will come true. . . .[20]

19.
N. Berdiaev, *Krizis iskusstva*, 23.

20.
O. Rozanova, Letter to A. Kruchenykh, [October 1914], private collection, Moscow.

21.
E. Guro, *Dnevniki poslednego perioda*, RGALI, f. 134. 1. 3.

Reading this letter one recalls a diary entry that artist and poet Elena Guro made not long before her death about "the admirable habit of recasting all bitter and sorrowful stimuli into transports of inspiration."[21] Rozanova was able to subordinate her nightmares and psychological pain to her ineradicable creative impulse. All of this manifested itself in her war linocuts as an incredible, tense synthesis of personal suffering and the philosophical aloofness of the observing artist—a brilliant fusion of spiritual power, pain, and pure talent. The world suddenly was unrecognizable and reversed in the human sub-conscience; it became alien, frightening, irrational—all the categories that one wants to repress in his perception.

Rozanova's color linocuts to Kruchenykh's poetry cycle *War* were conceived within the artistic current of futurism, but in many respects their poetics are nevertheless different. In her work there is an intense inner drama that *negates* the linear, absolute, real time expressed in the juxtaposition of psychological and historical, chronological time (the execution) and imaginary time (the miracle), each of which possesses its own reality and unreality. The base of the metonym of war is a synec-doche for the album *War* as a whole. It speaks of war as a total and uni-versal phenomenon, the unknown; cosmic war and historical war never intersect, but coexist in different dimensions. As one of the leading modernist writers of the twentieth century, Jorge Luis Borges, argues, "that does not mean that we shall never know, even approximately, the date of the dream; it means that the chronological determination of an event, of any event on earth, is alien and exterior to the event."[22]

Because it was overemphasized by historical circumstances, "being towards death," which in Paul Ricoeur's interpretation of the "polar opposition" of mortal time and cosmic time, is absolutized in avant-garde culture.[23] In the context of World War I, both historical time and "psychological time" were transformed by Rozanova and Kruchenykh into "poetic time," which has no chronological dimensions.

Rozanova planned her album as early as the winter of 1914 to 1915, but it was not until the summer of 1915, when Shemshurin agreed to finance the publication and print the engravings, that she returned to the idea. In her letter of 19 July she wrote Shemshurin, "I'll begin draw-ing and printing immediately. I'm thinking of preparing a large num-ber of copies on white paper. Even the cover will be white. As for colors, so far I've chosen cinnabar, blue, black, and green, if only I can find them in the shops. Each picture will be a combination of two or three of these colors. It seems most convenient to print only on white paper in several colors, and this will also give the work a smart look. But perhaps for variety's sake I'll do a few copies on colored paper. The pictures will probably be five-by-six or six-by-seven *vershki* in size. Thank you for wishing me luck. . . ."[24] By this time she had definitely chosen and tested the technique she would use—color linocuts. In another letter to

22.
Jorge Luis Borges, "New Refutation of Time," in *Other Inquisitions*, trans. Ruth L. C. Simms (Austin, Tex., 1993), 184.

23.
Paul Ricoeur, *Time and Narrative*, trans. Kathleen McLaughlin and David Pellauer (Chicago, 1988), 141.

24.
O. Rozanova, Letter to A. Shemshurin, OR GRB, f. 339. *Vershok*—old Russian measure of length equivalent to 4.4 cm.

Shemshurin she informed him that the cycle was to be "in the spirit of my playing cards," referring to the 1914 linocuts in which she first used this technique with a handinked stencil producing a rich and original texture. She applied paint with a brush and not a roller, so that each copy was handmade and unique. When completed, it was an album consisting of fifteen unbound pages, ten of which were linocuts on the war theme. The remaining five used the same technique to print Kruchenykh's verses. The work was completed in January 1916, at which time she informed Shemshurin, "Although I am keenly aware of my shortcomings in these books, I can say unwaveringly that this is the best I have produced thus far in the area of printed art. Technically it is stronger than anything before it, and it is also more substantive and more original."[25]

Her remarks here, of course, do not mean that her album can be treated separately from "anything before it." On the contrary, it is firmly rooted in her preceding experience with book design. *War* exemplifies the logical evolution of the futurist book, and is among its purest variants.

The modernity is treated in the album as an organism that from the depths of its being reveals a myth of its own, unknown and unparalleled, that its purpose and meaning can only be guessed. Rozanova draws strength and inspiration directly from the present, not retreating a step from her basic idea of art:

> Creation is a great act of contempt toward all that is within and outside us, toward the obvious, and a great act of attention toward that which is just beginning to take shape.
>
> . . . To produce a work of genius the artist must possess an acute awareness of reality and extraordinary will power to be able to renounce the past and avoid confusing its false, decrepit image with emerging newness.[26]

For Rozanova, as for the "futurians" poets Kruchenykh, Khlebnikov, and Mayakovsky, the theme of war arose from that same inner necessity that Kandinsky considered to be the principle criterion of art. This theme, treated symbolically, was inseparably connected with the concept of innovation and the destruction of old forms in the name of creation of the new. The struggle among the various currents in art was persistently associated with war, down to set rhetorical locutions in the manifestos of this century's first decade, such as the "Slap in the Face of Public Taste," or in the 1913 manifesto of the Union of

25.
O. Rozanova, Letter to A. Shemshurin, OR GRB, f. 339.

26.
O. Rozanova, "Suprematism I kritika," *Anarkhia* 86 (1918).

23. *BATTLE*. FROM THE PORTFOLIO *WAR* (*VOINA*), POETRY BY A. KRUCHENYKH,
LINOCUTS BY O. ROZANOVA. PETROGRAD, 1916. LINOCUT IN BLACK. 36.7 × 28.5 CM.
COURTESY OF THE JUDITH ROTHSCHILD FOUNDATION.

Youth: "we will never cease to disturb the slumber of the lazy as we enlist ever new forces in our eternally new and eternally beautiful struggle." Kandinsky was among the first to draw this parallel between the artist-creator and the mythological warrior or dragon slayer. Another leader of the Blue Rider group, Franz Marc, connected the abstract concept of war, which he approached like a heroic myth of classical antiquity, with the development of a new artistic language. The prewar poetry of the Russian futurists Khlebnikov and Kruchenykh developed a notion of war as a spiritual exploit, the conquest of the human self. The staging of *Victory Over the Sun* in 1913 represented the culmination of this idea:

> Be indignant:
> even the enemies of the Russian Futurists give them credit for their feats:
>
> Our Futurists seriously and perhaps not without reason claim the role of prophets in the present war . . . in their prophesy Wilhelm II himself in the opera is the main abductor of the sun. . . .
>
> It would not be bad if the Futurists would perform their opera again so that the public could see firsthand how raving . . . can suddenly find analogous echoes and colors in our contemporary bloody and nightmarish reality.[27]

In their attacks on traditional values and academic art, many avant-gardists underscored this parallel with expressions such as "word-shots," "revolution," "combat," and "futurist battles."

In 1913, Kandinsky created his famous *Improvisation No. 30*, in which many people perceived a prophesy of war. He himself wrote that he

27.
Kruchenykh put this passage from K. Barantsevich's article on the last page of *Secret Vices of the Academicians* (Moscow, 1915; dated 1916 on the cover).

24. *FRAGMENT FROM NEWSPAPER REPORT: DURING THE EXECUTION. . . .* FROM THE
PORTFOLIO *WAR* (*VOINA*), POETRY BY A. KRUCHENYKH, LINOCUTS BY O. ROZANO-
VA. PETROGRAD, 1916. LINOCUT IN BLACK. 37.4 x 27 CM.
COURTESY OF THE JUDITH ROTHSCHILD FOUNDATION.

anticipated the war, aware that a monstrous struggle was ripening in the
spiritual sphere. Indeed, in some sense World War I was no surprise to
the avant-garde artists; for them it merely marked a welcome boundary between epochs that presaged the end of the old times and
announced the wait for the new, a shift of traditions and cultures. The
year 1914 was to many the symbolic beginning of the new millennium.
From this point of view it is interesting to note that many artists wanted
retrospectively to connect their pre-1913 works with World War I.

War, in Rozanova's linocuts and Kruchenykh's poetry cycle, is
not only disaster and destruction, but also the agonizing birth of an
unknown, violent new age of terrible power. She intuitively expresses
her premonition of the future of Russia, which, according to Blok,
"rushed out of one revolution to look greedily into the face of
another that is perhaps even more terrible."[28] Her symbolism is subjective and elusive, free of superfluous allegorical content. Like a

28.
A. Blok, in his essay "The Flame"
("Plamen'"), first published in the
newspaper *Day* (*Den'*),
28 October 1913.

25. *FRAGMENT FROM NEWSPAPER REPORT: REMEMBERS WITH HORROR. . . .* FROM THE PORT-
FOLIO *WAR (VOINA),* POETRY BY A. KRUCHENYKH, LINOCUTS BY O. ROZANOVA. PETRO-
GRAD, 1916. LINOCUT IN GREEN, 37 x 25.7 CM.
COURTESY OF THE JUDITH ROTHSCHILD FOUNDATION.

testimony elevated to the level of an epic symbol, Rozanova's and
Kruchenykh's *War* strikingly conveys a sense of the author's active
participation. It is a poetic mythologization of the time generated by
a fantastic juxtaposition of reality, the stringent documental quality
of the wartime everyday, newspaper chronicles and the grotesque,
and original metaphors "without exclamation points and drumbeats."[29] On the folios of *War*, as in Khlebnikov's and Mayakovsky's
"war" poetry, there are iconographic motifs connected with evan-
gelical themes (even more specifically, with the Crucifixion) but it is
not they that determine the character of the work. Rozanova bases
two sheets of the *War* portfolio on lines taken directly from the newspapers, entitling them, in fact, *Fragments from Newspaper Reports* (figures
24, 25). What explodes into visual form is not poetry, but the deliberately impersonal, nameless laconic documentary discourse of the
chronicle. The word made visual freezes a composition shot through

29.
V. Khovin, "Futurism i Voina,"
Ocharovannyi strannik
6 (1914).

26. *AIRPLANES OVER THE CITY*. FROM THE PORTFOLIO *WAR* (*VOINA*), POETRY BY A. KRUCHENYKH, LINOCUTS BY O. ROZANOVA. PETROGRAD, 1916. COLLAGE, LINOCUTS IN BLACK AND RED ON GRAY PAPER. 23 X 16 CM. COURTESY OF THE JUDITH ROTHSCHILD FOUNDATION.

with dynamics and rhythm, thereby introducing a sense of the eternal and nontransitory into the general context. Taken out of their usual context these newspaper excerpts compel the viewer to listen to the genuineness of a tragedy that has been restored to the line. In an image of the execution of peaceful civilians (figure 24), which Rozanova created as an almost cinematic montage of two simultaneously depicted planes, the path of a bullet fired from a rifle emphasizes the halted eternity of the moment. In the mind of the modern-day viewer, this page may have contained allusions to Borges's story "The Secret Miracle," in which time stops for the hero as he faces the firing squad:

30.
Jorge Luis Borges, "The Secret Miracle," trans. Harriet de Onis, in *Labyrinths: Selected Stories and Other Writings*, ed. Donald A. Yates and James E. Irby (New York, 1996), 93.

The sergeant shouted the final order.

The physical universe came to a halt . . . the men who were to kill him stood motionless. The sergeant's arm eternized an unfinished gesture. On a paving stone of the courtyard a bee cast an unchanging shadow. The wind had ceased, as in a picture. . . .[30]

Thus a sparsely worded passage from a newspaper report grows into a visible tragedy viewed in horror, and a scene of death is transformed into one of immortality. That which is ordinary and usually nameless in a military chronicle can in essence never be ordinary and nameless. It is difficult to imagine a more powerful, dramatic and simple embodiment of this truth.

The theme of the victim is a central one in Rozanova's *War* linocuts, and it appears on one of the first pages in *Airplanes over the City* (figure 26). The symbolism or image of the airplane attracted many twentieth-century artists and poets, especially the futurists. David Burliuk once mentioned that Khlebnikov became interested in aviation from the point of view of "verbal creativity." Wassily Kamenskii was a pilot. Malevich created several drawings of airplanes, including his famous painting *Aviator* (1914; now in the collection of the Russian Museum). Perhaps the symbolism of the airplane represented in part the freedom of innovation and in some respect intersected with the purely Russian futurist theme of the humanized machine. In Kzuchenykh's poem it is "Man Leaping from Airplane," a flattened human hieroglyph, that oddly repeats the outline of his double, the airplane in scarlet resembles the pose of a crucified human being. This image–symbol, one that has acquired the precision of a hieroglyph, will reappear almost identically, later, in the sheets *Fragments from Newspaper Reports*, *Battle in the City*, and *Duel* (figure 28), the last of which is among the most symbolic and lyrical compositions in the album *War*. The theme echoes the Crucifixion stories of the Bible, which are most clearly referred to in the image of "Crucified by the Germans" (figure 25), in which a soldier is plunging a bayonet that looks like an ancient spear into his crucified victim. Rozanova operates with a dual reflection of reality: the immediate statement of the fact in the newspaper text and her own subjective, emotionally open reading or revelation of the text. It resembles Kruchenykh's seemingly "eyewitness testimony," which is expressed as a poetic interpretation of a line from the newspapers:

> with closed eyes
> > I saw the bullet
> it slowly
> > stole toward a kiss[31]

Although she bases the composition on documentary texts, Rozanova's work avoids becoming documentary itself, successfully

31
с закрытыми глазами
видел пулю
она тихонько
кралась к поцелую

resisting the allure and false reverence for the topical that in one way or another is experienced by all artists who turn to facts and history for their material.

In the "open eyes" of the newspaper she reads a new tragedy of the modern myth. She needs no distant associations, for the newspaper becomes the new apocalypse, and assumes the infallibility of the Bible. The daring and emotional confessional nature of her innovation is similar to that of Mayakovsky, about whom Pasternak once said: "the novelty of the time was climatically in his blood."[32]

At the time, Rozanova was likely familiar with cubist and Italian futurist collages in which real newspaper clippings were included to provide an aura of concreteness and contemporaneity . In her linocuts for *War* she does not directly follow this example, but carves her texts, as well as the picture, by hand. This is text she has read and rewrote, experienced, and suffered through; much as the futurist poets aspired in their works to restore to the word its primordial purity and power and to each sound its autonomous valence. Rozanova restores to the visual image of the word that sense of the preciousness and weight of each letter that is found in early examples of the Old Russian lubok, in which the text generates a special complex texture and organizes the compositional and rhythmical visual structure of the page. In the lubok xylography, from the middle and end of the seventeenth century, word and image are equivalent and are not separated in the perception of the artist and spectator. The most important task is to make the text an important visual element in the creation of the overall composition, so that the readability of the text is not absolutely necessary and therefore is secondary. Words are arranged in expanding squares, and are in some respect reminiscent of carved stone slabs filled with letter ornamentation; the lack of intervals between words contributes to this impression.[33]

The composition of the text in this linocut and even the script bear a resemblance to the Old Russian lubok popular prints. The textural quality of some compositions is almost analogous to that of primitive woodcuts—uneven and shaggy, and concealing imperfections that do not strike one as irritating defects but harmoniously blend into the overall structure of the work. Rozanova considered a separate table of contents and several poems by Kruchenykh that had been erroneously printed at the typographer's as one of the most serious failures in the album: "It is a pity that the main, accidental shortcoming—the verses in the table of contents—evidently cannot be

32.
Boris Pasternak, *Izbrannoe*, vol. 2 (Moscow, 1986), 233.

33.
In this connection one recalls the talented poet Nikolai Burliuk, who maintained that one and the same word "sounds different" on stone and on copper:
... the poetic word is emotional. Correspondingly, it changes its properties depending on whether it is written or printed or thought. It affects all our feelings....
The position of the text on the paper is enormously important. (Nikolai Burliuk, "Poeticheskie nachala," *Futuristy. Pervyi zhurnal russkikh futuristov* 1–2 [Moscow, 1914].)

27. *DESTRUCTION OF THE CITY*. FROM THE PORTFOLIO *WAR* (*VOINA*). POETRY BY A. KRUCHENYKH,
LINOCUTS BY O. ROZANOVA. PETROGRAD, 1916. LINOCUT IN BLACK. 36 × 27 CM.
COURTESY OF THE JUDITH ROTHSCHILD FOUNDATION.

corrected. These verses came to me later than those printed on individual sheets, and I had no possibility of printing them, but it was also
a shame to leave them out, since I thought they were no less interesting than the first ones. . . . I have no idea how to get rid of this now
and I have no way of doing so, but printing these verses at the typographer's is to my mind even worse, since they have no simple, good
fonts, the texture is entirely different, and because there are more
lines in the verses they will have to make the letters smaller, and a
conflict will arise between the earlier artistic technique of the first
verse and the later one lacking an artistic presence. . . ."[34]

Rozanova's interpretation of the lubok was probably influenced
by Kandinsky's graphics. The whole question of his impact on her
style in *War* is rather complex, but there is a fairly clear connection
with individual works of his, in particular some of the xylographies in
Klänge (1913). Kandinsky identified the engraving with lyrical poetry,
speaking of equivalences between color and music, line and rhythm,

34.
O. Rozanova, Letter to A.
Shemshurin, OR GRB, f. 339

28. *DUEL*. FROM THE PORTFOLIO *WAR* (*VOINA*), POETRY BY A. KRUCHENYKH, LINOCUTS
BY O. ROZANOVA. PETROGRAD, 1916. LINOCUT IN GREEN. 36.8 × 28.3 CM.
COURTESY OF THE JUDITH ROTHSCHILD FOUNDATION.

and object and word.[35] He and Rozanova were most probably not acquainted or in professional contact at this time, but more likely simply shared a common thematics and were moving in a similar direction. The analogy may also appear surprising in view of the fact that in late 1915 and early 1916 Rozanova's own experiments brought her to suprematism, and many of her works were done under Malevich's influence.

In *Battle* (figure 23), and particularly clearly in *Duel* (figure 28), Rozanova turns to the *Klänge* xylographies in which Kandinsky develops his arche typical motifs of the rider and battle. Themes of struggle and duel becomes the leitmotiv of her series, from the destructive battle containing the concentrated dynamics of life and the moment, expressed in the hard broken contours and erratic rhythm, to the one-on-one combat in the symbolic *Duel*, which is eternally frozen in an abstract triangular arc of rainbows. The triumphal polyphony of *The Battle in Three Spheres* plays like an apotheosis in which red is the color of the new life and regeneration.

35.
See W. Kandinsky and F. Mark, eds., *Blaue Reiter. Almanach*, new documentary edition with an introduction by Klaus Lankheit (New York, 1989), 147–87.

The theme of battle is intimately interwoven with the themes of the city and the machine in the interpretation of the Futurists, who poeticized the laconic functionality yet hidden elemental uncontrollability of the inner power of the machine, the city, and the combat.

In Rozanova's portfolio the essence, or soul, of war is embodied in battle, parallel to which there is the theme of the city—the city of evil. Empty, fantastic, and gloomy, her city, or rather her image of the urban Moloch, possesses the autonomy of a living organism. Once again she resorts to this image, attracted not only by the dynamism of its structure, but also by the special "new realism" of the life of the big city. Sometimes covertly hostile, at others, as in *Destruction of the City* (figure 27) the image seems to be a suffering, frightened creature. In one of her own poetic drafts the subject is treated as follows:

> Like a stiffened corpse
> The dead eye of the windows
> Looks blindly
> The slate-gray steed has covered
> The earth with its black mane.[36]

The death of the city is portrayed as being as tragic as human death, and there is an element of self-destruction. The eye of the spectator cannot immediately distinguish the cannons in the composition, for they seem to be a part of the city organism—the unstoppable, fateful pagan force of a rebellious machine. Here there is no place for human beings—only for projectiles exhaled by the cannons, and the sunken buildings. It is a battle of machines, elemental forces, conveyed in Kruchenykh's verses through an alliterative series of the Russian consonant sounds "zh," "z," "s"reminiscent of grinding metal:

> The iron rings, the iron
>   whistles
> Let the iron live too.[37]

Rozanova's war-torn city becomes an iron mousetrap for its human inhabitants.

The artist reduces the form of the object to a visual sign. The self-sufficiency of color, texture, and materials was a primary area of concern in the "new art" of the early part of this century. According to Rozanova's Union of Youth colleague Markov (Valdemar Matvei),

36..
Трупом застылым
Глядит незримо
Мертвое око окон
Черной гривой
Покрыл землю аспидный
        конь.

37.
Железо звенит, железо
        свистит
Дайте пожить и железу

whose 1914 book on texture gained considerable attention, each pure color pigment has its own structure, its own "skin," or texture.[38] The colors Rozanova uses—black, red and green—bring to the work a very expressive, vivid, and unique texture. Black is very contrastive and produces a strong, dynamic and uniform quality. Green, by contrast, is an abstractive, luminous, transparent nuance that yields a very plastic texture; a color that flows obediently, it does not allow clear contours but instead demands to be used in spots or color surfaces. It is found in the most symbolic and abstract pages: in the print *Facing Death*, for example, it contributes to a transparent, unreal image of the entire slain Russian corps that evokes associations with Old Russian miniatures.

Depending on how thickly the paint is applied, red has an especially varied texture. Rozanova had a strong feeling for this color and its nuances. In the portfolio it is the "color of clotted blood" in *Airplanes over the City*, while in *Battle in the City* it takes on a trembling, elevated and solemn tonality. In this latter work all three colors are combined in a carefully orchestrated polyphonic crescendo. The composition is divided into three triangular color zones. Color acquires a saturated emotional nuance as its symbolic nature comes to the fore in the dissonance of three themes. There is first the concentrated destructive power of the cavalry conveyed through the repeated staccato rhythm of bristling bayonets and teeming horsemen. The theme of the victims is rendered in a falling, mixed, erratic rhythm of green lines, and there is a red triangle rising up in a mass of flaming buildings. Red is used as a leitmotif evoking associations to blood, fire, and scarlet sunsets.

In her aspiration to register as universally as possible the motif that again and again returns to her and resonates in her mind and "credo," parallel to the painterly image Rozanova creates a poetic one of sound. In one of her poems of 1916, which is full of neologisms, she enters into a poetic dialogue with Kruchenykh.[39]

Her poetry is subject to the same style as the engravings: the visualized object is still present in them and evokes a vibration of semi-conscious recollections, allusions, and visions, but all of it is weightless and immaterial, like an unclear reflection on water. The usual link between objects in the engravings and words in the poetry has been severed. Object and word are subordinated to the same formative element of rhythm, and it is this connection that creates the organic dynamic entity of both poetry and drawing.

38.
V. Markov, *Printsipy tvorchestva v plasticheskikh iskusstvakh. Faktura* (St. Petersburg, 1914). On Markov see also I. Buzhinska, ed., *Chteniia Matveiia. Sbornik dokladov I materialov* (Riga, 1991).

39.
Rozanova's poem in the original runs:
Из убравно скатерно
Дымно четких плит
Звук копыт
Лязгает
Под подковами ломко
    Свод
    Гнет
    Стелет
Накренясь камнем
шамкает
Ломит вызкую мглу
Сумерек гнилистых
    Низ
    Верх
Стонет заревом
Стынет багряно
Рвя занавес
В небе обрызганных звезд
Рвет гам криков

29. *ABSTRACT COMPOSITION*, 1915.
COLLAGE ON PAPER. 12.5 X 8 CM.
COURTESY OF THE RUSSIAN STATE ARCHIVE OF LITERATURE AND ART.

Rozanova also finds other means of realizing and recreating her subjective vision. In *War*, color crowds out line, and by means of these color surfaces the paper collages generate a new spatial dimension.

While working on collages for the album, Rozanova experimented with what were for her new techniques and new media as she prepared for the *0.10* exhibition. She wrote Kruchenykh of her doubts, discoveries, and failures, sending him sketches of her collages (figure 30) and asking for his advice:

> I've done quite a lot of work for the exhibition. Physically and technically sometimes very difficult work due to the lack of certain tools. I'm glad that you liked my collages. Can you draw me what you have in mind?
>
> Besides compositions using various materials I'll paint some oils. But probably not more than five. . . .
>
> I'm thinking of writing Pougny in a few days, since of course he didn't get my first [letter]. . . .[40]

40.
O. Rozanova, Letter to A. Kruchenykh, 1915. Private collection, Moscow.

30. DESIGN FOR A COLLAGE ON PAPER WITH A FRAGMENT OF A TRANSRATIONAL POEM.
C. 1915. WAX CRAYON. 22 × 17.5 CM. INSCRIBED BY THE ARTIST IN BLACK INK:
RHYMES OF CONSONANTS: ZBRZHAEST ABAGATAN / ZHP.
COURTESY OF GMURZYNSKA GALLERY, COLOGNE.

41.
A. Kruchenykh, Letter to
A. Shemshurin, 19 December
1915. OR GRB, f. 339. 4. 1.

42.
A. Kruchenykh, Letter to A.
Shemshurin, [1915]. OR GRB
f. 339. 4. 1.

43.
This important publication, whose
contributors included Kazimir
Malevich and his friend and future
fellow suprematist Ivan Kliun,
was published in Moscow while
Kruchenykh was spending the
summer 1915 with Malevich at a
dacha in Kuntsevo near Moscow.
Kliun not only contributed an article but also designed the book,
which Kruchenykh had orginally
intended Rozanova to do. Her
watercolor sketch of the cover
bearing the caption "Sleepy
Whistlers" is in RGALI 1334. 1.
1309. Kruchenykh may have been
thinking of entitling the entire collection just that (after the title of
his article there) but then settled
on the final variant. "I'm already
publishing my article on style, I've
added some....
" Kruchenykh wrote Shemshurin
on 2 August (referring to one of
the sections of his article subti-
tled "Tel' ale stil' literatorov"
(A. Kruchenykh, Letters to
Shemshurin, 1915, OR GRB f. 339.
4. 1.) To symbolize their turn
toward the future the coauthors
decided to date the book "1916"
on the cover.

Theirs was a real collaboration in letters. As well, Kruchenykh shared his opinion of Rozanova's work with Shemshurin:

I'm not wasting my time here, and if all goes well I'll bring back quite a bit from Batalpashinsk!
Got some of the engravings from O. R. Overall they are simply superb! And in private life I am a severe critic. . . .[41]

Armed with Malevich's theories of nonrepresentational or "non-objective"art, with which he had become acquainted as early as the summer of 1915, Kruchenykh was working on the same problems. His work on collages of colored paper for his own album *Universal War* (it is this Rozanova was referring to when she asked him to "draw what [he had] in mind") was moving along ("I'm working a lot on the painterly side of my new book," he wrote Shemshurin in late September).[42]

Although he was far from the capital, Kruchenykh tried to keep abreast of the latest in literature and art. As usual, besides his active correspondence with his friends, he was working on a great many plans and ideas—the publication of new books, and an article for the collec-tion *The Secret Vices of the Academicians*.[43] By this time Malevich had already begun to develop his theory of suprematism (although the term itself did not yet exist), defining the new and absolutely nonrepresentational in art. He still carefully concealed these ideas from his rivals, but he shared them with his tried and true friends and collaborators Kruchenykh, Matiushin, and Kliun. "What was done unconsciously is now yielding extraordinary fruit," he wrote Matiushin in late May, 1915, about his famous drawing for the curtain of *Victory Over the Sun* (*1913*), in which he now discerned the prototype of suprematism and anticipated *Black Square*.[44]

Kruchenykh personally witnessed the birth of this new theory. He was powerfully influenced by his conversations with Malevich (which are partially reflected in their correspondence of 1915 to 1917, devoted to the quest for structural parallels between poetry and painting) and their collaboration on the book. His own thesis on the "non-objective" in poetry developed parallel to the concept of suprematist geometrical abstraction in painting. All of this is reflected in his article "Sleepy Whistlers" in *The Secret Vices*, and in his daring proposal for *Universal War*, a unique album combining transrational poetry and abstract visual forms, which a letter to Shemshurin indicates he began working on precisely at this time.[45]

The very air in the summer of 1915 seemed to be seminal and charged with Malevich's profound energy.[46] The idea of "moving beyond zero" was partially realized in the declarations by Malevich, Kliun, and Kruchenykh in *The Secret Vices of the Academicains*:

> Because they are unnecessary I reject the soul and intuition. At a public lecture on 19 February 1914 I rejected reason.
>
> I warn of the danger—now reason has locked art into a four-walled box of dimensions. . . . (K. Malevich)[47]
>
> Taking as our starting point the straight line, we have arrived at the ideally simple form: straight and round planes (in verbal art—sound and letter). The simplicity of the form also depends upon the profundity and complexity of our tasks. (I. Kliun)[48]
>
> Man already sees that the words existing before him have died, so he tries to refurbish them, turn them inside out, patch them . . .
>
> Poetry has reached an impasse, and the only honorable way out is not to use worn out images, epithets and words—to switch to transrational language. (A. Kruchenykh.)[49]

Malevich's new ideas are a prominent topic of discussion in Rozanova's and Kruchenykh's correspondence. The independence of

44.
See Malevich's letters to Matiushin published in E. F. Kovtun, *Ezhegodnik rukopisnogo otdela Pushkinskogo Doma na 1974* (Leningrad, 1976), 186.

45.
"Just now I'm preparing the coming book, perhaps by Christmas the drawings, collages, etc. will be ready." (A. Kruchenykh, *Letters to Shemshurin*, 1915, OR GRB, f. 339. 4. 1.)

46.
He again looked for support and wanted to resurrect the old "futurist trinity" with Matiushin and Kruchenykh. While *The Secret Vices* was being prepared for printing he conceived of publishing a journal, appealing to Matiushin for his cooperation: We're thinking of doing a journal and are starting to discuss the what and how of it. Since in it we intend to reduce everything to nothing we decided to call it *Zero*. We ourselves, of course, will later go beyond zero.
It would be very good if you could also offer some useful advice. . . . It would also be good if you could come here—there's a room and it's quiet. Only the menu is birch bark and lilies, with air for dessert. Thoroughly primitive conditions, but then the thing would go even better. Best wishes. Yours, K. M.
See Malevich's letters to Matiushin, in E. F. Kovtun, *Ezhegodnik*, 186.
According to Kovtun, this was the germ of the idea of publishing the suprematists' journal *Supremus*, which, however, was never realized.

47.
A. Kruchenykh, K. Malevich, and I. Kliun, *Tainye poroki Akademikov*, 31.

48.
Ibid., 29-30.

49.
Ibid.

Rozanova's views can be judged by her somewhat skeptical reaction to Malevich's and Kliun's contributions to *The Secret Vices.* Reacting to them in the same letter to Kruchenykh she writes:

> Flat colors (without the illusion of three dimensions provided by a painting) were familiar even to the ancient Greeks (urns). It is the basis of almost all *panneaux*. Relief there is in any event limited. Japanese and Chinese painting and the French nineteenth-century artists Maurice Denis, [Pierre-Cécile] Puvis de Chavannes, [Édouard] Vuillard, etc., show the same aspirations.
>
> Of Malevich I would say "he wants to seem educated and talks about unintelligible things." Moreover, in his art there is more calculation and clever posing than anywhere else. For someone else that is not a vice, but for a man who "rejected reason at a public lecture" it doesn't seem quite "it."[50]

Yet Rozanova indubitably shared the substance of these ideas. Kruchenykh's remark that she was the one who introduced transrational painting is fully applicable to her 1915 collages,[51] and her work in this area to some degree anticipated and coincided with the transition to suprematism (figure 29, plate 30). It was extremely important to her, for it was the creative laboratory whose small forms provided her with an opportunity and conditions for artistic experiment.

Rozanova created her collages for the album *War* (the cover and the composition *Airplane over the City*) after the engravings, finishing them in December 1915 upon her return from Vladimir to St. Petersburg. In them she clearly applied her recently acquired knowledge of suprematism. However, a traditionally futurist mentality dominates *Airplane over the City* (figure 26), which is without a doubt one of the most dramatic compositions of the cycle and is enhanced by new technical achievements in the areas of form and texture. On the lilac cardboard sheet are joined together three small prints—an airplane flying over a city, and the small ciphers of a man and an airplane. A black circle cut out of paper pulls together the composition and is seen as almost a three-dimensional black sphere or enormous point in inert space that is a kind of paraphrase of Malevich's *Black Square*.

The cover of the album (figure 22), by contrast, is done in a purely suprematist key and constitutes the first, classic suprematist experiment in book design. The laconicism, and solemn simplicity of the colors (white, blue, black) and shapes (rectangle, square, circle, and triangle), allow this work—perhaps Rozananova's first in the new style—to be compared with Malevich's best works at the *0.10* exhibition. Yet

50.
O. Rozanova, letter to A. Kruchenykh, 1915. Private collection, Moscow.

51.
A. Kruchenykh, "Predislovie," *Vselenskaia voina* (Petrograd, 1916), 1.

31. *WRITING DESK*, 1915.
   OIL ON CANVAS. 66 × 49 CM.
   COURTESY OF THE STATE RUSSIAN MUSEUM, ST. PETERSBURG.

there was not a single painting by Rozanova at this exhibition that could
unconditionally be called suprematist. This apparent incongruity,
however, can be explained by the fact that she came to suprematism by
way of the collage, a path that was for her logically unavoidable and
predetermined by the entire previous evolution of her art.

   The rich potential of the collage as a method explains the significant
role it played in the development of art from cubism to constructivism
and beyond, down to the "new realism" of the late twentieth century.

The collage principle underlies the very philosophy of the avant-garde, whose investigative "linguistic consciousness" aspired to penetrate reality by actively studying the internal laws of art apprehended through the internal laws of the material "as such." The first step was taken by the cubists, who focused on including fragments of real objects into painterly compositions and experimented with combining various textures and elements. In their paper collages they proceeded on the same principles as in painting. In Georges Braque's many still lifes the collage (usually of playing cards or pieces of labels or wallpaper) figures above all as a thing or object introduced into the context of the author's drawing. The cubist variant of the collage is the most classic variant of the method. It shares a certain semiotic kinship with the eighteenth- and nineteenth-century *trompe l'oeil*, which focused on a precise imitation of various textures of represented materials and objects.

In futurist collages there is a tendency to juxtapose not only the painterly surface and inserted real material details of objects (such as paper, textiles, wood, etc.), but also to place together visual images and substantial fragments of printed texts. Instead of the separate letters, numbers, and figures that are so often inserted into cubist collages, futurist compositions could contain entire newspaper columns. These newspaper clippings acquired visual expressiveness and served to indicate the reality of the present moment and incarnate "the present day." Here the typographical sign functions as a complete drawing done by a machine. Severini's 1915 collages and Carra's famous 1914 "Manifestazione interventista" are structured entirely on newspaper clippings. Handwritten patriotic war slogans were the only elements drawn over the printed text by the artists in these compositions.

This approach may be said to characterize the first stage in the evolution of the collage, before it was separated from figurative art. At first Rozanova used this technique in the same manner, borrowing from the cubists and futurists. Her *Pub (Auction)* (Plate 21), for example, is done in the manner of the classic cubo-futurist picture, including material elements such as fragments of newspapers and wallpaper, and separate letters cut from newspaper text. Alongside this there are illusionary painted images of the same elements, which, however, have now been deprived of their "object" reality and exist only in the space of the picture, so that their genuineness is "counterfeited," as it were, by the artist. Irena Bolotina, an expert on the Russian still life, notes, "It is interesting that in twentieth-century Russian art there are works, of, for example, Rozanova, which resemble the illusionist still lifes of the eighteenth century with respect to compositional principles and selection of objects (but not manner of execution). This similarity tends to be an external one. . . . The depiction of flat objects in . . . [Rozanova's *Workbox*] was a way of bringing them onto a plane and was done for formal and decorative rather than illusionistic purposes: the play with materials on the boundary of the genuine (collage) and the illusory whose meaning is precisely the destruction of the illusory world of the 'old' picture."[52]

In some of her still lifes and interiors from 1915 Rozanova exaggerates this latter device and no longer resorts to the insertion of disparate material fragments. Her compositions *Cupboard with Dishes*, *Workbox*, *Perfumery (Barbershop)* (all in the Tretyakov Gallery), *Writing Desk* (figure 31), *Room* (plate 22), and *In the Street (The "Modern" Théater)* (plate 20) are structured on the principle of collage in the sense not of a technical device but an artistic method. In these works the object or its individual details appear in a new function as a sign or pure visual form.

In Rozanova's 1915 works we find a certain "projection" of all possible future directions of her art. There is suprematism in the autonomy of planar color forms that generally constitute the background in these compositions, and there are "shoots" of *tsvetopis'* discernible in her intense interest in the translucent, semitransparent planes, depictions of glass, and the introduction of fragments of rays of light on a rainbow spectrum (as, for example, in *The "Modern" Théater*). Here in the recoding of the object or thing set in an unexpected or alien context and stripped of its usual everyday meaning, there is a foreshadowing of the future Dada.

The landscape and portrait are practically absent from her painting at this time, or more precisely, they have lost their generic specificity. One example is *The "Modern" Théater*, which is reduced to a painterly construction consisting of color planes that serve as the background for accidental objects and details caught by the eye of the passerby. Entirely absent here, however, is any futurist intonation accentuating dynamism and simultaneity. These compositions bring to mind the "alogical" period of Malevich's cubo-futurism in 1914, particularly such works as *Lady at the Poster Column* or *Englishman in Moscow*. The fragmentary visual structure of the painting and the inscriptions included in these compositions (usually a transformed painted shop

52.
I. S. Bolotina, *Problemy russkogo i sovetskogo natiurmorta*, (Moscow, 1989), 53, 57.

sign with missing letters, making it read like a line from a transrational poem) are identical. The profound analysis of transrational poetry in one of Malevich's letters to Matiushin records the elusive transition of the rational "objective" world ruled by the laws of logical meaning, to the domain of abstract form and the poetic and intuitive: "First there were no letters, there was only sound . . . out of sound came the word. Now out of the word comes sound. This return is not a step backward. Here the poet has abandoned all words and their purpose. . . . And the letter is no longer a symbol for expressing things, but a sonic note."[53]

It is fully applicable as well to the painting of this transitional period at the stage of alogism.[54] In Malevich's *Aviator* (1914), as in Rozanova's canvas *Clock and Cards* (1915), the card is among the elements of the "alogical" context. In these compositions, which consist of abstract color planes serving as the background to realistically depicted individual objects or details that seem to have been torn out of the context and to have lost their ordinary semantic connections, there is within the painterly construction a kind of metaphysical speculative picture resembling a transrational rebus made up of different, and at first glance arbitrary combination of objects and fragments offered to the spectator. In this game, however, there is no absolutely and uniquely correct, winning answer, because the rebus is not amenable to any rational mechanism, as Kruchenykh, the "creator" of transrational language, acknowledged in one of his letters: "It's a riddle. . . . The reader is above all curious and sure that the transrational means something, that is, that it makes some logical sense, which, in fact, is absent here. So that the reader is hooked on the bait—a riddle, a mystery. . . . Man . . . is secretive, greedy, a creator of mysteries. . . . Whether the artist is deliberately hiding in the soul of zaum, I don't know."[55]

Any connection between these objects transformed into empty signifiers and removed from their usual context and therefore devoid of any content of their own and open to any interpretation is irrational, free, and associative. The significance and meaning of each of them is mobile and ambivalent, and slips away and changes depending on all possible associations, personal intuition, and reminiscences of the spectator. Objects in these constructions are like words in transrational poetry: they can accumulate an entire scale of meanings, from everyday details to metaphysical symbols. Malevich's aviator holds in his hand an ace of clubs, and this card (which in fortune telling signifies a government building that depending on the situation may be interpreted as a

53.
See Malevich's letters to Matiushin, in E. F. Kovtun, *Ezhegodnik*, 186.

54.
In 1913 and 14 Malevich created the series of paintings he called *Alogism* or *Transrational Realism*. As Kovtun notes, "In using alogism Malevich tried to go beyond the boundaries of common sense. . . . What was closed to common reason would now become accessible through intuition, allowing the deliberate extraction of ideas from the unconscious. Malevich's "Cow and Violin" (1913) is the earliest manifesto of alogism. On the back of the canvas Malevich wrote: "Alogical comparison of the two forms—violin and cow—as an element in the struggle against logic, natural order, and philistine meaning and prejudice." (E. F. Kovtun, "Kazimir Malevich: His creative Path," in *Kazimir Malevich 1878–1935* [exhibition catalog] [Amsterdam, 1989], 154.)

55.
A. Kruchenykh, Letter to Shemshurin [1916], OR GRB, 339, 4, 2.

prison, a barracks, or even, more generally, military service), is read as a kind of key sign that sets a certain mood for the entire picture (especially within the historical context of World War I, which was in progress at the time). The same occurs in Rozanova's *Clock and Cards*, where the objects hover in a kind of frozen metaphorical space or reversible galaxy of signifiers and are open to endless interpretations as visual symbols, much as in the dream scenes of surrealist films, or those of early Ingmar Bergman. (It is no mere coincidence that at the Samara Art Museum, in which the picture is presently located, it was for a long time listed under the title *Gambler's Dream*.) The face of the clock, stopped a few minutes before midnight, and the three cards that seem to soar on a background of green cloth produce a contrast between the intuitive and the rational—arbitrary and elemental as the game, and eternal and immutable as time.

Rozanova depicts objects "as such," depriving them of an everyday context as though to restore to them their phenomenological and autonomous essence represented by the pure physical features of texture, form, and color. One typical still life of this sort is *Writing Desk* (figure 31), which is structured on a dual illusion. Using no materials other than paint, she cleverly "forges" the texture of various materials such as wood, cloth and paper, much in the manner of eighteenth- and nineteenth-century *trompe l'oeil*. But her imitation is very much in the mocking spirit of a naive, obvious "counterfeit" that is easily detected by the viewer.

The writing desk itself, however, is perceived as a synthesis of various things invariably associated with it in our consciousness: a book with an old-fashioned marbleized cover, sheets of paper with printed and handwritten text, a ruler, a barometer, the large black signature of the owner, a fragment of an inscription inserted into the composition (Rozanova's favorite device). All of these objects seem to be acting out before us a drama called *Writing Desk*. In the purely painterly sense, however, in these still lifes everything is reduced to the interaction of color planes. Color composes space, so that the rhythm and dynamic composition of the picture are based on the consonance of the large color planes of the background—a black square below, a red rhombus, and a brown triangle.

The formal composition in all of these works done in the style of alogism is structured with mathematical precision approaching that of a blueprint. It is especially noticeable in works such as *Cupboard with*

32. PAGE FROM KRUCHENYKH'S LETTER TO SHEMSHURIN WITH HIS OWN AND
ROZANOVA'S POEMS. 1916.
COURTESY OF THE RUSSIAN STATE LIBRARY, MANUSCRIPT DIVISION, MOSCOW.

Dishes or *Clock and Cards*, whose objects very nearly approach simple geometrical shapes. They are painted in local color without a hint of
chiaroscuro, which produces the impression of a repellent, varnished
surface resembling the texture of collages of glossy paper. The way in
which Rozanova arrives at suprematism differs substantially from that
of Malevich. She comes to geometrical abstraction through the thing
"as such" and an intent, attentive focus on its "thingly" nature, or
more precisely, on texture and color. "Abstract art has been born of a
love for color . . . figurative art, of a love for the object," she wrote in
her 1917 article "Cubism, Futurism, Suprematism." By abstracting the
very concept of "thing" and stripping it of everyday concreteness and
its logical *raison d'être* in her 1915 canvases, she came to replace the object
with color forms in her move toward suprematism.

The theory and practice of Malevich's suprematism was determined to a greater degree by rational, artificial, and logical constructs.
In its initial conception it represented his own explosive reaction to the
alogism of the preceding years, which spilled over into the "intuitive
reason" of suprematism. Malevich noted of the role of things in cubo-
futurism that they "contain a great many moments of time; their
appearance differs, so the painting of them consequently differs. All of
these appearances of the time of things and their anatomy . . . became
more important than their essence and were apprehended intuitively
as a means of constructing a picture. These means were construed in

such a way that the unexpectedness of the meeting of two anatomical structures would produce the most charged dissonance possible."[56]

The great attention to detail in seemingly realistic representations of the thing are inevitable in the structure of such a painterly construction, because what produces the necessary alogical dissonance is precisely the combination of the naturalistically depicted detail separated from the object with the cubo-futurist rupture or shift of forms. These works have nothing in common with the traditional still life: their apparent figurativeness, which misled even perceptive critics of the time such as Abram Efros, is deceptive. Efros's remarks on the feminine "intimacy" and "coziness" of Rozanova's talent, which he perceives even in the selection of themes such as *Workbox*, *Cupboard with Dishes*, and so on, is easy to refute, for all of these themes have counterparts in the cubo-futurist works of Malevich (whose style can hardly be called "intimate"). Malevich's *Vanity Case* (1913; Tretyakov Gallery, Moscow) corresponds to her *Workbox*, his *Desk and Room* (1913; Stedelijk Museum, Amsterdam) corresponds to her *Writing Desk*, and so on.

The similarity in the choice of these themes and the way in which they are treated has to do not so much with the masculinity or femininity of the artist, as Efros suggests, but with the fact that precisely such seemingly intimate motifs focused entirely on the object and thing freed of any content are so eminently suited to the avant-garde goal of overcoming the logic of figurative art. The next step in the development of this painterly construction is the transformation of the anatomical structures of things and the substitution for them of abstract shapes. This in fact occurred in Suprematism, particularly in Rozanova's 1915 collages. In her collages of colored paper she violated the traditional scheme, in which plastic forms presume a certain content.

The next stage in the evolution of the collage principle was also reflected in the ideas embodied in Marcel Duchamp's readymades and Tatlin's counter-reliefs, and in Dadaist collages, particularly the colored paper collages of Jean Arp first shown at an exhibition in Zurich in 1915,[57] and the similar works of Man Ray and Max Ernst. These works possess a special quality distinct from later Dadaist photomontages. Arp's collages are completely abstract, structured on a combination of rectangles of colored paper arranged on the page like a mosaic. Each piece of paper is endowed with the force of a simple sign or primary element. These collages, which have no documented connection with

56.
See Malevich's letters to Matiushin, in E. F. Kovtun, *Ezhegodnik*, 190–91.

57.
It is interesting to note here that the Dadaist Jean Arp, who began working with colored paper collage in 1915, was at the same time making sketches for embroideries and appliqué, and in his notes even associated these two tendencies. The coincidence with Rozanova's development, in which collage also led to suprematist sketches of embroideries and appliqué for the Verbovka exhibition, is striking. On Arp's work in embroidery and collage see Roszika Parker, *The Subversive Stitch: Embroidery and the Making of the Feminine* (London, 1989), 191:
Take the case of the Dada movement. The movement started in Zurich during 1915. Committed to combat materialism and over-intellectualisation, the artists involved rejected oil painting for all it connoted. Sophie Tauber, member of the group … introduced the painter Jean Arp to embroidery. He later wrote about their work together:
The Renaissance taught men to arrogantly exalt their reason. Modern times with their sciences and technologies have consecrated ment to megalomania. The chaos of our eras is the result of that overestimating of reason. We sought an anonymous and collective art. In 1915 Sophie Tauber and I embroidered and did collages. Jean Arp's contribution to the first issue of the magazine *DADA* in July 1917 was an embroidery, but a poem Arp wrote reveals that he valued embroidery not for its qualities as an artistic medium but for its stereotypical associations with intuition, feeling and above all with nature.

Rozanova's colored paper collages of the same period, nevertheless have a great deal in common with them, for they no longer presume the "rhetorical effect" typical of cubist and futurist works. Underlying both Arp's and Rozanova's collages are new theories of color, although Arp proceeds from Robert Delaunay's simultaneism, whereas Rozanova bases herself on Malevich's suprematism. Another interesting coincidence is that neither artist became an orthodox follower of either of these currents. Implemented in their works instead is an individual variant of a new synthesis that logically resulted in Rozanova's discovery of *tsvetopis'*, which she referred to as a new, "transfigured" color scheme.

Rozanova was working in her 1915 collages with problems similar to those treated in Pougny's and Udaltsova's abstract compositions of 1916 and 1917, and in Popova's 1917 collages. These included how to bring out the properties of color surfaces, the effect of their interaction, and the dominants of rhythm freed from figurativeness. In Rozanova's collages, paint pigments are supplanted by material possessing its own coloring; color is not only abstracted from the object but is itself "objectivized." The texture of the paper or cloth is used exclusively to characterize color, so that in the completed collage the character of the material itself becomes indifferent and the paper loses its status of "thing." Structurally her collages are in some sense close to reliefs, the color surfaces conveying a special sense of space.

These works by Rozanova, some of which are in Shemshurin's and Kruchenykh's archives, served as the prototype for the latter's album *Universal War*, published in 1916. All the elements of Kruchenykh's aesthetics—nihilism, absurdism, the dehumanization of art—propelled him in the direction of Dadaism. That movement, which is aptly captured in Georges Batailles's phrase "I am war," was in the cultural sphere an event equal in significance to the war. Operating with the elementary abstract categories of pure rhythm, form, and color, Kruchenykh creates in his book a suprematist model of a Universal War of 1985. One of the outstanding merits of the album—a Dadaist work in the fullest sense of the word—is its successful realization of Kruchenkyh's concept of collage as an artistic method transcending mere technique and capable of meteaphorically expressing the "discordant concordance" of the age. (It appeared at the same time as the works of Jean Arp's Dadaist colleagues and thirty years before Matisse's celebrated *Jazz* series.) Kruchenykh noted in the foreward:

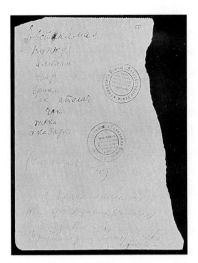

33. PAGE FROM KRUCHENYKH'S LETTER TO SHEMSHURIN WITH HIS OWN AND
ROZANOVA'S POEMS. 1916.
COURTESY OF THE RUSSIAN STATE LIBRARY, MANUSCRIPT DIVISION, MOSCOW.

These collages were born of the same source as transrational language—
the liberation of creation from unnecessary conveniences (through
nonobjectness). Transrational painting is becoming predominant. Olga
Rozanova produced some examples of it earlier, now several more artists
are working on it, including Malevich, Pougny, and others, under the
rather uninformative name of "suprematism."

But I am glad for the triumph of painting as such. . . .

Transrational language, of which I am the first representative, holds out
its hand to transrational painting.[58]

Kruchenykh interpreted suprematism in accordance with his own
ideas as transrational painting based on Malevich's notion that "the
new painterly realism, absolute creation" transformed every painted
surface into a "living, real form . . . every form is a world."[59] Form,
which is inseparably linked to the structure of the material, functions
like the self-sufficient word (*samovitoe slovo*) in transrational poetry.

The structure of the album is quite unlike that of the futurist books
discussed earlier. Perhaps all they share is an explicit impression of
being handwritten or handmade, which leads to the notion that everything touched by the hand of the artist is already a work of art.
Shemshurin aptly noted the growth of this principle, saying that "The
futurist in Goncharova depends entirely on typography. . . . In
Rozanova [the *War* album] typography has already been banished, but
there is still something mechanical, since the paint is set on one and
the same stencil. In your works, on the other hand, the only remaining mechanical feature is a pair of scissors."[60]

58.
A. Kruchenykh, "Predislovie," 1.

59.
Malevich, *Ot kubizma i futurizma k suprematizmu* (Moscow,
1916), 11.

60.
A. Shemshurin, letter to A.
Kruchenykh. This passage from a
letter located in Khardzhiev's
archive is quoted by him in his
article "Poezia I zhivopis'" in
Khardzhiev's, Malevich, and
Matiushin, *K istorii russkogo
avangarda*, 61.

The unity of word and image is embodied not in their interpenetration, but in their parallel implementation as equivalent systems subject to the same rhythm and combined within the same covers. The transrational word and the sound contained within seek out an exact equivalent in the abstract geometrical shape, in color, and in the correspondence of units of construction, so that the color form is structured on an analogy to the phoneme. Elaborating on the overall idea of the album, Kruchenykh stated in a letter, "I was not writing about a union of transrational painting and poetry, but about their generic similarity."[61]

A close examination of the work reveals two different devices in its construction. Some of the collages, despite their generally abstract expression, still allow certain allegorical associations with some sort of object, image, or phenomenon. Their principal expressive details are the contours and outlines of the color plane, which variously resemble human beings or a crown. Compositionally these collages are the least monolithic and exact. Three of the most textual (in the broadest sense) such examples are among the images of the "future world and interplanetary wars" on the last compositions of the album with contemporary themes: *Zealous Germany*, *Germany in Ashes*, and *Military State*. In Kruchenykh's description, "The military state, that is, Germany, is depicted conventionally as a spiked brass helmet and its shadow, which resembles a black panther. . . . *Germany in Ashes* and *Zealous Germany* are shown in a primitive style as an angular soldier with a head like a wooden block. First he danced aggressively, then he fell on his face and was crushed by a shrapnel shell from above."[62]

The inner necessity of such a "literary" plot runs counter to the structure of Rozanova's collages, while a number of others—*Battle of the Futurist*, *Battle with the Equator*, and *Destruction of the Gardens*—correspond typologically to them. One of the best compositions is *Heavy Artillery*, which is constructed entirely on the juxtaposition of classic geometric shapes and executed in a laconic, purely suprematist style.

Kruchenykh, incidentally, was very critical toward his own work: "In *Universal War* there is little true creativity, because it is the first experiment in (what was for me) a new style. . . !"[63] He proved to be an original and competent follower, however, and, in the words of Kirill Zdanevich, soon was "first among the Russian futurist artists in the area of paper collage."[64]

The actual authorship of the collages in *Universl War* undoubtedly belongs to Kruchenykh, but the idea of such paste-ons of colored

61.
A. Kruchenykh, Letter to Shemshurin [1916], OR GRB, f. 339. 4. 2.

62.
A. Kruchenykh, *O voinakh 1914–41 godov.* Manuscript. RGALI, f. 1334.

63.
A. Kruchenykh, Letter to Shemshurin [1916], OR GRB, f. 339, op. 4, ed. khr. 2.

64.
K. Zdanevich, "Kruchenykh kak khudozhnik," Kuranty, Tiflis, 1919, #3–4.

34. HANDWRITTEN PAGE FROM NESTROCHE WITH A POEM "HORSEWOMAN" SIGNED BY
ROZANOVA AND KRUCHENYKH. 1917.
PRIVATE ARCHIVE, MOSCOW.

paper came from Rozanova, whom he asked to edit his album in December 1915 while he was in the Caucasus.[65] Under his influence, it was during this period that she became seriously interested in transrational poetry. Kruchenykh always mentioned her among his fellow poets and followers:

> Better known to us other futurists who now (1917–1918) are appearing for the first time as poets.
>
> These are Ilya Zdanevich, Olga Rozanova, and Nikolai Chernyavsky.
>
> Olga Rozanova, the well-known artist, has written some interesting examples of transrational poetry. . . .[66]

Kruchenykh discerned and awakened the poet in Rozanova as early as late 1915, and as time went on her poetic experiments and her own attitude toward them became more and more serious. Her first reader and critic was, of course, Kruchenykh. He greeted the appearance of the new poet with sincere delight, and cunningly mystifying the credulous Shemshurin with mentions of an unnamed "new poet":

> A new, very interesting poet has been born. I'll introduce you. . . . My new poet is growing stronger, eats well, will soon be fully feathered and take flight! . . . Perhaps you will tell me your opinion of the new poet separately.

65.
Kruchenykh's authorship is fully documented in his correspondence with Shemshurin, the editor of the album. (fragments of these letters are cited in various places in the present study). The history of the publication of the album and arguments confirming Kruchenykh's authorship are discussed in detail in N. Gurianova, "Tsvetnaia klei," *Tvorchestvo* 5 (1989): 28–31. Both Russian and Western scholars have, however, until very recently attributed the design of the album entirely to Rozanova; this error has been corrected in the past few years.
See, for example, Susan Compton, *Russian Avant-Garde Books 1917–34* (Cambridge, Mass., 1991), 71: The collages for *Universal War* were attributed to Rozanova in the previous volume of this study, but books produced afterwards by Kruchenykh suggest that he made the earlier collages himself. Some copies of *1918*–published in Tiflis in 1917– include a handwritten list of previously published work, with the information: "A. Kruchenykh, Universal War, coloured collages, out of print", with no mention of Rozanova's name, though the joint authorship of other books is credited in the same list. See also R. M. Mason, *Moderne. Postmoderne*, 241–44.

66.
A. Kruchenykh, *Ozhirenie roz. O stikhakh Terent'eva i drugikh.* (Tiflis, 1918), 12–13.

It's very important to me, because he has not yet published and I want to introduce him—so, is it worth it?

As a person he is very devoted and true and orthodox.[67]

In 1917, Kruchenykh published some of Rozanova's poems in the hectograph collections *Balos* and *Nestroch'e* (figure 34). By this time their collaboration on books was already behind them, and an entirely new spiral of cocreation had begun. Fueled by the ambition to expand the boundaries of genre and discover universal, synthetic laws of creation, a paradoxical situation of mutual influence arose in which the poet was strenuously involved with the visual arts and the artist was shaping the new laws of poetry. Henceforth their collaboration took the form of a conversation (they would not produce any more joint works) in a correspondence between Moscow and the Caucasus.

Much as Rozanova "edited" Kruchenykh's collage experiments, he devoted the same serious attention to her poems (figures 32, 33). In his works of this period there are many veiled quotations of Rozanova— rhythmical discoveries that appealed to him, and unexpected consonances. *Nestroch'e* contains one untitled poem signed by both of them. The process of coauthorship can be reconstructed on the basis of the original of a letter to him, in which she jotted down her poem "The Horsewoman" ("Naezdnitsa"). He proofread the manuscript, and the result of his corrections were published in *Nestroch'e* (figure 34). He mercilessly deleted everything representational and descriptive—"elegance" of allusions and collocations about which Rozanova wrote in the same letter: "When I wrote you that I envy you for being able to take the element of horror to such a level of tension, I also mean that I am afraid that I am not free from "elegance," which is a kind of chain [*sic*]."[68]

Kruchenykh removed everything specific connected with the original image of the heroine on horseback with whom Rozanova may have associated herself. Gone as well are all logical links; of the line *naprolom opasnosti* ("breaching danger") all that remains in Kruchenykh's version is the word *prolom* ("breach, break, gap"), a word that in itself connotes alarm, danger, desperate daring. Similarly, of Rozanova's *chervonets uspekha priemliu* ("I will accept a coin of success"), only *charvonets* (an unusual spelling of the word for "coin") is left. Note here that he has changed one letter, which an orthographic mistake has given a new and resounding meaning. It is no longer *chervonets*—the prerevolutionary ten-ruble gold coin—but a sign of success that sounds in the word itself. The poet awakens the reader's subconscious and curiosity,

67.
A. Kruchenykh, letter to , 19 July 1916 (OR GRB, f. 339. 4. 2). Rozanova's authorship was determined by identifying the poem "Vul'garkh bul'varov…" of the "new poet" in Kruchenykh's letter. (OR GRB, f. 339) Under the title "Spain" ("Ispaniia"), it was published in a posthumous selection of her verses in *Iskusstvo* 4 (1919). The typed original of another poem, "zbrshest dzeban . . ." has been discovered in Rodchenko's archive among her poems ready for publication in 1919 and 1920. Kruchenykh himself mentions yet another transrational poem, "le fante chiol," in a reference to Rozanova in his book *Ozhirenie roz*. At first Rozanova probably did not wish to reveal her name. In a letter to Kruchenykh she wrote, "I'm using the pseudonym R. Vasilev. I like it better than the one you suggested. I can't think up anything myself—no talent." (Undated letter [1916], collection of Aleksandr Parnis, Moscow).

68.
O. Rozanova, letter to A. Kruchenykh, [1915], private archive, Moscow.

preventing him from enjoying the beautiful rhyme. According to his theory, art is at once work and play, and the reader must accept its rules.

Rozanova's poetry is heterogeneous. There are poems written under Kruchenykh's immediate influence, and perhaps his involuntary "pressure," that are "twins" of his works. Gradually, however, her own voice emerges—rich, musical, vivid; tender and delicate like her painting.[69] Kruchenykh distinguished several types of zaum, and these can also be found in Rozanova's works. There are first of all the poems structured on a "mistake" or incorrectness and emotionally connected with some object; such, for example, is "The Horsewoman."

Among the most vivd and "theatrical" of her works is "Spain" ("Ispaniia"), published in a posthumous selection of her poetry in the newspaper *Art* (*Iskusstvo*) in 1919. An ornament of consonances (or "goblet" of consonances, as she herself called one of these studies) is woven into the rhythm of a tarantella. The principle upon which consonantal and vocalic rhymes are structured is reminiscent of the unexpected color combinations in her paintings. Resonant, "loud" nouns here are like sound coordinates—boulevards, Hussars, Arabs, Algiers, Gitan, tarantella, rentier, antiquary, phantom, grimaces—while transrational derivatives from these, in which Rozanova lovingly polishes the sound texture, join them into a unified chain. The end of the poem contains its title poetic theme woven into the overall fabric of sounds imitating a traditional trite romance about life, love, and the "dance of death."

In "Is this a dream . . ." ("Son li to . . ."), another poem of this group focused on poetical descriptions of different shades of red, the sound and uneven rhythm of the verses resemble a fire flickering in shades of red, from ruby to scarlet.

As in her painting, Rozanova shies away from representational, figurative, obvious images, reminiscences or objects. In "Gasta—aluminum bowl" ("Gasta—aliuminovaia chasha") she creates new names for objects as a child would do.[70] The main feature of her poetry is its inimatible tonality rather than the visually shaped image of the verses (in which Kruchenykh was so interested at the time—his visual poetry of 1916–1917 are often called "quiet," "soundless" suprematist zaum).

Typically, Rozanova was very casual about jotting down poetry, whether by hand or on a typewriter, as if she had forgotten her artistic experience. Judging by her letter answering him, in 1915 Kruchenykh wrote a work called "Poem of Numbers" ("Poema tsifr").

69.
On Rozanova's poetry see Janacek, *Zaum*, 181–95, and N. Gurianova, "Aleksei Kruchenykh i Olga Rozanova: Vzaimosviaz' poezii I zhivopisi v russkom futurizme," *Europa Orientalis* 11 (1992): 49–108. The latter work includes as an appendix a selection of Rozanova's poems, many of them published for the first time. See also O. Rozanova, *Stikhi* (Moscow, 1997), a small, reproduced collection of one hundred copies, for bibliophiles.

70.
The typed original of the poem is in the A. Rodchenko and V. Stepanova archive, and published in N. Gurianova, "Aleksei Kruchenykh Olga Rozanova," 105.

71.

O. Rozanova, letter to Kruchenykh, cited by Khardzhiev in "Poezia I zhivopis'," 57.

72.

In the same letter to Kruchenykh in which she included "The Horsewoman" there is another fragment of an untitled poem designated in parentheses as "abstract":

af - arrest

ard - ag - gest

dar - khim

Lamanee

Shal - om - ezd

Mim.

Certain poetic studies of this group were originally structured on simple imitations of various sounds. One such interesting example appears in her manuscripts almost unchanged three times, but each time with a new title, which makes the poem itself sound different. In the first variant, entitled "Caucasian Etude" ("Kavkazkii etiud"), the sound series seems to be a simple imitation of Caucasian speech. (There is an analogy in "Finland," one of Guro's first transrational poems, structured on the principle of onomatopoeia.) In the second variant a "mistake" is introduced into the invented title "Crimesian" ("Krymskaia")—a grammatically incorrectly formed adjective from the noun "Crimea." Here there is a kind of semi-allusion to mystify the reader. Finally, in the third variant, the title undergoes its last metamorphosis and becomes "Kromkaia," a transrational word. The ambivalent "riddle" it contains evokes a number of individual, particular associations. These changes in title place the poem itself into an entirely different set of coordinates, as from an onomatopoetic work it takes on a transrational, self-sufficient quality. Liberated from all logical motivation, the sound series is apprehended as purified sound "as such."

This example of soundless visual poetry, which was to have been designed by Rozanova, has been lost. Apropos of "regarding poetry as pure graphics" she wrote him in August 1916, "I think this is interesting as an individual case, one aspect of poetry, but not the entire art of it as a whole, since poetry is not only beheld, but also read aloud. . . ."[71]

This quality is especially prominent in the "second" type of zaum that may be distinguished in her poetry, which consists of abstract poetic forms structured on the principle of euphony.

Even in the paintings from her final "abstract" period of 1916 to 1918, Rozanova did both suprematist works and "real" (as she called them) paintings from nature. The same process—working simultaneously in various styles—also takes place in her poetry.[72]

TRANSFIGURATION
exploring color

Olga Rozanova's individual style, and her poetic yet rational, profoundly professional and thoughtful interpretation of key problems of avant-garde painting, offer new insights into the overall development of the theory of color in twentieth-century abstract art.[1] Her own theory of color, in which she distanced herself from Malevich's suprematism, was logically concluded in her discovery in 1916–1917 of *tsvetopis'*. A series of paintings were thus labeled at her posthumous exhibition (December 1918–January 1919).[2] Probably belonging here as well is the abstract composition from the Baku Museum of Fine Arts (Azerbaijan) (plate 28) in which a deep philosophical symbolism and the asceticism of suprematism are combined with the new "liberated" (her term) color. Literally translated, *tsvetopis'* means "color painting." It is difficult to say whether it was Rozanova who coined the term, but it is interesting to note that together with *svetopis'* ("light painting, painting in light," in connection with photography), it occurs in Khlebnikov's manuscripts in the 1910s. Rozanova's

1.
The typological parallels between Rozanova's color compositions and postwar abstract expressionism (and the works of Mark Rothko and Barnett Newman) may seem at first glance exaggerated, but in fact they are well founded and deserving of further research. See *Russian Avant-Garde Art: The George Costakis Collection*, 54, and also the exhibition catalogu: Marc Rosenthal, *Abstraction in the Twentieth Century: Total Risk, Freedom, Discipline* (New York, 1966), 271.

2.
Gosudarstvennaia vystavka. Posmertnaia vystavka kartin i risunkov O. V. Rozanovoi. Katalog. (Moscow, 1919).

interest at this time in the theory of color was quite logical, since color has always been a central concern in the theory and practice of abstract painting; suffice it to mention the experiments in this area of Kandinsky, Robert Delaunay, Yakulov, Guro, Matiushin, and Kliun in this century's second and third decades. At the *Tenth State Exhibition: Nonobjective Art and Suprematism*, in 1919, after Rozanova's death, indeed a boundary was drawn between suprematism and abstract works focused entirely on the experiments with color. (Even Malevich remarked in this exhibition's catalog on the problem of color in suprematism.) Besides Rozanova's works, the exhibition featured color compositions by Kliun, Menkov, Rodchenko, and Aleksander Vesnin, and it is worth noting that followers of Malevich such as Menkov and Kliun, who also exhibited Suprematist works, distinguished these in the catalog from their own color abstractions.

Varvara Stepanova, who described the posthumous exhibition from the point of view of a professional artist sincerely and deeply interested in Rozanova's work, noted that "Rozanova's suprematism is opposite that of Malevich, who constructs his works on the basis of square forms. Rozanova uses color instead. In Malevich color exists only to distinguish one plane from another, whereas in Rozanova a composition serves to reveal the full potential of color on a painterly surface. To suprematism she contributed a suprematism of painting, not of the square. Of special interest is the room containing her suprematist works and the abstract works of her final period. Here, unlike other periods, color does not play upon the brilliance of its nuances, but is stripped to its essence. These pictures are structured on mutual color relationships. . . ."[3]

Rozanova's essay "Cubism, Futurism, Suprematism" partially expresses her ideas on the nature of color and its function in abstract art:

> We respond optically to any painted surface, we see it as color. But as we look at the painted object, we see this or that color within the dimensions of the surface it is occupying (the pink blush of the apple, these green roofs) as well as in connection with the material nature of the object (its construction, its pigment quality, etc.). In this way we materialize the immaterial essence of the color. . . .
>
> The texture of the material gets in the way of the probable nature of color.
>
> It is a surrogate for pure painting.
>
> . . . texture, imitating material . . . impeded the creation of painting in which color, not imitation, is the aim and objective.[4]

3.
Varst (V. Stepanova), "Vystavka O. Rozanovoi," *Iskusstvo* 4 (22 February 1919).

4.
Rozanova, "Cubism..." in this volume, 197.

35. SKETCHES, C. 1916.
    PENCIL. 29.2 × 25 CM.
    COURTESY OF A. RODCHENKO AND V. STEPANOVA ARCHIVE, MOSCOW.

This passage clearly shows why she turned to collages of materials possessing a minimum texture such as transparent colored paper. In these works, which generally eschew elements of different textures, the combination of color planes creates a special sense of plastic unity and wholeness. In constructing her collages Rozanova in some sense also approaches the relief (as was mentioned in previous chapters, she was in fact at this time experimenting in that area).[5] Underscoring the two-dimensional nature of her suprematism in painting (in contrast to Malevich's spatial departure into a "new dimension"), Rozanova did not reject but also did not accentuate the fact that the sum of the painterly planes of different forms creates the illusion of a sculpted relief, an illusion that seems to issue from within the planar system itself. An unpublished watercolor sketch (c. 1916, 19.4 × 11 cm. Fedorovsky collection, Berlin) of a curious composition depicting a kind of semispherical three-dimensional form could quite easily serve as a draft of a relief. As such, it sheds some light on Rozanova's work in this genre. The composition—which gravitates toward three-dimensionality and, besides the semispherical black-and-white center, consists of planes in semitransparent light green, dark green, black, violet and brown tones that seem to

5.
I have in mind here the reliefs "Automobile" and "Bicyclist," and two compositions that have not survived of "clay and crystal objects." These two *Compositions* were shown at the *Exhibition of Leftist Trends* at the Dobychina Art Bureau. See *Vystavka kartin Levykh Techenii* (Petrograd 1915), catalog nos. 91–92.

hover and touch in space—is very reminiscent of her collages of colored paper. The margin of the drawing is covered in notes such as "detach and raise figure." Experts on the Russian avant-garde as different as Larisa Zhadova and Christina Lodder emphasize the connection between the appearance of the suprematist relief in some of Rozanova's, Pougny's, and Kliun's works and the development of the collage in Russia. As Lodder notes, "The collage technique has its own history in Russian art independent of Tatlin."[6] And Zhadova remarks in her analysis of Rozanova's collages and reliefs that "Rozanova cleverly combined abstract color work with painting, and a sense of spaciousness with a concrete approach and a tactile treatment of the medium in dealing with individual elements of her composition. Matiushin described her painted and sculptured reliefs—abstract work in various materials—as 'jolly things for junior Martians.'" She goes on to describe the occasional use of the relief by Rozanova and Pougny: "The curious reliefs (or 'painted sculptures') which appeared among Puni's as well as Rozanova's works at the *0.10* exhibition . . . are important because they foreshadow Suprematism's advance into real space. They also point to a junction with Constructivism and the possibility of a fruitful combined Suprematist-Constructivist movement in the future."[7]

In contrast to Malevich's "surface in general," Rozanova was most interested in the compositions of structures and the individual color-form internal kinetic tension the artist attempts to bring out.

As is well known, Malevich regarded suprematism as a "dominance" *over* the reality of earthly life (a meaning he concealed even in the very name of his theory)—the liberation of the spirit, a new cosmic perception of universal laws. According to Malevich and his followers, suprematism was to effect a synthesis of painting, poetry, music and architecture. Here we find expressed with new force the nostalgia of the avant-garde for universalism and a new "great" style capable of uniting all forms of art.

Upon moving for good to Moscow in late 1916, Rozanova became an active member of Malevich's Supremus (from this time on, she participated in all exhibitions "under the flag" of this group).[8] Both in her painting and in her articles she enthusiastically developed new ideas of "creating from nothing," as Berdiaev ironically and aptly defined the spirit of suprematism: "brand-new currents such as suprematism are incisively formulating the long-since-matured need to free once and for all the purely creative act from the power of the natural objective world. . . . This is not only the liberation of art from

6.
Christina Lodder, *Russian Constructivism* (New Haven, Conn.: 1985), 9.

7.
Larissa Zhadova, *Malevich: Suprematism and Revolution in ussian Art, 1910–1930* (London, 1982), 63, 65.

8.
However Rozanova was invited to participate in the famous Tatlin's *Store* exhibition in Moscow in 1916 but was not able to send her works in time: "The Muscovites invited me to take part in their exhibition *The Store*, but rail transport is so slow these days that I couldn't send any pictures." (Letter of O. Rozanova to A. Shemnshurin, 31 March 1916. OR GRB, f. 339. 5. 14.)

figurative and narrative qualities, but a liberation, based on creation from nothing, from the entire created world."[9]

Born again in the philosophy of suprematism (if it is in general permissible to combine these two notions) was the great illusion of "life-building," which aspired to generate the "creation of new life" and new beauty. To a considerable extent, it also carried further the aspiration of the cubo-futurists of to discover the laws unifying the new "liberated" painting, poetry, and music.

Malevich and his group intended to plant the first seeds of this universal "creation of new life" in the journal *Supremus*. Rozanova described the proposed publication to Matiushin in a letter as a "strictly partisan" periodical to which would contribute the members of Supremus—Udaltsova, Popova, Kliun, Menkov, Archipenko, Rozanova, Vera Pestel, Natalia M. Davydova, and others: "Its program: Suprematism (in Painting, Sculpture, Architecture, Music, the New Theater, and so on). Articles, a Chronicle, letters, aphorisms, poetry, reproductions of Suprematist pictures and applied art. Articles of a scholarly, artistic-scholarly nature, etc."[10]

The first issue of the journal never appeared, although practically all of its contents were ready for printing. Among other contributions by different authors, these included Matiushin's article "On the Old and New in Music," Malevich's article on suprematism, Rozanova's "Cubism, Futurism, Suprematism," Kruchenykh's poetry, and a revised version of his "Declaration of the Word as Such."[11] To this text, which Kruchenykh reworked in 1917, he added two new points: one proclaimed the "highest and definitive universality and economy (*eko-khud*)" of transrational poetry, while in the other he attempted to illustrate the process of the creative poetic act, concluding it with the formula "in music—the sound, in painting—color, in poetry—the letter (thought = vision + sound + line + color)."[12]

Kruchenykh enlisted Rozanova to help him in his attempt to test his theory in some models of visual poetry, proposing that she do her own graphic sketches of the poems, and, in the capacity of painter color them. In Shemshurin's archive there are several unique pages of "color poetry in which the word, the line and the drawing have fused, so that the impressions conveyed by one or the other are not separated by time and space."[13] These sketches were intended for Kruchenykh and Rozanova's book, which was, however, never published (figure 36, 37). (Kruchenykh used some of the black-and-white variants of

9.
Nikolai Berdiaev, *Krizis iskusstva*, 14–15.

10.
Letter of O. Rozanova to M. Matiushin, May 1917. IRLI, f. 656.

11.
See Part 2 of this book, "A Chronology of the Life and the Works of Olga Rozanova," 167–69.

12.
Iz Literaturnogo naslediia Kruchenykh, 203–04.

13.
Letter of A. Kruchenykh to A. Shemshurin, 1916. OR GRB, f.339. 4. 2.

these compositions in his book *Learn, Arters!* (*Uchites' khudogi*), designed by Kirill Zdanevich.) Kruchenykh wrote that he himself "merely outlined approximately how the drawing was to be combined with letters. Olga Rozanova carefully redrew and colored it, and there you have the sketches of my drafts. . . . Perhaps in that (colored) form we will somehow manage to publish them."[14]

"The following is ready for publication," Rozanova wrote to Nadezhda Udaltsova,

> 1. my article
> 2. Kruchenykh's play
> 3. "Declaration of the Word"
> 4. the poetry collection *Balos* and
> 5. *Blue Eggs*

> My two poems are here as well; tell Malevich that I don't object to including them. . . .[15]

Under the direct influence of Malevich (and mindful of Marinetti's experiment with "sign" poetry), during this period Kruchenykh became interested in "mute" poetry that was not intended to be read aloud or recited, but to be apprehended purely visually. As early as 1916 Malevich (who also wrote poetry himself) thought that "the new poets have waged a struggle with the thought which has enslaved the free letter: the letter is no longer a sign for expressing things, but an audial note (not a musical one). And this note-letter may even be more delicate and expressive than musical notes . . . we tear the letter out of the line, out of one direction, and give it the possibility of free movement. . . . Consequently, we arrive at . . . a distribution of masses of letter-sounds in space which resembles that in suprematist painting."[16]

It is important to note here that Malevich is speaking of suprematism only in connection with the visual poetry. Like Kruchenykh, he presumes an analogy between the phoneme and the color form, between sound and color. In his remarks on poetry Malevich is thinking not in time but in space, comparing the page of a book to the surface of a canvas on which are arranged, in his own words, "compositions of verbal masses." As he presented his ideas to Kruchenykh, "letters in the new poetry are bereft of their primordial functions, and the poet fills them, so that these groups of accumulations result in "bumgch," "ollos," "achki," "oblygglamgly." In this last "oblyg" of yours there is a great mass of sound that can be unrolled in which the final

14.
Ibid.

15.
See Part 2, "A Chronology of the Life and the Works of Olga Rozanova," 168.

16.
K. Malevich, "Pis'ma k M. V. Matiushinu," in E.F. Kovtun, ed., *Ezhegodnik*, 190–191.

36. O. ROZANOVA, A. KRUCHENYKH. VISUAL POETRY.
1916. BLACK INK, WATERCOLOR. 17 x 7.5 CM.
COURTESY OF THE RUSSIAN STATE LIBRARY,
MANUSCRIPT DIVISION, MOSCOW.

37. O. ROZANOVA, A. KRUCHENYKH. VISUAL POETRY,
1916. BLACK INK, WATERCOLOR. 18 x 6 CM.
COUTESY OF THE RUSSIAN STATE LIBRARY,
MANUSCRIPT DIVISION, MOSCOW.

letters deliver a powerful blow . . . so that letter groups can appear on
the page in various directions, as in suprematist painting."[17]

Rozanova's poetry under discussion here is dominated by the
"bared" device of euphonic zaum corresponding to the "intuitive reason"
of suprematism. It is interesting to note that the number of signs in the
sound series of her works is the same as that in the color spectrum of
some of her 1916 paintings—usually fifteen to seventeen sounds (or
colors) used in both her abstract poetical and her painterly compositions.

These compositions are unusually musical. Her transrational
poetry is always based on two or three phonemes that she varies and
arranges, playing on "vocalic" and "consonantal" rhymes, much as in
a musical étude. In her suprematism the same phenomenon occurs
with color, although on spatial rather than temporal coordinates. Her
suprematist works have the same compositional completeness and
uniform rhythm: the basic color forms are endlessly reflected in
supplemental, fragmentary forms filling space.

17.
K. Malevich. Letter to
Kruchenykh, [1916]. Private
archive, Moscow.

As we now move on to an analysis of Rozanova's abstract painting, it should be noted that these works are not uniform, as within her suprematist period, in 1915 to 1917, it is possible to distinguish several basic typological groups linked to each other by stylistic similarities. First of all, there is a set of works with a limited palette employing simple, lapidary forms (usually rectangles), or rather, broad, rich planes of color that seem to stick to the surface of the canvas. Such is the work *Suprematism* (c. 1917. Oil on canvas 39 x 31 cm), from the Tagil Art Museum, which uses an elementary structure of color-form of the three primary colors blue, red and yellow, and the *Abstract Composition* (figure 38) from the Russian Museum, whose painterly theme consists in a dissonant resonance of red and yellow (dissonance became a key concept in Malevich's Suprematism). In these works there is a very strong sense of a solid, heavy, color "mass." Allowing for the basic two-dimensionality of these compositions that distinguishes them from Malevich's spatiality (Rozanova thought that the flat reflective surface of the painting served at its best to convey a color), they are rather different from the initial stage of suprematism, although they approach the reserved color spectrum of Malevich's early suprematism.

The next and most extensive group in Rozanova's suprematist works consists of paintings in which her gift for color found its fullest expression. It was in these pictures, such as the suprematist compositions from the Nizhny Novgorod, Alma-Ata, Ekaterinburg (plate 26), and Slobodskoi museums, that she created her own special variant of suprematism based on the dominant role of color.

In her aforementioned article "Cubism, Futurism, Suprematism," most of which is devoted to color in abstract art, Rozanova enters into a "dialogue" with Malevich, in many respects basing herself on his theory and repeating a number of his positions on the sources and evolution of representational and nonrepresentational art.[18] If for Malevich however, "paint is the main thing," for Rozanova all abstract art is born of a "love of color."

These two words "paint" and "color" are by no means the synonyms they may appear to be at first glance, for in them is concentrated the essence of Malevich's and Rozanova's different and opposite approaches to abstract art.

When Malevich speaks of paint as the most important element in suprematism, he is saying that the concrete materiality of pigment is the principal means of expression (together with form and line), or the

18.
Here and following Malevich is cited from his book *Ot kubizma k suprematizmu. Novyi zhivopisnyi realizm* in K. Malevich, *Sobranie Sochinenii*, 5 vols., ed. A. Shatskikh and A. Sarabianov, (Moscow, 1995), vol. 1, 41, 50.

"instrument" of the artist. In his system these means are transformed and become the subjects or "components" of his painting. Even when he uses the word "color" in his writings ("the self-sufficient components of painting are color and texture") he still means "paint," the materiality of color contingent on texture. Moreover, speaking in one article about the spectrum of suprematist colors, which he divides into basic and supplemental, in most cases he simply gives the name of a particular pigment.

For Rozanova, by contrast, the essence of color is "in general nonmaterial." Color is not an instrument but a universal goal that the artist strives to achieve by all means of expression at her disposal: "Painterly form is the nature of realizing (embodying) color on a plane with the aid of material paints."[19] This approach to the question is reminiscent of many points in Kandinsky's theory, particularly his notion of abstract, symbolic color. In her article Rozanova speaks of color not as a property of the object or form, but as an independent quality that is not connected with any object; whence logically follows her statement that the texture of a material, like its volume and the atmosphere, contaminate the nature of color: "Realistic painting is concerned precisely with tone and not with color."[20] She justifies suprematism's rejection of "real forms" with the argument that they "do not hold color, which dissipates and fades," and perceives the merit of futurism not so much in the "beauty of speed" and a "new expression of contemporary life" (the view of the Italian futurists, and after them Malevich) as in the fact that these currents "removed color from the confines of trivial forms."[21] According to her, the task of suprematism is "to create quality of form in connection with quality of color," not the reverse, for she considers form as merely derivative from color.[22] (Later, in her final tsvetopis' period, in late 1916 and into 1918, she would arrive at the destruction of the pure geometrical form.) This is yet another important distinction between her and Malevich, who acknowledged the dominant role of "painterly form as such."

The disparity between Rozanova's and Malevich's methods will become obvious if we do a comparative analysis of two compositions with the same theme—Airplane Flying.[23] Three colors figure in Malevich's work: red, yellow, and black on a white background symbolizing the "nothing" of outer space. Corresponding to these are variations of three forms hovering in this space—a rectangle, a square, and a narrow

19.
Rozanova, "Cubism...",
in this volume, 199.

20.
Ibid., 198.

21.
Ibid., 195.

22.
Ibid., 199.

23.
See K. Malevich, Airplane Flying,
1915. Oil on canvas, 57.3 x 48.3,
The Museum of Modern Art,
New York.

strip stretched almost into a line. Only at one point does one form intersect another.

Seventeen colors—basic, supplemental and mixed—"resound" in Rozanova's composition (plate 25). The texture of the painted surfaces is not uniform, and in places brush strokes and thinning layers of paint are visible. Various geometricized shapes consisting of joined parts of triangles, circles, rectangles and other segments intersect each other in a rhythmical dissonance that seems to have exploded, scattering them around the center with enormous centrifugal force. Color variety is justified by a corresponding variety of painterly forms. On the background of this dynamic composition, three huge colored planes—blue, light blue, and yellow—have been united into a single static figure. They seem to have crowded out the white background, which remains only as narrow strips along the edges of the canvas. The structure of these three surfaces is somehow reminiscent of Popova's *Painterly architectonics*, particularly her 1917 picture with black, red, and gray forms from the Tretyakov Gallery, of which Sarabianov remarked, "Popova has selected three 'figures,' but has combined or 'tied' them into a kind of inseparable whole. . . . In contrast to Malevich, she concentrates painterly planes and fills in forms. At the very center is an overall 'figure' consisting of three parts. The edge of each of these is at some distance from the frame. . . . They stop, so to speak, and stand there supported on the corners of the canvas to form something resembling a pyramid."[24]

At the same time, the foreground of Rozanova's picture provides a strong contrast to all of these statics, and the dissonance dominating her structures constitutes the principal difference between her works and Popova's architectonics, which "seem to overcome the chaos of reality and to restore harmony."[25] Unlike Popova, in whose works color emerges in connection with the plastic, almost sculpted form of her architectonics, and unlike Malevich, who subordinates color to the scale and size of space in his pictures, Rozanova achieves a special painterly effect through contrast, dissonance, and sudden harmonies of color combinations determined by rhythm, dynamics, and mood (like sound in music). Classic examples are her two works *Suprematism* (1916. Oil on canvas, 66.5 x 48.5 cm. Nizhny Novgorod Art Museum) and *Suprematism* (1916. Oil on canvas, 55 x 36 cm. State Kazakh Museum) from Alma-Ata. The latter composition, one of the most atectonic in construction and rhythmically tense and expressive, might be called an example of

24.
D. V. Sarabianov, "Stankovaia zhivopis' i grafika L. S. Popovoi," in: *L. S. Popova: Katalog vystavki proizvedenii k stoletiiu so dnia rozhdeniia* (Moscow, 1990), 56.

25.
Ibid. 57.

1. *IN A CAFE*, C. 1911-1912.
   OIL ON CANVAS. 61 x 83 CM. COURTESY OF THE STATE RUSSIAN MUSEUM, ST. PETERSBURG.

2. *CAFE*. 1911.
   OIL ON CANVAS. 36 x 42.8 CM. COURTESY OF THE STATE RUSSIAN MUSEUM, ST. PETERSBURG.

3. *ON THE BOULEVARD.* 1911.
OIL ON CANVAS. 36.5 x 56.5 CM. COURTESY OF SAMARA ART MUSEUM.

4. *PORTRAIT OF A LADY IN PINK.* (ANNA ROZANOVA, THE ARTIST'S SISTER), C. 1911–1912.
OIL ON CANVAS. 113 x 139 CM. COURTESY OF MUSEUM OF FINE ARTS, EKATERINBURG.

5. *PORTRAIT OF LADY IN GREEN DRESS.* (E. V. ROZANOVA, THE ARTIST'S MOTHER), 1912.
OIL ON CANVAS. 140 x 89 CM. COURTESY OF ASTRAKHAN STATE PICTURE GALLERY.

6. *STILL LIFE WITH A VASE*, C. 1912—1913.
OIL ON CANVAS. 109 x 101.5 CM. COURTESY OF SAMARA ART MUSEUM.

7. *STILL LIFE*, 1912.

OIL ON CANVAS. 71 x 61 CM. COURTESY OF THE RADISHCHEV MUSEUM OF FINE ARTS, SARATOV.

8. *THE FACTORY AND THE BRIDGE*, 1913.
OIL ON CANVAS. 83.2 x 61.6 CM. COURTESY OF THE MUSEUM OF MODERN ART, NEW YORK. THE RIKLIS
COLLECTION OF MCCRORY CORPORATION PHOTOGRAPH. © THE MUSEUM OF MODERN ART, NEW YORK.

9. *BUILDING SITE*, 1913.

OIL ON CANVAS. 91.5 x 110 CM. COURTESY OF SAMARA ART MUSEUM.

10. *CITYSCAPE (FIRE IN THE CITY)*. C. 1913—1914.
OIL ON TINPLATE. 71 x 71 CM. COURTESY OF SAMARA ART MUSEUM.

11. *CITYSCAPE (EMBANKMENT)*, 1913.
OIL ON CARDBOARD. 66 x 51,3 CM. COURTESY OF THE THYSSEN-BORNEMISZA COLLECTION.

12–13. ILLUSTRATIONS FOR *DUCK'S NEST . . . OF BAD WORDS* (*UTINOE GNEZDYSHKO . . . DURNYKH SLOV*),
BY A. KRUCHENYKH, ST. PETERSBURG, 1913.

LITHOGRAPHS, HAND COLORED WITH WATERCOLOR AND GOUACHE ON TAN PAPER. COURTESY OF THE
JUDITH ROTHSCHILD FOUNDATION. PHOTOGRAPHY BY DAVID HEALD.

14. *PEGASUS*. ILLUSTRATION FOR *EXPLODITY!* (*VZORVAL!*) BY A. KRUCHENYKH, SECOND EDITION, ST. PETERSBURG, 1914
LITHOGRAPH, HAND COLORED WITH WATERCOLOR AND BRONZE PAINT ON GRAY PAPER. 17 x 12 CM.
COURTESY OF THE STATE MAYAKOVSKY MUSEUM, MOSCOW.

15. SKETCH FOR THE PAINTING *BOOKS AND CARDS* (OIL ON CANVAS, 62 x 38 CM, MUSEUM OF FINE ARTS, KRASNODAR. THIS PAINTING WAS ERRONEOUSLY LISTED IN THE MUSEUM INVENTORY AS "SIDEBOARD WITH DISHES"). 1915.
PENCIL, GOUACHE. 19 x 11 CM. COURTESY OF ALEKSANDR FEDOROVSKY, BERLIN.

16. *QUEEN OF SPADES*. FROM THE SERIES *PLAYING CARDS*, C. 1915.
OIL ON CANVAS. 77.5 x 61.5 CM. COURTESY OF MUSEUM OF FINE ARTS, SIMBIRSK.

17. *KING OF CLUBS.* FROM THE SERIES
PLAYING CARDS, C. 1915.
OIL ON CANVAS. 80 × 72 CM.
COURTESY OF REGIONAL MUSEUM,
SLOBODSKOI.

18. *QUEEN OF DIAMONDS.* FROM THE
SERIES *PLAYNG CARDS.* C. 1915.
OIL ON CANVAS. 81 × 64 CM.
COURTESY OF PRIVATE COLLECTION,
ST. PETERSBURG

19. *JACK OF HEARTS*. FROM THE SERIES *PLAYING CARDS*, C. 1915.
OIL ON CANVAS. 80 x 65 CM. COURTESY OF REGIONAL MUSEUM, SLOBODSKOI.

20. *THE "MODERNE" MOVIE THEATER (ON THE STREET)*, 1915.
OIL ON CANVAS. 101 × 77 CM. COURTESY OF REGIONAL MUSEUM, SLOBODSKOI.

21. *PUB (AUCTION)*, 1914.

OIL ON CANVAS. 84 x 66 CM. COURTESY OF MUSEUM OF FINE ARTS, KOSTROMA.

22. *ROOM* (*INTERIOR*), 1915.
   OIL ON CANVAS. 100 x 77 CM. COURTESY OF MUSEUM OF FINE ARTS, KRASNODAR.

23. SKETCH FOR AN ABSTRACT COLLAGE ON PAPER, 1915.
WAXCRAYON, 21.5 x 16.7 CM. PRIVATE COLLECTION, MOSCOW.

24. SUPREMATISM, 1916.
OIL ON CANVAS. 71 x 49 CM. COURTESY OF REGIONAL MUSEUM, SLOBODSKOI.

25. *SUPREMATISM (FLIGHT OF AN AIRPLANE)*, 1916.
OIL ON CANVAS. 118 × 101 CM. COURTESY OF SAMARA ART MUSEUM.

26. *SUPREMATISM*, 1916.
OIL ON CANVAS. 90 x 74 CM. COURTESY OF MUSEUM OF FINE ARTS, EKATERINBURG.

27. *ABSTRACT COMPOSITION* (COLOR-PAINTING). C. 1916–1917.
OIL ON CANVAS. 71 x 64 CM. COURTESY OF MUSEUM OF FINE ARTS, SIMBIRSK.

28. *ABSTRACT COMPOSITION* (COLOR-PAINTING), C. 1917.
OIL ON CANVAS. 84.5 x 62 CM. COURTESY OF MUSEUM OF FINE ARTS, BAKU.

29. *GREEN STRIPE*, 1917.

OIL ON CANVAS. 71.5 x 49 CM. COURTESY OF ROSTOV-IAROSLAVL MUSEUM OF ARCHITECTURE AND ART, ROSTOV.

30. *ABSTRACT COMPOSITION*, 1915.

COLLAGE ON PAPER. 22.5 x 15 CM. COURTESY OF THE STATE RUSSIAN ARCHIVE OF LITERATURE AND ART.

31. *ABSTRACT COMPOSITION* (COLOR-PAINTING), 1917.
    OIL ON CANVAS. 58 x 44 CM. COURTESY OF THE STATE RUSSIAN MUSEUM, ST. PETERSBURG

32. *SUPREMATIST DESIGN,* 1916.
    BLACK INK, WATERCOLOR OVER PENCIL. 25.1 x 16.8 CM. SIGNED IN PENCIL, *Ольга Розанова*; ERASED
    THROUGH STILL LEGIBLE INSCRIPTION IN PENCIL AT BOTTOM CENTER, *Декоративный мотив.* COURTESY
    OF THE JUDITH ROTHSCHILD FOUNDATION.

33. SUPREMATIST SHAWL DESIGN, 1917.
BLACK INK, WATERCOLOR. 32.5 x 32.5 CM. COURTESY OF A. RODCHENKO AND V. STEPANOVA ARCHIVE,
MOSCOW.

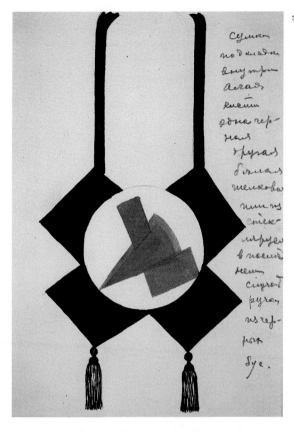

34. SUPREMATIST BAG. DESIGN FOR
    AN EMBROIDERY, 1917.
    BLACK INK, WATERCOLOR, PENCIL.
    19.2 × 13.3 CM. INSCRIBED BY THE ARTIST:
    BAG/UNDERCLOTH/MAKE CRIMSON/TASSELS
    MAKE ONE WHITE/ANOTHER BLACK/SILK OR
    GLASS BEADS/IN THE LAST CASE/HANDLES/
    FROM BLACK BEADS.
    COURTESY OF ALEKSANDR FEDOROVSKY,
    BERLIN

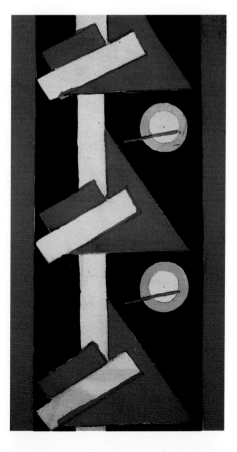

35. SUPREMATIST ORNAMENT. DESIGN FOR AN
    EMBROIDERY, 1917.
    BLACK INK, WATERCOLOR. 23 × 13 CM.
    COURTESY OF ALEKSANDR FEDOROVSKY, BERLIN.

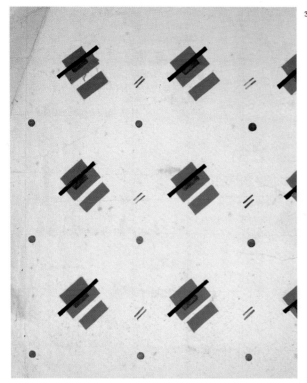

36. TEXTILE DESIGN, 1917.
   BLACK INK, GOUACHE. 29 x 20.3 CM.
   COURTESY OF ALEKSANDR FEDOROVSKY,
   BERLIN.

37. TEXTILE DESIGN, 1917.
   BLACK INK, WATERCOLOR, 21 x 13.2 CM.
   COURTESY OF ALEKSANDR FEDOROVSKY,
   BERLIN.

"romantic" suprematism. By means of colored hyperbolic and metaphoric combinations of vivid light and dull dark tones she introduces a qualitatively new dimension into the geometry of suprematism. This work embodies in full her notion that "dynamism in the world of colors is created by the properties of their values. . . . It engenders style and justifies construction."[26]

In some of her suprematist works Rozanova experiments with a direct and reverse perspective to create an atectonic painterly construction. She introduces an element of volume by combining some kind of color "facets" to achieve the illusion of mutually transforming planes and a three-dimensional form (such, for example, is *Abstract Composition (Suprematism)* (c. 1916. Oil on canvas, 85 x 60.5 cm.) with red, yellow, and brown from the Russian Museum). She gradually changes this illusory volume, however, and returns once again to a planar dimension by means of a reverse perspective that in the eyes of the viewer destroys and literally breaks the illusion of three-dimensionality. Tracing in accordance with its laws the outlines of these facets, she turns the volume inside out, as it were. Breaking off the line of the front facets, she continues the lateral ones, which join once again with the background and organically enter its plane as triangles of color.

This same Möbius strip effect also appears in the *Suprematistm* from the Regional Museum at Slobodskoi (plate 24), which could be considered a classic variant of suprematism were it not for the strips of color in its lower part, which clash with the overall wholeness of the work and disrupt its flat surface. Rozanova again uses two backgrounds: on the "soundless," indifferent white one a kind of centrifuge emerges that draws into itself the remaining shapes and colors—a round "hole" of a cold blue-green tone. Around it is an even larger deep, dark-green, almost black circle. These green circles, which take up most of the canvas, are demarcated from each other by a thin golden rim that reflects the light that seems to be circling on the surface. The light rays or strips of color on the first plane seem to penetrate the depth of the green circles and are reflected in it, although their shade has now become darker.

The theme of each of Rozanova's suprematist compositions is the birth of color, much as in her poetry it is the birth of sound in the dissonant, contrasting clashes of light and dark, harmonious and atonal. The luminosity of color in her painting corresponds to the openness and purity of sound in her transrational poetry. In her 1916 *Suprematism* (Oil on canvas, 102 x 94 cm.) from the Ekaterinburg museum we can see this

26.
Rozanova, "Cubism . . .",
in this volume, 200.

metamorphosis taking place before our very eyes. Only six colors act in the composition: black, white, yellow, blue, and two shades of gray. These are mutually complementary opposites. On the background of the gray—the color of nonbeing and amorphous primary matter (according to Kandinsky)—a white triangle in both color and form embodies the fullness and completeness of absolute soundlessness. A precolor chaos of black seems to penetrate this form. The contrast of black and white is the strongest dissonance; to some degree it is the archetype in our consciousness. (Characteristically, Rozanova called one of her 1916 collages *Perpendicular of Fullness and Negation in Supplemental [Colors] in the Sphere of Neutral [Colors]*, explaining on its label that "white is fullness, black is negation."[27]) Blue and yellow are likewise a contrastive pair, but filled with color. The color composition is dominated by a shift, an almost Gothic sweep—a flash of yellow-gold resembling lightning sprinkled over cooling fragments of blue. In her compositions, color achieves an almost impossibly penetrating acuteness, creating a physical sensation of overcoming the inertness of matter in a kind of spiritual act. This surmounting, which is equally significant in early avant-garde painting and poetry, was noted by Matiushin in his article "On the Old and New in Music" as a qualitatively new feature of abstract art: "The soul of the creator turns everything near and visible upside down and with its transformative power hurls it into infinity, where enormous layers of crude matter shine as stars and the perception of 'noises' makes us mighty, carried away, forces us to believe in the beauty of reality. . . ."[28]

There are three such experimental graphic sketches in pencil and watercolor (c. 1916) in the Fedopovsky collection in Berlin. In all three Rozanova draws color combinations of cold (green, blue) and warm (yellow, orange) tones within a circle. In two of the sketches she organizes separate tones that seem to spiral around the center, while in the third the circle, whose outlines are merely drawn in pencil is intersected by two colored stripes: a vertical blue one, and on its left a horizontal or slightly downward sloping yellow one going off to the side. An inscription in pencil in the margin notes: "Add perpendicular one later," and continues similarly to what was cited above: "Meeting of supplemental in sphere of color fullness." These experiments in the area of color may well have been directly connected with the development of her theory of *tsvetopis'*.

Rozanova's brilliant use of color was recognized by all her contemporaries and fellow artists in the leftist camp. She possessed

27.
Rozanova's collage is in the A, Rodchenko and V. Stepanova archive. I would like to express my gratitude to his family for access to these materials.

28.
M. Matiushin, "O Starom i Novom v muzyke" (1916). Mayakovsky Museum, no. 11865.

38. *ABSTRACT COMPOSITION (COLOR-PAINTING)*, 1917.
   OIL ON CANVAS. 62.5 X 40.5 CM.
   COURESY OF THE STATE RUSSIAN MUSEUM, ST. PETERSBURG.

the rare ability not only to declare her ideas, but also to implement them creatively. Malevich valued highly her independent mentality; the ideas on color she summarized in "Cubism, Futurism,

Suprematism" may have persuaded him to review his own position. Toward 1917 his color spectrum expanded, and sympathetic shades began to appear in his compositions. Of the artists in his group Rozanova was perhaps the only one he himself considered a "true" suprematist. In his review of the 1918 exhibition of the Left Federation of the Professional Union of Artist-Painters he declared categorically that "That which has been exhibited as abstract and designated in reports as suprematist does not correspond to the truth, except for Rozanova."[29] Rozanova injected a strong shot of color into suprematism, as it were; in a letter to Shemshurin she mentioned that "There is supposed to be a Suprematist exhibition in a private home during Easter. . . . If I have time, I'll bring some paintings with a 'transfigured' color scheme."[30] She added, in a later letter, "I found a new way of investigating color; if it isn't at variance with the 'transfigured' method it is possible in suprematist painting as well."[31]

In her last two years of life Rozanova attempted in effect to combine the principles of the two leading contemporary theorists of abstract art—Malevich and Kandinsky.

All of Malevich's suprematist compositions are structured on his own thesis that "art is the ability to create a construction that arises not from the mutual relationship of form and color . . . but on the basis of weight, speed, and direction of movement."[32] In his view of art as a "created construction" there is a contradictory union of a rational and an intuitively utopian approach aptly defined by Malevich himself as the "intuitive reason" (of suprematism).

In Rozanova's terms this is the rather nebulous "law of pragmatic inevitability,"[33] which, she derives from all of her theoretical premises, has clearly been influenced by Kandinsky's "law of inner necessity," according to which forms "are not fabricated and not constructed." The artist merely directs and controls what appears to his imagination. The phenomenon of Rozanova's late suprematism and *tsvetopis'* is concealed in this attempt to combine the mystical spiritual element in Kandinsky's theory of color with Malevich's utopian philosophy of form and space. Her ideal—to convey in painting the immaterial essence of color, its inner energy and luminosity—is realized in *tsvetopis'*, her color-painting.

"Here we can trace the transition from the planes of suprematism into color that is broadly thinned to liberate it from its dependence on form and plane," Stepanova wrote.[34] This evolution

29.
K. Malevich, "Vystavka profsoiuza khudozhinkov-zhivopistsev. Levaia federatsiia (molodaia fraktsiia)," *Anarkhiia* 89 (1918).

30.
Letter of O. Rozanova to A. Shemshurin, 18 February 1917 (OR GRB, f. 339 5. 14).

31.
Letter of O. Rozanova to A. Shemshurin, 9 August 1917 (OR GRB, f. 339. 5. 14).

32.
Malevich, "Ot kubizma k suprematizmu," 23.

33.
Rozanova, "Cubism . . .", in this volume, 200.

34.
Varst (V. Stepanova), "Vystavka O. Rozanovoi."

can already be observed in the three of Rozanova's abstract works from 1914 (V. Marinetti collection, Milano), and in some of the watercolors in the Fedorovsky collection in Berlin. In the 1917 canvases—the *Untitled* (plate 28) from the Baku Museum of Fine Arts, and *Green Stripe* (plate 29), from the Rostovo-Iaroslavl Museum—the luminous transparency of color is so great that the spectator gets the phenomenal impression of a projected colored ray of light refracted on the white ground of the primed canvas. In the Baku composition this ray seems to be focused on the surface of the "screen" of the canvas, and we see an expanding cone of light intersecting the suprematist colored shapes. This effect brings to mind a slide projected onto a wall, or the German avant-gardists Hans Richter's and Viking Eggeling's experiments with painted films in the 1920s. In his posthumous tribute to Rozanova, Rodchenko wrote in 1918:

> Was it not you who wanted to light up the world in cascades of color.
> Was it not you who proposed projecting color compositions into the ether. . . .
> You thought of creating color through light. . . .[35]

These lines refer to Rozanova's last projects, which remained unrealized, to the ideas to which she intended to dedicate her art in the future. There is no doubt that it was these that exerted some influence on Aleksander Rodchenko during this period, for in 1918 and 1919 he painted an entire series of paintings entitled *Tsvetopis'*.

In her 1917 compositions Rozanova achieves a maximum luminosity of texture through transparent color glazings applied in a very thin layer on the whiteness of the strongly reflective ground (plate 31). She gets away from the "materiality" of suprematist shapes sharply drawn on a plane, and in the flows of blue in her abstract composition from the Simbirsk Museum (plate 27) the contours are washed away, the figure and even the paint itself as a material substance seeming to dissolve in light.[36] Malevich achieves a similar effect in his suprematist works between late 1917 and 1919. Examples include his white on white (*Suprematism*, 1918) and yellow on white (*Suprematism*, 1917–1918) in the Stedelijk Museum in Amsterdam.

The principal property of color in Rozanova's "transfigured color scheme" is its luminosity, which recalls the transparent color harmony of medieval frescoes. Even the name she chose for this type of painting seems to presume the "transfiguration" of color into

35.
Alexander Rodchenko. *Experiments for the Future,* (Moscow, 1996), 65.

36.
This work was erroneously listed in the museum as belonging to B. Shaposhnikov. I was able to attribute it to Rozanova on the basis of an old photograph of the composition dating to the 1920s in Kruchenykh's archive in RGALI. On the back of the photo there is a note in Kruchenykh's hand identifying Rozanova as the author. The photograph is reproduced in A. Sarabianov, N. Gurianova, *Neizvestnyi russkii avangard,* 243.

light. As Stepanova put it, "a single color develops into an autonomous painting."[37] Rozanova's *Green Stripe* (plate 29) is among the treasures of twentieth-century abstract painting. The work seems a transcendence, an elusive, palpitating iconic radiance that pours, exhaling light, onto the canvas. There is some evidence that this composition was part of a triptych that also included *Yellow Stripe* (location unknown) and *Purple Stripe*. The latter composition, which consisted of a diagonal purple stripe on a white background, was in the Rostovo-Yaroslav Museum in the early 1920s. Inventory records in the museum archive indicate that it was later excluded from the collection as "a work of no artistic value"; its present whereabouts are also unknown.

More than anyone else Rozanova adopted Malevich's notion of suprematism in all its depth and breadth not only as a new method in painting, but as a "new religion" of art, a spiritual quest for synthesis. Malevich's search for new forms took him far beyond painting in his theory of abstract art. In his essays on poetry and music, in brochures and even in letters he is painfully seeking a new critical language capable of expressing the weight of his ideas. There is not a trace in him of the romantic passion of the futurist manifestoes or the style of absurd para-doxes and self-parody that characterized alogism, the Russian premonition of Dada. It is precisely Malevich's language and literary style, rather than his confused theoretical theses and ideas, that hold the key to an understanding of his theory. His suprematist style is categori-cal and dogmatic. The ecstatic tone of his essays calls to mind passionate, fanatical sermons. In this zealous attitude toward art and the word there is an element of religion, or more exactly heresy. His theory is something in which one must first of all "believe": "Who will leave behind the book of new laws of our tablets? . . . The New Gospel in painting. . . . Like Christ, who locked himself into this book of millenia, without this book the gates to heaven were locked. . . . Christ revealed heaven on earth, created the end of space, set two boundaries, two poles. . . . We will go past thousands of poles. . . . Space is larger than heaven, stronger, might-ier, and our new book is the doctrine of the space of the desert."[38]

Malevich's striving toward cosmic spirit, which at times was embell-ished by a very naive fanaticism, was tragic and in a way iconoclastic, for it was devoid of the image in return for which was given that regal and faceless "nothing"—the "space of the desert."

Of all the suprematists, in her *tsvetopis'* Rozanova was possibly the only one able to combine this "cosmic" disharmony with a human

37.
Varst (V. Stepanova), "Vystavka O. Rozanovoi," *Iskusstvo* 4 (22 February), 1919.

38.
Malevich, "Pis'ma k M. V. Matiushinu," 195.

dimension, and the spiritual, mystical, and mental with the emotional, intuitive, and sensual. In her last works she found—consciously or intuitively—her way out of the suprematist "impasse." There is still no image in her works, but instead of the faceless "nothing," there is a radiant light permeating her colors. If in the uncompromising, even totalitarian stance of his innovation Malevich perceived a new religion imbued with the poetics of dehumanization, and the zaum poets sought in it the possibility of unlimited creative freedom, Rozanova quite unexpectedly spoke of a new humanized beauty. "Most people are used to looking at works of painting as items of everyday domestic life—still a luxury for the few, but, ideally, for general consumption," she said. "But we protest against such vulgar utilitarianism. The works of pure painting have the right to exist independently. . . . To many, our efforts and endeavors—as well as those of our Cubist and Futurists predecessors—to put painting on a course of self-determination may seem ridiculous, and this is because they are difficult to understand and do not come with glowing recommendations. Nevertheless, we do believe that a time will come when, for many people, our art will become an esthetic necessity—an art justified by its selfless aspiration to disclose a new beauty."[39] These last remarks involuntarily bring to mind something E. N. Trubetskoi said in his study on icon painting, *Speculation in Color*: "Dostoyevsky said that 'beauty will save the world.' Elaborating on that thought [Vladimir] Soloviov proclaimed the ideal of 'theurgic art.' . . . And the very notion of the healing power of beauty has long lived in the idea of the revealed and miracle-working icon!"[40]

Paradoxical as it may seem, Malevich's voice also joins this choir. In his suprematist "manifesto" he writes:

Here is the Divinity ordering crystals to assume a different form of existence.
Here is the Miracle . . .
The Miracle must also be present in the creation of art.[41]

The avant-garde's utopian notion of "life-creating" tragically coincided with the Russian Revolution—yet another great illusion of the new art. Rozanova provides an expressive picture of her life at the time in a letter to A. Shemshurin, where she mentions that she is working, that she is

a member of the Trade Union Club [of Painters]
a member of the Cooperative
a delegate from Supremus

39.
Rozanova, "Cubism...",
in this volume, 200.

40.
E. Trubetskoi. *Umozrenie v kraskax* (Moscow, 1916), 41–42.

41.
Malevich, *Ot kubizma k futurizmu i suprematizmu*, 20.

and the secretary of the journal by the same name, . . . as soon as I get home from work I have to go to one meeting or another and from 7 to l in the morning listen to people talking nonsense.[42]

In addition to this bothersome and thankless work she attended sessions of the Artistic Enlightenment Commission attached to the Soviet of Workers' Deputies, and was a member of the young or "left" fraction of the Professional Union of Artist-Painters. She devoted so much time to this work that she was even obliged to spend the summer in Moscow. She wrote to Matiushin, "Our union is expanding. New members are joining, even Benois has announced he wants to join, because he is dissatisfied with the Petrograd organization [of painters]. The union will cover all Russia. Work is going according to plan. There will be a plenum meeting in the fall, and elections to the Council (60 members), since now there is only a temporary one of 15 members."[43]

This organizational work was tiring and clearly a burden to her, but as a "person of duty" Rozanova could not refuse the assignments she was given. Attending meetings was, for her, hard labor, above all because it robbed her of time for her art. Yet it was at precisely this time that she was developing her theory of *tsvetopis'*. How distant she was from the fuss of all these interminable meetings is evident from an invitation she received to one such gathering, which she covered in pencil with lines of verse, unusual metaphors that occurred to her, and sketches of others in the room.

At a plenum meeting of the Professional Union of Artist-Painters in June 1918—after the enormous trouble it had taken to found the organization—the entire left federation resigned its membership in protest over a decision to abandon division of the trade-union into federations. The following day the newspaper *Anarchy* published the "Resolution of the Left Federation," which largely shared the political views of the Moscow anarchists-syndicalists, signed by its chairman, Tatlin, and secretary, Rodchenko. On 2 July of that year, the same paper carried Rozanova's article "The Destruction of the Tri-Federational Structure of the Union as the Reason for the Withdrawal of the Left Federation." In this daily organ of the anarchists she also published her polemical articles "Suprematism and the Critics" and "Art—Only in Independence and Unlimited Freedom!" The title of the latter piece is symbolic.

Common to the early avant-garde texts, which are similar only in their dissimilarity, is the theme of the inner freedom of the individual and art: not so much the freedom to choose and to reinterpret tradition

42.
See Part 2, "A Chronology of the Life and the Works of Olga Rozanova," 169.

43.
Letter of O. Rozanova to M. Matiushin, 18 June 1917. IRLI, f. 656

39. *SELF-PORTRAIT*, 1917.
    PENCIL. 42 X 24 CM.
    PRIVATE COLLECTION, MOSCOW.

as freedom from the metaphysical rationalism that invariably manifests
itself in the creation of a canon or model in which reality is construed as
a closed system or finished, completed structure. The openly declared

theme of "free creation" had already resounded in Rozanova's manifesto "The Union of Youth," which called for the destruction of cliches and dogmas and the hierarchical standards of contemporary society.[44] In an article for *Supremus* written four years later, in 1917, she remained faithful to her original slogan, once again confirming her artistic credo: "We propose to *liberate* painting from its subservience to the ready-made forms of reality and make it first and foremost a creative, not a reproductive, art."[45]

All of these texts show that the aesthetics of the early avant-garde was founded on a view of the world that differed from the one expressed in the stereotypes of contemporary civilization. This outlook was acquired in the free creation of the spirit that underlay all the formal discoveries of Russian Avant-Garde. The influence of one of the chief principles of this new aesthetics, namely the "principle of free creation," as Vladimir Markov (Voldemar Matvei) put it, was felt throughout the entire early avant-garde movement.[46] This aspiration toward the unlimited inner freedom of the artist contains something that distinguishes the movement of the early Russian avant-garde from cubism, from Italian futurism (with its openly expressed interest in technology and its desire to found a dominant school and ideology), and from later movements in Russian art (suprematism, constructivism, and the futurism of the 1920s Lef group). This element may be defined as an element of anarchy, understood here as overcoming without destruction, rather a deconstruction of arche (αρχη)—of canons, bases, foundations—anarchy as an endless process of renewal and, at the same time, by removing the alien husks of the canon, a return to a deeper, hidden, inaccessible proto-essence of being. Features of aesthetic anarchy manifest themselves, first of all, in the very heterogeneity and organic multifariousness of the early Russian avant-garde—the terminological limitations of the notion "avant-garde" become obvious when an attempt is made to represent it as a single whole consisting of equal, mutually subordinate tendencies. Second, anarchy is apparent in the affinity of the new art for spheres and genres that seem completely to erase the traditional boundaries of the "space" of art. The very idea or "protoplasm" of the avant-garde movement found its spirit in the aesthetics of "ontological anarchy." Here it must be added that political anarchism related to utopianism (in which one order supplants another and one temporal foundation is destroyed in order to replace it with another) has little in common

44.
The manifesto, written by Rozanova, was published as a separate flyer on 23 March 1913.

45.
Rozanova, "Cubism ...", in this volume, 194.

46.
"Free creation ... always generates the independent principles that emanate entirely from it." (V. Markov, "Printsipy novogo isskusstva," *Soiuz molodezhi* 1, no. 2 (1912). For example, the theme appeared in the titles of Kulbin's article "Free Art as the Basis of Life" (1910) and in Livshits's "Liberation of the Word" (1913). In many of his works Kruchenykh emphasized the significance of transrational language as "*free* language."

with the notion of anarchy in the ontological sense, which from the outset rejects the foundation as a structural formation and ossified model that denies the freedom of arbitrary creation independent of the obligatory reigning principle of action in a given period.

Nevertheless, many avant-gardists undoubtedly shared some of the political views of the Moscow anarchists, and a few studies suggested the links between the Russian avant-garde and political anarchism.[47] There was in fact such a connection, and the futurists' and suprematists' obvious sympathy toward anarchism is there to see. In 1918, Malevich, Morgunov, Rozanova, Udaltsova and Rodchenko regularly published articles on art in the section Tvorchestvo (Creation) of *Anarchy*, the weekly paper of the Moscow Federation of Anarchist Groups published from 1917 to 1918.

If 1917 never became the epochal date in the change of landmarks of Russian art, in history it became a new datum point. The innovators welcomed first the February and then the October Revolution in the sincere belief that the long awaited opportunity for real action and the fusion of the space of art and life had arrived. But their initial euphoria soon passed, for the inner sense of freedom and the anarchist consciousness of the "futurists of the spirit" came into increasingly sharp conflict with a reality that was little by little being subordinated to new "masters of life" who were strikingly unlike the naive ideal of "creator-inventors of the new life." In 1918 the futurists published their articles in the anti-Bolshevik anarchist press, but in the 1920s their political disillusionment and tragedy became a farce, as many were obliged to "swear allegiance" to this same Bolshevik government at the price of their freedom and talent.

In her painting Rozanova tried to load herself to the limit, but beginning in early 1918 she had practically no possibility of working as an artist. The lack of a studio (she got her first ever a week before she died), poverty, health problems, and overall exhaustion were factors, but the main reason was her more and more burdensome activity in the Art and Production subsection of IZO (the section of visual arts of Narkompros, which was the People's Commissariat of Enlightenment). In the spring she became a member of the re-créated Moscow Art Collegium, and on 2 May she became the head of the Art and Production subsection, in which she worked less than six months. The sphere of responsibilities of an artist who had "never occupied an official post" (as she indicated in the application form),[48] included matters

47.
Basic works are Renato Poggioli's *Theory of the Avant-Garde* (Cambridge, Mass., 1968) and Donald Drew Egbert, *Social Radicalism and the Arts* (New York, 1970).

48.
Personnel file of O. Rozanova, 24 May-November 1918. TsGA Rossii, f. 2306. 55. 204. Personnel-related correspondence with Narkompros administration, 1918. TsGA Rossii, f. 2306. 23. 28.

40. *FASHION DESIGN*. C.1916.
    PENCIL. 45 x 30.6 CM.
    COURTESY OF THE STATE TRETYAKOV GALLERY, MOSCOW.

connected with industrial art throughout the country such as "the organization and development of handicraft production, the reestablishment and administration of existing arts and crafts schools throughout Russia," and even "equipping and furnishing the People's Houses" and "questions having to do with art and the manufacture of household objects, toys, etc."[49] During the three summer months she visited almost all of Podmoskov'e and the Vladimir province, Sergiev Posad, Ivanovo-Voznesensk, and Mstera. In her reports on her trips she not only described the poverty of the peasant craftsmen and the famine that forced them to leave their work and go to the cities, but also pointed out the most urgent needs and drew up a detailed plan for reconstructing and preserving handicrafts without force or interference on the part of the government. One of her main tasks was to resurrect traditional technologies by returning to old models once

49.
Ibid.

they had been purged of the mass clichés that had corrupted folk art in the twentieth century, and to found handicraft centers and workshops in the villages. Here as well she could not help but perceive the vital principle active in the Abramtsevo studio, nationalized in 1918. Unfortunately, her projects for reorganization of the crafts centers were destined from the beginning to remain just projects that could not be implemented under the conditions of those years.

Rozanova was especially interested in textile workshops, which inspired many of her sketches in a suprematist key using elements of folk ornamentation (plates 36, 37).[50] In fact, she had shown an interest in applied art, particularly costumes, as early as 1915. A letter to Kruchenykh in the fall of 1915 is interesting in this respect:

> The object of costume is 1) to hide imperfections of the body through the cleverness of the cut; 2) to bring out typical features of build; 3) to exaggerate these. Costume is a mask, costume is a mirror, costume is a crooked mirror? Women who dress badly are those whose costume serves only to cover their nakedness and nothing more, and those who have no idea of themselves naked. As for men, they dress too uniformly, too monotonously, too joylessly, but pragmatically and in material that doesn't soil easily. It's easier to jump into a moving streetcar in trousers than in a tight skirt, and it is easier to get stains out of the cloth used for men's clothes than out of women's elegant and coquettish ball gowns. Personally I find that modern women's clothing is ill-adapted to the realities of life, whereas men's clothing has come to a dead end in terms of inventiveness.[51]

In 1916 and 1917 she did a number of sketches of women's "fashions" (figure 40), handbags and embroideries for the Verbovka artel. According to Charlotte Douglas, women from the Ukrainian village of Verbovka were among several groups actively engaged in collaborating with professional artists and a revival of handicrafts that began even earlier, before World War I: "Organized with the help of Exter in 1912, the Verbovka women worked with both fine artists and folk painters and transferred motifs directly from original drawings and paintings to needlework charts. They also sewed articles of clothing—dresses, scarves, sashes, and handbags—and they intended eventually to move into printed textiles and decorative paper."[52]

The first exhibition of *Contemporary Decorative Art: Embroideries and Rugs on Patterns by Artists* took place in the Lemercier Gallery in Moscow in November 1915 (a month before the famous *0–10* exhibition in Petrograd) and featured works done by embroideresses from Skoptsy

50.
See Rozsika Parker: "Before the revolution Rozanova had been working with embroidery. For the magazine of the Suprematist artists, she prepared a design for an embroidery in three colors, declaring her determination to widen the definition of art beyond easel painting. She incorporated her embroidery designs into dress. Large patches of embroidery were placed on the dresses to accentuate the geometrical outline of the design, and to provide a sense of dynamism and rhythm." (Rozsika Parker, *The Subversive Stitch*, 194.)

51.
Letter of O. Rozanova to A. Kruchenykh [October 1915]. Private archive, Moscow.

52.
Charlotte Douglas, "Suprematist Embroidered Ornament," *Art Journal* 54, no. 1 (Spring, 1995): 42.

53.
See further Douglas, "Bezpredmetnost' i dekorativnost'."

and Verbovka from sketches by Malevich, Pougny, Boguslavskaia, Exter, and Yakulov.[53] The second Verbovka exhibition was held in Moscow in December 1917 and showed some four hundred works of applied art, mostly embroideries and textile prints. Besides a few goods by folk artisans (the peasant E. Pshechenko and others) decorated with traditional plant ornamentation, there were a great many works done on the sketches of professional artists from the Supremus group, such as Malevich, Popova, Exter, Pougny, Rozanova, Udaltsova, and Davydova, who organized and participated in the exhibition.[54] According to an anonymous reviewer in the daily *Early Morning*, the 1917 Verbovka exhibition was "free from vulgar clichés, almost everything bore the stamp of the personal taste of the artist." Almost all the works executed from professional sketches by peasants from Verbovka were "very nearly exact copies of suprematist paintings . . . an exultant brilliance of blinding colors and silks joined in the most daring combinations."[55] Especially enhancing the exhibition were works done from Exter's sketches, including dolls, and "suprematist" pillows on drawings by Malevich, Pougny and Davydova. The exhibition was housed in an art gallery on Bolshaya Dmitrovka 11, a hall that more than once had hosted the sensational shows of the new art, usually accompanied by lectures and papers. On 17 December (*Old Style*), Mayakovsky gave a paper at the second Verbovka exhibition. Contemporaries considered the exhibition one of the most significant events of the year. Rozanova showed over sixty works, including printed cloth (plate 33), ribbons, bindings, and handbags (figure 41, 42), of which Zhadova remarks, in her monograph on Malevich, "[Rozanova's] handbag designs are strikingly fresh and might easily find a place in a fashion magazine today."[56]

Many works were purchased at the auction organized during the exhibition, and it is therefore practically impossible now to determine their location, but many of the sketches have been preserved. Some of these and the goods produced from them were shown again at Rozanova's posthumous exhibition in the winter of 1918 and 1919. Reproductions of some of her suprematist designs were supposed to be included in the decorative arts section of the journal *Supremus*. Recently, notebooks containing over thirty sheets of sketches of compositions intended for the Verbovka exhibition were discovered (Aleksandr Fedorovsky collection, Berlin). This is a sensational find for researchers, as until now only a few such sketches by Rozanova were known. There are several variants of handbag designs with detailed

54.
As Natalia Adaskina notes, "Natalia Mikhailovna Davydova organized an art enterprise in the village of Verbovka in the Ukraine, where peasant women produced embroideries to designs by avant-garde artists from the capital … L. Zhadova mistakenly calls her Natalia Iakovlevna, confusing her with N. Ia. Davydova (1873–1923), who was connected with the Abramtsevo circle and also was involved with folk art." (Natalia Adaskina, "Constructivist Fabrics and Dress Design," *The Journal of Decorative and Propaganda Arts* 5 [Summer 1987]: 144; see also Wendy Salmond, "The Solomenko Embroidery Workshops" in the same issue, 131.)

55.
Po vystavkam," *Rannee utro* [8 December 1917].

56.
Zhadova, *Malevich*, 34

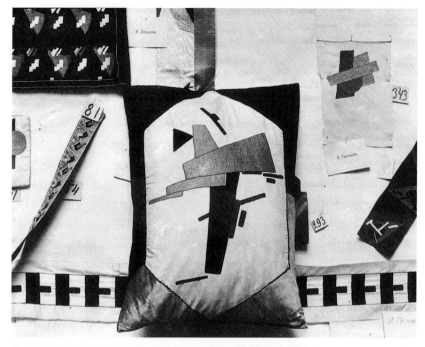

41. DISPLAY OF WORKS DESIGNED BY ROZANOVA, UDALTSOVA AND DAVYDOVA ON
"VERBOVKA" EXHIBITION IN MOSCOW. ORIGINAL PHOTO BY DAVID SAYLER. 1917.
COURTESY OF CHARLOTTE DOUGLAS, NEW YORK.

indications of the materials, including the color and quality of the
lining, that bear witness to Rozanova's constant concern with the
texture of the objects she designed (plate 34). Her instructions indicate
that she supplemented geometrical combinations of variously colored
silks with decorative elements such as silk tassels and beads.

Rozanova's sketches of ribbons are among her most interesting
and complete variants of abstract ornaments (plate 35). These not only
employ purely geometrical abstractions of suprematist forms, but also
include elements of traditional ancient Greek ornamentation and
geometricized plant motifs. In other sketches intended for embroidery
in satin-stitch on silk rather than for appliqués, she attempts, as in her
tsvetopis', to dissolve forms in color by avoiding clearly delineated
contour borders and playing on color tints.

Rozanova's sketches of book covers deserve particular attention,
because in these compositional constructions she most closely
approaches the laws of painterly structure. Many of them resemble
sketches for canvases, something to which their rectangular format is
probably also conducive. Moreover, these sketches give us reason to
believe that some of them may have provided the impetus for certain of
her suprematist paintings (plate 32).

With a natural elegance possessed by no one else, Rozanova was able to combine universalism and the severe grandeur of theoretical suprematism with a human dimension of beauty; she adjoined the spiritual and mystical with emotions and irony and incarnated the "nonobjectness" of suprematism in *objects* of art.

Suprematism became a laboratory whose experiments led Rozanova to realize her innovative ideas in two seemingly opposite embodiments: in the area of "high art"—in the creation of *tsvetopis'* or, as she put it, a "painting of transfigured color far from utilitarian goals"—and in honest craftsmanship that boldly transforms the everyday into a living environment for art.

To all appearances, Ivan Kliun was not exaggerating when he noted that "all Moscow admired Davydova's decorative exhibitions and embroideries on sketches by Rozanova."[57] Before the opening in October 1918 of SVOMAS (the Free State Art Workshop), a group of students compiled a list of leaders in which Rozanova was indicated as the head of the special textile studio.[58]

There are several sketches for textile designs that repeat the same pattern but vary its colors. It is interesting to note that this same pattern (although also with an entirely different treatment of color) occurs in Liubov Popova's works, which seems to indicate not only that these two artists were in close contact during these years, but also that there may have been a kind of a collective, "workshop" collaboration among the artists who came together in Verbovka. Another of Rozanova's sketches (plate 36) is interesting in that as an ornamental element it cleverly uses none other than the motif from her aforementioned *Abstract Composition* with red on a yellow background (figure 38). In this case it is difficult to determine which is first—the painterly composition or the suprematist ornament—as both works are absolutely equivalent aesthetically. In all of these sketches one senses the enormous creative potential that subsequently developed in the 1920s in the works of Stepanova, Popova, and other masters of textile design.

Rozanova was attracted by a wide variety of potentials inherent in all the genres of art in which she felt she could find a place for her imagination and free experimentation.

In late September 1918 she began working on preparing the airport at Tushino for the first anniversary of the Russian Revolution. She was interested in going beyond the framework of easel painting and using in the design not only traditional forms but also search-

57.
I. Kliun. *Predislovie k katalogu Posmertnoi vystavki kartin, etiudov, eskizovi risunkov O. Rozanovoi.* (Moscow, 1918), 3.

58.
Perepiska otdela IZO . . . TsGA Rossii, f. 2306. 23. 28.

42. SUPREMATIST BAG DESIGNED BY ROZANOVA ON "VERBOVKA" EXHIBITION IN
MOSCOW. ORIGINAL PHOTO BY DAVID SAYLER. 1917.
COURTESY OF CHARLOTTE DOUGLAS, NEW YORK.

lights in order to master the enormous space of the airport as artistic
space by transforming it into a kind of "living environment" and
embodying the dimension of art in the dimension of reality.
Somewhat earlier she had worked together with Malevich, Morgunov,
Udaltsova, and others on decorating Moscow for the May First celebration in 1918, following the Soviet government decree of 12 April,
"On the Monuments of the Republic," which established specific tasks
for visual propaganda and revolutionary commemoration.[59] If the
artists worked mainly in the genre and stylistics of decorative panneaux
for the May event, in the later October anniversary they made ample
use of elements of performance, illumination and fireworks in the
center of the city:

> Dusk falls quickly and the lights of the illuminations go on all over the city.
> . . . The streets are lit as though it were peacetime. The buildings shine
> in multicolored lights, and the sky, illuminated by searchlights and full of
> fluffy pink clouds, seems strangely mysterious and beautiful.[60]

On 7 November, the day her work was to be displayed, Rozanova
died in the Botkin Hospital from diphtheria resulting from a chill she
caught while working on the airport. In December her first solo—and

59.
Sovetskoe dekorativnoe iskusst-
vo. Materialy i dokumenty
1917–1932. Agitatsionno-
massovoe iskusstvo. Oformlenie
prazdnestv (Moscow: Iskusstvo,
1982), 52. "The artists and craftsmen who designed and created
these public events were faced
with complex tasks, and they discovered opportunity for bold, creative experiments and pursuits.
The very scale of the work was
unusual, as whole towns were
decorated and there were thousands in the crowds of participants. The artists' creations were
not displayed in enclosed museum galleries . . . but on the open
spaces of squares and streets. . . ."
(Vladimir Tolstoy, Irina Bibikova,
and Catherine Cooke, *Street Art*
of the Revolution: Festivals and
Celebrations in Russia 1918–33
[London, 1990], 17.)

60.
Izvestiia (9 November 1918). Cited
in Tolstoy, Bibikova, Cooke, *Street*
Art, 65.

posthumous—exhibition opened in Moscow, initiating a cycle of state-sponsored showings. Stepanova and Wladyslaw Strzeminski (who prepared lectures for her exhibition), and Kliun and Aleksander Drevin, were directly involved in organizing it. More than 250 of her works were on display, from early school studies to her last experiments with *tsvetopis'*. During the three months it ran, the exhibition attracted seven thousand visitors and aroused considerable comment, including short articles by Stepanova, Kliun (who edited the catalog), and Efros. IZO began preparing a collection of articles and materials devoted to Rozanova and an edition of her poetry, in which some critics even managed to glimpse "a threat to the existing order."[61] The first Free Artistic-Artisan Workshops in Ivanovo-Voznesensk, which she had helped organize, were named in her honor. Almost all of her works found a place in the "museum of a new type" in Moscow—the Museum of Painterly Culture, as well as in the Museum of Artistic Culture in Petrograd. In the early 1920s, however, both the political and artistic situation changed.

One of the most original, fascinating, and distinguished artists of the Pleiad of the early Russian avant-garde, Rozanova is unfortunately still not well known; her premature death in 1918 prevented her from receiving her rightful place in history. After her death her paintings shared the fate of most prerevolutionary avant-garde art and in the late 1920s were sent to provincial museums or destroyed. Almost all of her archive perished, so that for many years her name was a mere "legend" for scholars. It was not until the 1970s that her work began enjoying a rebirth. Her paintings appeared in various exhibitions of the Russian avant-garde, and some of her articles on art were translated for the first time into English. George Costakis, who was one of the first collectors of Russian avant-garde art, once commented as follows on her work *Green Stripe*: "Shortly after the end of the Second World War, by accident I encountered some avant-garde art. The painting I saw first was done in 1917, yet it might easily have been a revolutionary work of about 1950. Indeed, it might almost have been mistaken for a canvas by Barnett Newman, who, to be sure, had no knowledge of its existence. Olga Rozanova was the artist, and she died in 1918. It was her work that opened my eyes to the existence and compelling power of the avant-garde."[62]

61.
"In No. 138 of the *Evening News* (*Vechernie izvestiia*) comrade Friche bitterly complains that *Art* (*Iskusstvo*) publishes Rozanova's poetry, which he does not understand and which he is almost inclined to view as a threat to the existing order." (*Iskusstvo* 5 [1919]: 2.)

62.
Russian Avant-Garde Art: the George Costakis Collection, 54.

PART II

г. Меленки.   Казанская улица.

MELENKI. KAZANSKAIA STREET. POSTCARD. 1910S.

CHRONOLOGY
of the life and work of olga rozanova

1886

22 June (4 July). Born near Vladimir, in the small town of Melenki, to Vladimir Iakovlevich Rozanov, a district police officer, and Elizaveta Vasilevna Rozanova, née Orlova, the daughter of an Orthodox priest. Olga was their fifth child. She had two sisters, Anna and Alevtina, and two brothers, Anatolii and Vladimir, the latter of whom died in 1898.
    (GAV f. 14, op. 7, d. 524.)

26 June (8 July). Christened in the Cathedral of the Intercession (Pokrovskii sobor) in Melenki, not far from the wooden Rozanov home on Kazanskaia Street.
    (Birth registry, 26 June 1886, GAV ZAGS Pokrovskii sobor g. Melenki, no. 101.)

1896–1904

Enrolled at the Vladimir Women's Gymnasium. At this time the Rozanovs moved to Vladimir and settled in a house owned by her mother's family on Borisoglebovskaia (now Muzeinaia) Street.
    (GAV f. 459, op. 2, d. 132; f. 433, op 1, d. 169).

43. OLGA ROZANOVA (FIRST ROW, CENTER)
    WITH HER SISTERS ALEVTINA, ANNA, AND
    HER MOTHER, ELIZAVETA VASILEVNA.
    EARLY 1890S. COURTESY OF ALEKSANDR
    FEDOROVSKY, BERLIN.

44. OLGA ROZANOVA, 1898.
    PHOTO BY M. KORENEVA, VLADIMIR.
    COURTESY OF ALEKSANDR FEDOROVSKY,
    BERLIN.

45. O. ROZANOVA, *MELENKI*. VIEW OF KAZANSKAIA STREET. P. V. ROSHCHIN'S HOUSE.
    C. 1904-5. PENCIL. 13 X 25, 6. COURTESY OF ALEKSANDR FEDOROVSKY, BERLIN.

Rozanova's father died in 1903.

> *They say that Vladimir is a "piece of Moscow." "Long forgotten piece" would be more like*
> *it. . . .*
> *. . . in Vladimir it's more like spring than in Moscow, and it even seems hotter and the air*
> *is springlike, and somehow you hardly even notice the houses, but you do notice the sky—*
> *sparkling and naive in a provincial kind of way. All in all, very heartwarming landscapes.*
>   (Letter of Olga Rozanova to Andrei Shemshurin. [1917]. OR GRB, f. 339,
>   op. 5, ed. khr. 148.)

1904–1906

Upon finishing at the Vladimir Women's Gymnasium in 1904, Rozanova
went to Moscow to study painting . Her brother Anatolii was already living there and studying law at the University of Moscow. She rented a
room on 3–ia Tverskaia-Iamskaia Street (the Tikhonov building), and
enrolled in the Bolshakov Art School.

> *The "Private Art School of Painting and Sculpture" run by Anatolii Petrovich Bolshakov*
> *(1870–1937) was officially permitted to open in 1900 (document of 19 July 1900*
> *signed by General-Major Trepov, Governor-General of Moscow). First located in the*
> *Nemchinov building B in Miasnitskii proezd near Krasnye vorota, it later moved across*
> *the street to the fifth floor of building 4, apartment 15, where it remained until it was*
> *closed in 1920. . . . Besides Bolshakov himself, teachers at the school (in the order in*
> *which they worked there) included V. I. Komarov, N. S. Ulianov, the sculptor Matveev,*
> *Pyrin, P. Petrovichev and S. I. Frolov. There were courses in nudes, portrait painting, and*
> *flowers (the latter two not always offered). Morning classes ran between 9 and 3, those*
> *in the evening (except Saturdays) from 5 to 8. Bolshakov, who taught little himself, was*
> *highly regarded for his open-mindedness and his ability to relate to and communicate*
> *with his students.*
>   (Bolshakov's biography, as communicated by his widow, E. S. Avdeeva. Zapis',
>   30 August 1940. OR GTsTM im. A. A. Bakhrushina, f. 34, ed. khr. 19.)

1907

Rozanova audited classes at the Stroganov School of Applied Arts,
applying in August for admission. She was not accepted, however,
but began attending the private art schools of Konstantin Iuon and
Nikolai Ulianov.

> *The time she spent at the Stroganov School . . . was very brief, for she was entirely dis-*
> *satisfied with the wretched system of instruction there. During this period she was inter-*
> *ested in literature, poetry, music and sculpture.*
>   ("Pamiati O. V. Rozanovoi" [obituary], *Iskusstvo* I [1919].)

1907–1910

Rozanova continued at Iuon's private school in Moscow.

After graduating from [Valentin] Serov's studio in Moscow in 1900, together with my friend I. O. Dudin I set up a private art school which managed to win the recognition of Moscow society and become very popular. . . . During the eighteen years it existed, three thousand pupils studied there, among them well known names such as the sculptors V. I. Mukhina and V. A. Vatagin, the painters and graphic artists A. V. Kuprin, S. Iu. Sudeikin, V. A. Favorsky and G. B. Yakulov, and architects such as the Vesnin brothers. . . .
(Konstantin Iuon, *Ob iskusstve* 2 [Moscow, 1959]: 211–12.)

Also studying drawing and painting there at the time were Rozanova's future comrades Popova, Udaltsova and Kruchenykh. In 1909, Popova left to study painting in Paris and began a brisk correspondence with Rozanova on her observations and impressions there.

1911

At the beginning of the year Rozanova joined the St. Petersburg Union of Youth, which was founded in early 1910.

On 16 February 1910 the Union of Youth society of artists was entered in the St. Petersburg registry of organizations as no. 503.

I. Name and Goals of the Society

    1. The goal of the Union of Youth is to acquaint its members with contemporary cur-rents in art, to develop their aesthetic sensibilities through collaborative work in drawing and painting, to exchange views on artistic questions, and to further con-tacts between persons interested in art.

    2. St. Petersburg is the geographical area of activity of the Society.

    3. The founders of the Society are the signers of the present Bylaws.

II. Activities

    4. . . . the Society has the right, in accordance with established rules:

        a) to have its own studio for joint projects among its members;

        b) to arrange for members gatherings in the studio at which they can draw, exchange views on questions relating to art, etc.;

        c) to organize exhibitions and auctions of works of art, musical gatherings, concerts, theatrical productions, and fund-raisers to promote art;

        d) to arrange public readings on questions relating to the objectives of the Society;

        e) to organize artistic competitions awarding prizes and honors;

        f) to publish various works of graphic and typographical art;

        g) to establish relations with art museums on questions relating to the objectives of the Society.

III. Membership

    6. Membership is open to all except minors, students, low ranking civil servants, cadets on active military duty, and persons on trial or under investigation.

IV. Initiation and Termination of Membership

    7. Dues of 1 ruble paid upon admission, 1 ruble monthly dues thereafter.

    8. Members are elected by the Plenum on the recommendation of the Board.

V. Administration of the Society

. . . is delegated to

a) the Plenum;

b) the Board; . . .

21. The Board consists of 5 members and 2 candidate members and is elected by the
Plenum.

22. Members of the Board are elected for a term of one year.

24. The Board elects from among its members a Chair, a Secretary, and a Treasurer.
      (Bylaws of The Union of Youth. OR GRM, f. 121, ed. khr. 2.)

Not counting the ubiquitous Burliuks, it was of course . . . Rozanova who held the cen-
tral position in the Union of Youth. She was a strong personality, a person who firmly
knew what she wanted in art and who pursued to her set goal along a special path of her
own that resembled no one else's. All their disagreements notwithstanding, artists of
irreconcilable tastes such as Goncharova and Exter seriously reckoned with her.
      (Benedikt Livshits, *Polutoraglazyi Strelets* [Moscow, 1933], 140.)

April

Rozanova debuted at the second Union of Youth exhibition in St.
Petersburg with two canvases, *Nature-morte* and *The Cafe* (*Katalog 2—i vystavki*
kartin Obshchestva khudozhnikov "Soiuz molodezhi" [St. Petersburg, 1911], catalog
nos. 80, 81).

Artists are abruptly on, ahead, away from established tastes. The beauty of the colors of
the latest painting and their novel, sometimes brilliant, sometimes refined harmony can-
not be denied. You only have to visit any exhibition of young painters and surrender to
purely color impressions, and "ordinary" painting will seem boring, black and inert.
Here the value of the new achievements is indubitable and very rich.
      (A. Rostislavlev, "Vystavka 'Soiuza molodezhi'," *Rech'*, 24 April 1911.)

December

Opening on 27 December of the All-Russian Congress of Artists in St.
Petersburg, which continued until 5 January 1912. On 29 and 31
December, Nikolai Kulbin read, for the first time in Russian,
Kandinsky's treatise "On the Spiritual in Art," which had been published in German in Munich at the end of December (it was written in
1910). This work exerted considerable influence on the development
of the theory of the avant-garde movement in Russia.

Opening in late December in St. Petersburg of the Stray Dog café,
which would become a favorite meeting place of the futurists from
1913 to 1915.

At the very end of 1911, N. Kulbin, N. Evreinov, and B. Pronin established a perma-
nent meeting place for the new forces in the capital—the Stray Dog basement café. It was

frequented by artists, poets, writers, actors, and audiences that came to see and hear them. Gatherings would begin there around 10 or 11 in the evening and end at 4 or 5 in the morning.

(Mikhail Matiushin, "Russkie kubo-futuristy," in N. Khardzhiev, K. Malevitch, and M. Matiushin, *K istorii russkogo avangarda* [Stockholm, 1976], 145.)

Rozanova moved to St. Petersburg.

1912

At the beginning of the year, Rozanova studied briefly at the well-known St. Petersburg art school of I. E. Repin's pupil E. N. Zvantseva, whose instructors included many masters of Russian art nouveau.

She went to St. Petersburg and worked at Zvantseva's school. During these years she clearly leaned toward cubism and futurism . . . the school could not satisfy her demands and she dropped out.

("Pamiati O. V. Rozanovoi" [obituary], *Iskusstvo* 1 [1919].)

Her eternally inquisitive soul and extremely well-developed intuition could never get along with old forms and continually protested against repetitions both in everyday life and in art.

A keen observer of life, she was able to sense in time the newborn nerve that was destined on the morrow to become the exponent of the time, the mirror of the present day.

(Ivan Kliun, Predislovie k katalogu *Posmertnoi vystavki kartin, etiudov, eskizov i risunkov O. V. Rozanovoi. 1918–1919* [Moscow, 1919] 1.)

On 4 January, opening of the next Union of Youth exhibition, at which Rozanova showed her *Portrait* and *Still-Life*.

(*Katalog vystavki kartin Obshchestva khudozhnikov "Soiuz molodezhi"* [St. Petersburg, 1912], catalog nos. 67, 68.)

This exhibition marks the first appearance of Larionov's Moscow group, which called itself The Donkey's Tail.

Dear Levky Ivanovich,

I just got Larionov's letter, which I am sending to you. The conditions set forth there seem entirely acceptable to us, the only unpleasant thing being the name "Donkey's Tail." Although we will also have another name, still, in the same building. . . .

(Letter of Iosif Shkolnik to Levky Zheverzheev, 14 December 1911. OR GTsTm im. A. A. Bakhrushina, f. 99, ed. khr. 95.)

Rozanova traveled to Moscow with a number of Union of Youth artists to negotiate future joint projects between the Moscow and St. Petersburg groups. The negotiations, however, failed to establish relations between the Union of Youth and the Moscow groups.

In 1912 our group went to Moscow to talk with the Muscovites about future projects. It consisted of Olga Rozanova, Spandikov, Shleifer, Shkolnik, Ballier and me. It was there

I first met Malevich, whose works made a deep impression on me, and also with
Mayakovsky and Kruchenykh.

  (Mikhail Matiushin, *Tvorcheskii put' khudozhnika.* Mayakovsky Museum, [manu-
  script, 1934], 76.)

March

An exhibition of works by artists in the groups the Donkey's Tail and the Union of Youth
opened on 11 March in Moscow in the new building of the Institute of Art, Sculpture, and
Architecture. Participants were, in the Donkey's Tail: V. K. Anisimov, V. S. Bart, S. P.
Bobrov, N. S. Goncharova, K. M. Zdanevich, I. F. Larionov, M. F. Larionov, M. V.
Le-Dantu, K. S. Malevich, A. A. Morgunov, E. E. Rogovin, E. Ia. Sagaidachnyi, I. A.
Skuie, V. E. Tatlin, A. V. Fonvizen, M. Chagall, A. V. Shevchenko, A. S. Iastrzhembskii
and others. In the Union of Youth: V. D. Varvarova, K. V. Dydyshko, A. M. Zelmanova,
L. M. Kurchanova, P. I. Lvov, S. Nagubnikov, Novodvorskaia, P. Potipaka, O.
Rozanova, E. K. Spandikov, I. S. Shkolnik, S. Ia. Shleifer, M. Iasensky, Filonov, V.
Markov.

  (*Soiuz molodezhi* 1[1912] 24.)

Vladimir Markov (pseudonim of Voldemar Matvei) took the initiative
in organizing the first two issues of the journal *Union of Youth*, which was
published in April and May 1912. They carried Markov's article "The
Principles of the New Art," which exerted an enormous influence on
his comrades. In the summer, Markov went to France and Germany on
behalf of the Union of Youth to establish a museum and library
attached to the organization and to set up permanent ties with Western
European artists.

Kandinsky, to organize an exhibition here, is also prepared to send [his painting] I am mak-
ing purchases for the museum, increasingly of such works as would also suit the journal.

  (Letter of Voldemar Matvei to Levky Zheverzheev, 26 July 1912. OR GTsTM
  im. A. A. Bakhrushina, f. 99, ed. khr. 59.)

In 1912, Shkolnik, the secretary of the society wrote to its chairman,
Zhverzheev, describing the situation there as follows:

I got a letter . . . from Malevich, who writes that they are interested in our affairs in
Moscow, especially the museum of modern art, and the artists there want to become
involved with that project immediately. I'm again being invited to Moscow to explain
everything once and for all, so that soon we can perhaps begin accepting pictures. . . .

  I'm often troubled by many problems in our society; it is particularly clear that its
existence is exclusively indebted to your material support. At the moment our artists are
growing stronger; the letters I get tell me that everyone is working a lot and wants to do
something. It would be very sad if we were not able to realize at least some of our plans.

  I would also like to tell you that in contributing to the establishment of the museum
or by helping our society you are promoting an entire group of artists—a deed that will in
any event be remembered.

  (OR GTsTM im. A. A. Bakhrushina, f. 99, ed. khr. 99.)

On 20 November in St. Petersburg a debate organized by the Union of Youth featured David Burliuk's paper "What is Cubism?" and Mayakovsky's "On the Latest Russian Poetry." Attending the event in the Troitsky Theater, besides Rozanova, Shkolnik, Spandikov, and other members of the society, were Evreinov, Kulbin, Benois (Benua), Dobuzhinskii and others. Benois published his reactions in his article in *Rech'* (23 November), "Cubism or Effrontery?" ("Kubizm ili kukishizm?").

December

Rozanova participated in the next Union of Youth exhibition (4 December 1912 – 10 January 1913), which included works of Ballier, the Burliuks, Goncharova, Larionov, Malevich, Matiushin, Mayakovsky, Pougny, and Tatlin, Voinov, and Dydyshko. It was here that Larionov first introduced Rayism [Luchizm], the first attempt at abstract art in Russia. Rozanova exhibited eleven works, including *Portrait of A. V. Rozanova* and *The Smithy* (*Katalog vystavki kartin "Soiuz molodozhi"* [St. Petersburg, 1912], catalog nos. 68–78.)

On 9 December she wrote to her sister Anna:

> *Your portrait caused a furor among the artists!.. Today I made a most interesting acquaintance: David Burliuk. Now I'm in love with him. We shook hands. He really likes my pictures and says that in me he's discovered a star. He also especially likes your portrait. And the houses in the landscapes. Burliuk is lecturing on art and wants to photograph my pictures and show them to the audience on a screen. He's traveling around various cities giving his lectures. Good for him! Beautiful body! But he's just a bit impudent. Tomorrow there's a lecture in St. Petersburg, and he gave me a free ticket. Oh, David!*
>
> *The critics, that is the trashy papers, are tearing me apart, they have even carried a reproduction of my "Smithy" and wanted your portrait as well, but Shkolnik refused.*
>
> *If you only knew how amusing these critics are! Burliuk laughs and says "they smear me as well, and I like seeing our names mentioned together."*
>
> *So far my pictures are not selling well, but they are enormously popular among the artists. One painter from the World of Art introduced himself to me at the exhibition and said it was an honor to meet me. Petrov-Vodkin's female students play up to me, Madame Zvantseva herself spoke to me at the exhibition and likes my pictures. . . . I'm making new friends, some of them interesting, but I'm swallowed up in the artistic milieu and artistic interests, and that's what is dearest to me. . . . Now I read the whole time about art in French and hang out at the exhibition. My pictures are hanging in the very best spot. David is leaving soon, alas!*
>
> (Letter of O. Rozanova to A. V. Rozanova, 9 December 1912. Cited from a handwritten copy made by N. I. Khardzhiev. Foundation Cultural Centre Khardzhiev-Chaga, Amsterdam.)

Publication of the futurists' first programmatic collection of poetry, "A Slap in the Face of Public Taste," containing the manifesto of the same name by Khlebnikov, Mayakovsky, David Burliuk, and Kruchenykh.

In the course of the year Kruchenykh began to publish his litho-graphed futurist books.

1913

January–February

On 3 January Rozanova, Shkolnik, Zheverzheev, Matiushin, and Ballier were elected to the Board of the Union of Youth. At this meeting Matiushin, David Burliuk, Morgunov, Malevich, Tatlin, and Varvara Bubnova were also reelected as members of the society. (Minutes of the 3 January meeting of the Union of Youth. OR GRM, f. 121, ed. khr. 1.)

Other meetings of the society discussed the preparation of the third issue of the journal and the publication of a book on cubism by Albert Gleizes and Jean Metsinger, the translation of which was assigned to Matiushin, Rozanova, and Ballier.

At the beginning of the year Ilia Repin's painting *Ivan the Terrible and his Son Ivan, 16 November 1581* (1885. Tretyakov Gallery) was slashed by the mentally ill A. Balashov. The press accused the futurists of instigating the incident, which evoked a number of protests on their part. (Repin later acknowledged that the futurists had nothing to do with the vandalism.) On 24 February, David Burliuk refuted the charges at a debate organized by the Jack of Diamonds. Rozanova's response was a note titled "The Reborn Rocambole" intended for the chronicle section of *The Union of Youth*.

> *Since the days of the Wanderers* [Peredvizhniki] *Russian art has passed through so many vital and important movements that anyone the least acquainted with art rightly considers the Wanderers deceased. Therefore the destruction of Repin's picture, although perhaps significant if only because it was fated to happen, should not have raised the ruckus that it did. Only a passive attitude toward art can explain this addictive relapse into the art of the Wanderers. Because it mechanically accepts artistic currents one after the other and therefore masters none of them, the Russian public in the broad sense has not yet realized the necessity of studying art actively. A purely external incident suffices to put it at a loss and lead it to turn to something that requires no active attention: the art of the everyday, the Wanderers. Idle minds that feel no need of living food for thought are most often satisfied by sensational novels appealing to the emotions. They have a favorite type of novel in which the hero dies and is resurrected several times over the course of many volumes. The deceased art of the Wanderers presents us with an analogy from real life . . . with tears of tender emotion in their eyes they accept the resurrection of their rocamboles at face value.*
>
> (Olga Rozanova, "Voskresshii Rokambol'," 1913. OR GRM, f. 121, ed. khr. 82.)

46. MEMBERS OF *HYLAEA*: FUTURIST POETS A. KRUCHENYKH, D. BURLIUK, V.
MAYAKOVSKY, N. BURLIUK, AND B. LIVSHITS. 1913

March

Rozanova finished her essay "The Basis of the New Art and Why it is
Misunderstood." It was read at a meeting of the Union of Youth, where it
was decided that it should be published in the third issue of the journal.
On 8 March the Union of Youth joined with the Hylaea group of futurist poets (which included Khlebnikov, Guro, Mayakovsky, Kruchenykh,
the Burliuks and B. Livshits) as an autonomous poetical section "for collaboration on the journal, in debates, and at exhibitions."

(Minutes of the meeting. OR GRM, f. 121, ed. khr. 1.)

Rozanova wrote a note on this meeting to Spandikov:

> *. . . come to Matiushin's at 3 today. There is a Board meeting there to which N. Burliuk*
> *and E. Guro have been invited as representatives of the Union of Youth literary section.*
> *The section is the subject of the meeting.*
> (Undated letter of Olga Rozanova to Eduard Spandikov, [March 1913]. OR
> GRM, f. 121, ed.khr. 62.)

Publication of the third and final issue of *The Union of Youth*, which
contained Rozanova's programmatic "The Bases of the New
Creation and Why it is Misunderstood," together with articles by
Spandikov, Ballier and Nikolai Burliuk, and Matiushin's "On
Gleizes' and Metsinger's Book."

> *Indomitable spring was alive in the "land of the futurists." The combined Union of Youth*
> *society of poets and artists was working energetically in St. Petersburg, publishing under*
> *this title journal collections with leading articles, in one of which Olga Rozanova wrote:*
> *"Each new age in art . . . develops a new codex of artistic formulae."*
> (Vasilii Kamenskii, *Put'entuziasta* [Perm': 1968], 167.)

> *In March 1913 the Hylaea group of Futurist poets . . . joined the Union of Youth for collab-*
> *orative ideological and practical work. The first thing we undertook was the publication of the*
> *third issue of* The Union of Youth, *whose first two issues were rather poor. In no. 3 we*
> *printed a number of articles, poems, and drawings. Prior to this our group had put out the sec-*
> *ond collection of* A Trap for Judges *(Khlebnikov, Guro, Mayakovsky, Kruchenykh,*
> *Livshits, the Burliuks, E. Nizen, drawings by Larionov, Goncharova, the Burliuks and Guro).*
> *We insisted that leftist Moscow artists be invited to contribute to the journal, but eclectics*
> *headed by Shleifer and Spandikov protested and were supported by Zheverzheev.*
> (Matiushin, "Russkie kubo-futuristy," 147.)

The collection was illustrated with engravings by Rozanova and
Shkolnik. It also carried an announcement of a forthcoming but never
realized album of drawings by these two artists.

On 23 and 24 March the Union of Youth organized public debates
in the Troitsky Theater in St. Petersburg. At the first—"On Modern
Painting"—the manifesto written by Rozanova was read. The preceding
evening it had been read at a meeting of the society, which decided to
"accept, print and read at debates O.V. Rozanova's text."
> (Minutes of the meeting. OR GRM, f. 121, ed. khr. 18.)

Also presenting papers at the debate were Malevich ("On the Jack of
Diamonds and the Donkey's Tail") and David Burliuk ("The Art of the
Innovators and Nineteenth- and Twentieth-Century Academic Art").

> *The two public debates organized by The Union of Youth on 23 and 24 March in the Troitsky*
> *Theater are especially interesting, because they brought out the essence of our tendency.*
> (Matiushin, "Russkie kubo-futuristy," 147.)

"The militant character of our public appearances needed a direct connection with every-thing that was young and fresh and had not been suffocated by the bureaucratic mold of the capitals. . . .

The first debate was chaired by Matiushin, and participants included myself, Burliuk, Malevich, and others. The audience behaved scandalously. That evening I spoke about the crisis and death of easel art (anticipating the advent of the poster and photographic montage?). Malevich, who gave a paper, was harsh. He threw out things like:

"That untalented bawler Chaliapin . . ."

"You driving along in your cabriolets, don't come chasing our futurist automobiles!"

He went on, I seem to recall, as follows:

"'The cubists and futurists are unintelligible? But what is so surprising if Serov shows. . . ." And he turned to the screen on which in the meantime a picture had appeared from a fashion magazine. There was an unbelievable roar, the police guard demanded that the meeting be adjourned, and we had to break off the proceedings.

Present at the second debate onstage and in the wings was almost the entire Union of Youth.
(Aleksei Kruchenykh, "Nash vykhod. K istorii russkogo futurizma" In: *Iz literatunogo nasnlediia Kzuchbenykh:pamiat' teper' mnogoe razvorachivaet.* Ed. Nina Gurianova (Berkeley, 1999), 65.

At the second debate, "On the Latest Russian Literature," held the following day, papers were given by Nikolai Burliuk ("The Fairy-Tale Myth"), Mayakovsky ("Arrived Myself"), Kruchenykh ("Demasking of the New Art"), and David Burliuk ("Graphic Elements of Russian Phonetics"). The theses of the last paper proclaimed "the notion of descriptive and graphic poetry":

1) [the Futurists] . . . have shaken the syntax of Russian speech. . . . 2) We have begun to ascribe content to words according to their graphic and phonetic characteristics. 3). . . b) consonants are the bearers of color and notions of texture; c) vowels are time, space, and the notion of plane. 4) We have forgotten orthography in favor of chance. 5) We describe the noun with all parts of speech. 6) We have created books written by hand. 7) We combat musical rhythm. 8) We are admirers of verbal innovation. Our hearts harbor hatred toward the language of the literature of our century and notions of "good taste" and "the beautiful."

This time witnessed the appearance of the extremely remarkable collections *A Slap in the Face of Public Taste, A Trap for Judges II, The Croaked Moon, Three, Mare's Milk, Roaring Parnassus,* and others. Also launched then were Mayakovsky's *I, his Tragedy* and "Cloud in Trousers," Khlebnikov's first three volumes of poetry, and books by Elena Guro, David Burliuk, and others.

From 1912 to 1915—a period of innumerable public appearances—we also wrote and published a great deal.

Our readings were overflowing, our books were snatched up, they all fought for a piece of us, inviting us to literary soirées, debates, chats about art with students.

Our artistic success was apparent to all.
(Kruchenykh, "Nash vykhod," 71.)

June

Early June saw the publication of Kruchenykh and Khlebnikov's *Forestly Rapid*, and Kruchenykh's *Let's Grumble!* and *Explodity*, with Rozanova's lithographs. The collaboration that began at this time soon grew into a close, lifelong partnership.

> *Upon arriving home I did about 40 drawings for the poet Aleksei Kruchenykh (very good, he's a Futurist) and recently he sent me no less than three books of poetry and prose illustrated with drawings by me and other artists. The books are* Let's Grumble, Forestly Rapid, *and* Explodity *(i.e. a bomb). The first of them contains some prose dedicated to me—"To O. Rozanova, the best artist in Petrograd."*
>
> *So far I've done very few pictures for the exhibition, just 4 and they are small, and that makes me sad, because for some reason I'm tired and just don't have any energy to work, yet the critics have already noticed me and the thick journals throw my name around when they talk about my article. David Burliuk also mentions me respectfully in his recent article, but I'm having a hard time getting any pictures painted. Of course, it's early in the summer, so things could still get better. . . .*
>
> (Letter of Olga Rozanova to Anna Rozanova (June 1913). Cited from a handwritten copy made by N. I. Khardziev. Foundation Cultural Centre Khardzhiev-Chaga, Amsterdam.)

July

At Matiushin's dacha in Uusikirkko, Finland, Malevich and Kruchenykh had a meeting they subsequently called the First All-Russian Congress of Futurists. They published the manifesto of this gathering in one of the summer issues of the journal *The Past Seven Days* (*Za sem' dnei*). Matiushin wrote that the meeting was connected with the decision by the joint committee of the Union of Youth and Hylaea to organize the "Futurist" ("Budetlianin") theater. It was there at Uusikirkko that work was begun on the opera *Victory over the Sun* (text by Kruchenykh and prologue by Khlebnikov, with music by Matiushin, and Malevich's costumes and sets).

Rozanova vacationed at Yalta in the Crimea, bringing back with her several notebook sketches.

> *Ialta, Crimea*
> *Sotninskaia 16, Druskin cottage, apt. 1*
> *Dear Olga Vladimirovna, you probably feel good there in the midst of beautiful nature. I love the Crimea, think about it all the time, but I'm not likely to get there this year. Are you working—do you intend to paint there? I have a lot of things, but they're all terrible because I don't feel well. I'll stay here another three weeks or so and leave for somewhere near Moscow. Shleifer will soon be in the Crimea, staying in Bakhchisarai;*

I recommend visiting the city, a lot of charming things there. I'll write in more detail in a few days, until then wishing you good luck and all the best.

I. Shkolnik

I'd be very grateful if you would write and tell me how and what you are doing.

(Letter of Iosif Shkolnik to Olga Rozanova, 30 July 1913; private archive.)

October

Rozanova exhibited her work at the *Permanent Exhibition of Contemporary Art* that opened on 3 October at N. E. Dobychina's Art Bureau (Moika 63). The exhibition was called "permanent" even though it was changed every three weeks.

The Gallery has as its goals:

to serve as a living link between artists and the public with respect to the sale of works of art and the execution of all manner of artistic projects. . . .

to offer collaboration in the selection and production of theatrical plays, concerts, operatic works, musical and literary soirées, etc.

to communicate information on various questions of art. . . .

(Announcement of the opening at the Dobychina Art Bureau Leaflet. OR GRB, f. 420, op. 1, ed.khr. 3.)

At the same time, Rozanova was busy working on her canvases for the forthcoming Union of Youth Exhibition, which was scheduled for the end of the year.

My address: Vasilevskii Ostrov, Line 9, building 58, apt. 21.

I have to do a ton of pictures for the exhibition [the Union of Youth], I haven't been to see anyone or told anyone I'm here, and although it is very important for me to know what is going on in our artistic affairs, I sit at home, because I'm afraid that people will bring me bad luck, give me the evil eye, or take up a lot of my time. Tomorrow, though, if I have a productive morning I'll drop in on Shkolnik in the evening, but I'll ask him not to tell anyone I'm in town. . . .

I've planned a lot of pictures, and nothing interests me more than art at the moment. It's just a pity that the exhibition is coming too soon.

The many wooden toys I bought in Vladimir, the colorful pillows on the chairs and the beautiful icons make my room quite cozy.

(Letter of Olga Rozanova to Anna Rozanova (October 1913). Cited from a handwritten copy made by N. I. Khardzhiev. Foundation Cultural Centre Khardzhiev-Chaga, Amsterdam.)

November–December

Rozanova participated in the final Union of Youth exhibition (10 November 1913–10 January 1914). Larionov's group did not take part, for it had definitively broken with the St. Petersburgers.

47. RECEPTION IN HONOR OF MARINETTI AT THE KALASHNIKOV BOURSE IN ST. PETERSBURG, 1 JANUARY 1914. SITTING IN THE FIRST ROW, CENTER, ARE: A. LURIE, F. T. MARINETTI, N. KULBIN. ROZANOVA IS IN THE SECOND ROW, FIFTH FROM THE RIGHT. NEXT TO HER IS N. BURLIUK.

Exhibitors included the Burliuks, Grishchenko, Kliun, Morgunov, Matiushin, Pougny, Spandikov, Tatlin, Filonov, Shkolnik, Exter, Natan Altman, and Lasson-Spirova.

Malevich presented his "transrational realism" of 1912 (*Peasant Woman with Pails, Knife Grinder*, and others) and the "cubo-futurist realism" of 1913 (*Reaper, Samovar*, and others). Rozanova had the canvases *Port* and *Building site* and the series of pictures *Trajectoglyphs of Mental Movements* ("Puti-pis'mena dushevnykh dvizhenii").

(*Katalog vystavki kartin "Soiuz molodezhi."* [*St. Petersburg, 10 November 1913–10 January 1914*], catalog nos. 102–18.)

The Luna Park Theater in St. Petersburg featured Mayakovsky's tragedy *Vladimir Mayakovsky* (2 and 4 December), which was designed by Filonov and Shkolnik; and Kruchenykh and Khlebnikov's opera *Victory over the Sun* (3 and 5 December). In the scenery and costumes of the latter, Malevich first used abstract geometrical shapes. Rozanova and David Burliuk created the playbills.

Posters announcing the Futurists' plays were put up throughout the city. One of them—a huge lithograph by Olga Rozanova in which prisms refracted the colors white, black, green and red to form a revolving advertisement—could not help but arrest the eye. The text was short:

For the first time anywhere
Futurist theatrical productions
2, 3, 4, and 5 December 1913

Luna Park Theater. Ofitserskaia 39.
(Kruchenykh, "Nash vykhod," 75.)

Kruchenykh caused an incident at one of the performances when he
proposed announcing to the audience before the play began that he
was not being paid by the Union of Youth. This scandalous prank
resulted in a break between the Union of Youth and the literary section
of Hylaea. A letter signed by Rozanova and many other members of the
former to society chairman Zheverzheev declared that it was "unadvis-
able" to continue collaboration with Hylaea. The members of the society found Kruchenykh's prank "offensive" not only to their chairman,
against whom it was directed, but also to their general constituency.
(Letter from the artists of the Union of Youth to Zheverzheev, 6 December
1913. OR GRM, f. 121, ed. khr. 72.)

On 22 December at the Stray Dog in St. Petersburg, A. Smirnov
delivered a paper on new trends in French painting. Blaise Cendrars
and Sonia Delaunay-Terk's simultaneist book *La prose du Transsibierien*
(1913) was shown at the lecture. Among those invited were Filonov,
Kulbin, Rozanova, and Nikolai Burliuk. "On Light," a lecture in
response by Yakulov, was supposed to be held on 30 December.

A number of futurist books were published during the year in Moscow
and St. Petersburg, including *Prayerbook of Three*, *Forest Boom*, *Explodity*, *Let's
Grumble!*, *Three*, *The Devil and the Speechmakers*, and *A Duck's Nest of Bad Words*, illustrated by Malevich, Rozanova, Kulbin, and others; the collection *A Trap for
Judges II* with drawings by Guro, Goncharova, the Burliuks and others;
Kruchenykh's books *The Hermits*, illustrated by Goncharova, *Half-Alive*, with
illustrations by Larionov, and *Pomade*, the last project undertaken jointly by
the futurist poets and Larionov's group. Mayakovsky's first book of poetry,
I! was designed by L. Zhegin and V. Chekrygin.

*Aleksei Kruchenykh and I have illustrated some books together which are selling very
well, so we should clear quite a bit on them.*

*I hang out at the Stray Dog. One night there was a kind of "apache evening," an
unusual Saturday, and I sat there the whole night through from 12:30 to 7:30 AM. So
I got there on the last tram and left on the first. Such are my labors and pleasures! Today
I'm going to the Dog again, but I don't plan on staying so long. . . .*
(Letter of O. Rozanova (9 December 1913). Cited from a handwritten copy made by
N. I. Khardzhiev. Foundation Cultural Centre Khardzhiev-Chaga, Amsterdam.)

1914

January

The disintegration of the Union of Youth.

Soon the Union of Youth broke up. The fourth issue of the journal never appeared, for Zheverzheev stopped subsidizing it. The only publication was Victory over the Sun *and some musical fragments. . . .*

The organizational meetings of our group took place periodically every year. In the winter or spring the Burliuks and Kamensky would arrive. Until 1916 Khlebnikov wintered in St. Petersburg.

In 1913 and 1914 the cubo-futurists were notorious, and people everywhere wanted to see and listen to them. The middlebrow critics brought to the lecture halls a lot of people who wanted to understand and learn.

(Matiushin, "Russkie kubo-futuristy," 153.)

February

Italian futurist leader F. T. Marinetti arrived in Moscow on 26 January. His first lecture was on 1 February in St. Petersburg. A second lecture followed on 4 February. A celebration honoring him was held at the Stray Dog.

In February 1914 Kulbin organized a reception for Marinetti at the Stray Dog. Kulbin revered the West and its culture.

When Marinetti arrived in St. Petersburg, Khlebnikov blurted out his famous interjection to the "muttonheads of hospitality bedecked in the lace of servility" (barany gosterpriimstva v kruzhevakh kholopstva).

Khlebnikov and Benedikt Livshits came together and distributed a leaflet to the audience. Khlebnikov never took part in our literary soirées and would sit quietly on the stage, but at Marinetti's reception he became so angry that he almost struck Kulbin.

Marinetti impressed me as a talented writer with a skillful command of language. He gave a good description of the noise of a propeller, explosions, and drumbeats, which were evidently meant to demonstrate the coming war in Europe. But in general all of this struck me as so many gimmicks.

(Matiushin, "Russkie kubo-futuristy," 154.)

Today some natives and the Italian colony on the Neva are falling at Marinetti's feet out of personal considerations, thereby betraying the first step of Russian art on the path of freedom and honor and bending the noble neck of Asia under the yoke of Europe.

As in the shameful days of Verhaeren and Max Linder, people who do not want a collar on their necks will be the serene observers of a dark deed.

The free stand to the side. They recall the law of hospitality, but their bows are drawn and their brows are creased in anger.

Alien, remember to what land you have come.

The lace of servitude on the muttonheads of hospitality.

(Leaflet on the occasion of Marinetti's visit. St. Petersburg, 1913.)

I remember the following from the time of Marinetti's visit to Russia: I showed him a copy of Te li le *with Olga Rozanova's unusual drawings and asked him: "Do you (Italians) have anything similar to this on the surface?"*

"No!" he said.

"Then if you don't have anything similar on the surface, you don't have anything similar in substance either!

Marinetti and his Italian friends were shocked.

(Letter of Aleksei Kruchenykh to A. Ostrovsky, 1927–1931. OR GPB, f. 552, ed. khr. 90, l. 6.)

Marinetti suggested to Kulbin that a Russian section be organized at the permanent gallery of the futurists in Rome (the Sprovieri Gallery). Kulbin invited a number of St. Petersburg and Moscow avant-garde artists, including Malevich, to participate, and Rozanova helped him. Malevich's answer to her has been preserved:

Dear Olga Vladimirovna,

Thank you very much for your notice on participating in the exhibition. I will, of course. Give my regards to Nikolai Ivanovich and thank him for the courtesy. Write and tell me who else will be taking part from our poor Union . . . Morgunov and Tatlin and I have completely dropped our memberships. . . .

(Letter of Kazimir Malevich to Olga Rozanova, 21 February 1914; OR GRM, f. 134, ed. khr. 71.)

The permanent Russian section at the gallery never materialized, but Russian artists did participate in the *First Free International Futurist Exhibition* held in Rome on 13 April–25 May.

April–May

The *First Free International Futurist Exhibition* was held at the Sprovieri Gallery. Participating on Marinetti's invitation were Archipenko, Kulbin, Rozanova, and Exter. Rozanova had four works in the same show (*Port, Man on Street (Passerby)*, *Dissonance*, and *Factory and Bridge*), together with a watercolored copy of Kruchenykh's *Duck's Nest of Bad Words*, and Klebnikov and Kruchenykh's book of poems *Te li le*, printed on colored hectograph.

August

Russia entered World War I on 1 August, and many avant-garde artists were drafted to, or volunteered for, the front.

Caught up in this hurricane were Konchalovskii, [Konstantin] Rozhdestvenskii, Larionov, Livshits, Kamensky . . .

Today is in fact the winter of the arts—who has time for art now, when human life is in danger. . . ?

(Letter of David Burliuk to Andrei Shemshurin, 1914; OR GRB, f. 339, op. 2, ed. khr. 8.)

Rozanova, from Vladimir, corresponded with Kruchenykh, who had received a deferment from front-line service because he was on standby reserve.

48. "FUTURIST EASTER" IN PETROGRAD. SITTING, FIRST ROW: N. KULBIN, O. ROZANOVA, A. LURIE, V. KAMENSKII, I. PUNI (POUGNY) AND V. MAYAKOVSKY ARE HOLDING GEORGII YAKULOV'S PORTRAIT. 1915. PHOTO FROM THE PERIODICAL *SINII ZHURNAL* (*BLUE MAGAZINE*), NO.12, MARCH 1915.

Autumn

Contemporary Popular Prints (Segoniashnii lubok) in Moscow published the wartime *lubok* posters of David Burliuk, Malevich, Lentulov, and Mayakovsky, all of whom were amply represented at the *War and the Press* exhibition in November.

Appearance in Moscow of Nataliia Goncharova's album of lithographs, *Mystical Images of War* (published by V. N. Kashin).

1915

February

Rozanova helped design the collection *The Archer* (*Strelets*), published by Aleksandr Belenson, which in addition to her lithographs contained illustrations by David Burliuk, Kulbin, Lentulov, and Siniakova.

Belenson was a St. Petersburger, a lawyer, the publisher of the futurist collection The
Archer. *He was also a poet, but there was no futurism in his works. In* The Archer
they tried to combine fire and water, Kruchenykh and Blok and Vilkina.

(A. Shemshurin, *Vospominaniia o moikh korrespondentakh,* 1920s; OR GRB, f. 339,
op. 6, ed. khr. 11.)

A party was held at the Stray Dog to celebrate this collection, in which
symbolists and futurists first appeared together.

*The Stray Dog was the favorite corner—tavern—theater—monster of Poets, Artists,
Composers, Actors. . . .*

Here at the Dog there was a lavish celebration of the appearance of the big collection
The Archer (*edited by Belenson, the exotic gentleman wearer of light blue trousers*)
and it was on this occasion that Maxim Gorky gave his speech acknowledging futurism.

(Vasilii Kamenskii, *Ego—imia biografiia velikogo futurista* [Moscow, 1918], 137.)

*Blok and Burliuk, Sologub and Kruchenykh, Kuzmin and Mayakovsky, Z. Vengerova
and Khlebnikov. . . .*

*You of course expect editorials, forewords, reservations; you expect them because
you remember, you remember splendidly, the irreconcilable and hostile attitude of the
writers who so unexpectedly joined together in the first* Archer *collection. But perhaps
the entire intriguing charm of the book, its seemingly accidental and innocent public
appeal lies in the very fact that it has no reservations or forewords. . . .*

Thus perhaps some of the contributors to The Archer *sacrificed to art their pop-
ularity, and their balance, and their claim to general recognition, whereas others sur-
rendered their very impressive pose of irreconcilable innovation and rebellion? . . .*

*If this is really so—is it sacrifice or merely a new page in the life of "would-be youth-
ful oldsters" in the one case, and, in the other, the "last" antic of eccentrics who have
exhausted themselves? . . . What is* The Archer—*a major literary phenomenon or
merely . . . a minor literary escapade?*

(Viktor Khovin, "Bezotvetnye voprosy," *Ocharovannyi strannik,* vyp. 7
[Almanakh vesennii] (Moscow, 1915), 10.)

Nor were the two Archer *collections published in 1915 and 1916 by Belenson with
Kulbin's intimate collaboration able to break out of the old frame of aestheticism. They
were the funeral procession of cubo-futurism.*

(Matiushin, "Russkie kubo-futuristy,"156.)

March

In Petrograd, the *First Futurist Exhibition "Tramway V"* (for the benefit of the
Art Workers' Infirmary) was held in the Little Auditorium of the
Imperial Society for the Encouragement of the Arts. Participants
included Malevich, Morgunov, Tatlin, Pougny, Boguslavskaia, Popova,
and Udaltsova. Rozanova displayed her 1914 works *Street, Fire in the City,*
and two portraits.

(*Katalog "Pervoi Futuristicheskoi vystavki kartin 'Tramvai V'"* [St. Petersburg, 1915], catalog nos. 60–63.)

April

Rozanova participated in the *Exhbition of Leftist trends* at the Dobychina Art Bureau in Petrograd (Field of Mars 7). She showed sixteen works, among them the eleven-picture cycle *Playing Cards*; and the works *Clock and Books*, *Tavern*, *Composition of Shiny Objects* (on tin), and *Composition of Clay and Crystal Objects*. (Katalog *"Vystavki kartin Levykh Techenii"* [St. Petersburg, 1915], catalog nos. 78–94.) Also participating in the exhibition were Altman, the Burliuks, Grishchenko, Kamenskii, Kandinsky, Kulbin, Pougny, Shkolnik, Udaltsova, G. Yakulov, Robert Falk, and Martines Saryan.

Running simultaneously with this exhibition was *1915*, which featured representatives of all the Moscow avant-garde groups. It was organized by Iurii Kandaurov and included works by David Burliuk, Chagall, Grishchenko, Goncharova, Kandinsky, Konchalovskii, Larionov, Lentulov, Mashkov, and Falk.

June

Shemsurin agreed to Kruchenykh's request to finance an engraving by Rozanova on the theme of the war. From Vladimir, where she was spending the summer, she wrote Shemshurin:

Dear Andrei Akimovich,

Aleksei Eliseevich Kruchenykh recently wrote me that you are proposing to publish engravings on the theme of the war in the style of my Playing Cards, *and that you have expressed a desire to support this publication financially. I would be very grateful for your kind assistance—this past winter I very much wanted to publish in this manner (engravings on linoleum) drawings on war themes, but unfortunately at that time I had neither the means nor the time. In the summer I am always freer and would be happy to begin working in this direction. In last year's* Cards *there were ten cards of various names and each had 150 impressions. Thus in all there were 1500 sheets.*

Each engraving was 4 x 5 vershki [1 vershok = 4.4 cm.] in size, and the publication cost a total of about 25 rubles. Engravings on the war in the same quantity and dimensions on the same type of paper in one color would cost the same, but since the theme is more complex technically (not portraits, as in the case of the cards) and fine lines cannot be made on linoleum, I would like to enlarge their size to 6 x 7 vershki including the margins. For the sake of variation it would be good to do some drawings in 2 or 3 colors.

. . . One drawback of printing by hand, unfortunately, is that some prints turn out very sloppy, but the method has the advantage of producing an excellent texture.

I don't know how books are sold in general these days, so I don't know how large the edition of these engravings should be. Perhaps it would be sufficient to publish 150 albums (1500 shots?) as we did last year.

If it is not too much trouble for you, I would be very grateful if you could send me the money for the work . . . I am in Vladimir now and will probably remain here to the end of the summer. I think I can get hold of the needed materials. Engraving on linoleum is extraordinarily interesting just now. At Golike's and Volborg's typography they told me that in Russia engravings are done exclusively on metal, and that they don't even have any (electric) machines for linoleum. That alone is especially good. It's good to be spreading an unusual rather than ordinary method of printing.

I will expect to be hearing from you here in Vladimir . . . this is in fact my permanent address.

Respectfully,

O. Rozanova

(Letter of Olga Rozanova to Andrei Shemshurin, 1915. OR GRB, f. 339, op. 5, ed. khr. 14.)

July–November

In Vladimir, Rozanova worked on her album of colored linocuts *War* (*Voina*), which were to accompany Kruchenykh's verses.

It seems that my work will soon be over. The only delay now is that it dries very slowly, so that you have to wait and can't print every day. All the tables, chairs and everything possible is covered in engravings. And it's a lot of fun to watch and work. I've already done about 600 sheets, but still more remain.

(Letter of Olga Rozanova to Andrei Shemshurin, 7 November 1915. OR GRB, f. 339, op. 5, ed. khr. 14.)

During this period Rozanova began work on her first compositions using collages of colored paper. She was in continual correspondence with Kruchenykh, who told her about Malevich's new ideas, and she was busy preparing new compositions for the *0–10* exhibition conceived by Pougny.

There's quite a bit of work on compositions for the exhibition. And physically and technically it is sometimes very difficult owing to the lack of certain materials and tools. I'm very happy that you liked my paper collages. Could you draw me a sketch of what you have in mind?

Besides compositions of various materials I'll be doing some oils, but probably not more than 5 . . . I intend to write Pougny a letter in the next few days, since of course he didn't get my first one.

(Letter of Olga Rozanova to Aleksei Kruchenykh, fall 1915; private archive.)

Presently I can only paint things that are either **entirely** *realistic or* **abstract,** *I can't allow anything in between, since I think that there are no links connecting these two arts, no comparisons and nothing in common, they are even farther from the similarity between the craft of a shoemaker and a tailor, etc. I now profess that objectness and non-objectness (in painting) are not two different* **tendencies** *within a single art, but* **two different arts**—*I even think it sensible to substitute projections on a screen for paint in non-object art. No connection at all!*

(Letter of Olga Rozanova to Aleksei Kruchenykh (summer 1915). Foundation Cultural Centre Khardzhiev-Chaga, Amsterdam.)

Rozanova contributed to Kruchenykh's article "On Feminine Beauty" (published 1920 in Baku). "I'm working a lot on the painterly aspect of

the new book and to some extent on 'feminine beauty' . . ."
Kruchenykh wrote Shemshurin on 29 September 1915.
(OR GRB, f. 339, op. 4, ed. khr. 1.)

Responding to Kruchenykh's request, Rozanova expressed her views
on the theme:

> There is a book entitled **Feminine Beauty from Ancient Times to the
> Present**. It's a publication of a new journal of foreign literature, 1901. It has a lot of
> pictures of various beautiful women as painted by famous artists. There is Gioconda,
> and Messalina, and Venus, and Titian's women, and the courtesans Pompadour,
> Marion Ninon Lanclos, Marion Delorm, Boticelli's **Spring**, Mademoiselle Recamier,
> Marie Antoinette, etc., etc. But . . . of course they are clothed. So all they illustrate is the
> beauty of the face, not of the body.
>
> Venus de Milo, as everyone knows, is Madame Mathematics incarnate, and every-
> thing about her is proportional. Goya, on the other hand, liked to portray women with
> small but thick legs and elongated torsos (his **majas**). Legs like pillars.
>
> I find that Titian's women look apoplectic, and Giaconda's enigmatic and "divine"
> smile has more delicate depravity than anything else. The busts of Rubens's beauties
> are reminiscent of French bread rolls.
>
> Besides natural beauty there is beauty exaggerated by means of powders and paints,
> obviously false or painted eyebrows, and dyed hair, for all of this produces a special
> "texture." I've heard that in America they wanted to use artificial teeth made of dia-
> monds. And I seem to recall that the "Song of Songs" is not without interest as a trib-
> ute to beauty.
>
> Everything that I've been chattering on about to you here may be just "useless non-
> sense," not what you expected of me. But for the time being I can't add anything in words
> to what I've said.
>
> Will you be looking into clothed or nude beauty, and if clothed, will you touch
> upon the principles of dress? The object of costume is 1) to hide imperfections of the body
> through the cleverness of the cut; 2) to bring out typical features of build; 3) to exag-
> gerate these. Costume is a mask, costume is a mirror, costume is a crooked mirror?
>
> Women who dress badly are those whose costume serves only to cover their naked-
> ness and nothing more, and those who have no idea of themselves naked. As for men,
> they dress too uniformly, too monotonously, too joylessly, but pragmatically and in
> material that doesn't soil easily. It's easier to jump into a moving streetcar in trousers
> than in a tight skirt, and it is easier to get stains out of the cloth used for men's clothes
> than out of women's elegant and coquettish ball gowns. Personally I find that modern
> women's clothing is ill-adapted to the realities of life, whereas men's clothing has come
> to a dead end in terms of inventiveness.
>
> (Letter of Olga Rozanova to Aleksei Kruchenykh, fall 1915; private archive.)

Rozanova did a few watercolor sketches of women's dresses and ball
gowns. She would return to work on costume in the following two
years as well in sketches using suprematist embellishments.

49. O. ROZANOVA, K. BOGUSLAVSKAIA, K. MALEVICH AT THE EXHIBITION *0.10*.
PETROGRAD, 1915.

In the fall Malevich and his group (Menkov, Kliun, and others) prepared to participate in the *Last Futurist Exhibition 0.10*.

> *The exhibition has taken final form and will open on 1 December in Petrograd. . . . They're beginning to agree with me in Moscow that we have to appear under a different flag. What is interesting, however, is will they provide a new form? It seems to me that suprematism is the most suitable thing, because it means supremacy.*
>
> (Letter of Kazimir Malevich to Mikhail Matiushin, 24 September 1915, *Ezhegodnik rukopisnogo otdela Pushkinskogo doma na 1974* [Leningrad, 1976], 185.)

> *In Moscow my idea is already clearly taking shape and in our group they are already talking about making an appearance. About doing a suprematist section already at this exhibition. Pougny doesn't know yet.*
>
> (Letter of Kazimir Malevich to Mikhail Matiushin, 31 October 1915, *Ezhegodnik rukopisnogo otdela Pushkinskogo doma na 1974*, 181.)

December

Rozanova returned from Vladimir to Petrograd, where she participated in the *Last Futurist Exhibition 0–10*, organized by Pougny. Malevich's suprematism was first displayed here. Rozanova participated with his group, showing eleven works, including *Metronome*, *Cupboard with Dishes*, *Sewing Box*, and *Writing Desk*, together with two reliefs, *Automobile* and *Bicyclist*.

> (*Katalog "Poslednei futuristicheskoi vystavki 0–10 (Nol'-Desiat')"* [St. Petersburg, 1915], catalog nos. 121–131.)

Malevich's brochure "From Cubism to Suprematism: The New Painterly Realism" was timed to coincide with the exhibition.

> *The suprematists—Malevich, Pougny, Menkov, Kliun, Boguslavskaia, and Rozanova— led the struggle to liberate things from the obligations of art.*
>
> (Kazimir Malevich, *Ot kubizma i futurizma k suprematizmu* [Moscow, 1916], 30.)

The Futurist Exhibition

It is impossible to deny that art is witnessing a change of forms, perhaps even a very major shift, and that the so called cubo-futurist movement has already acquired a very definite and even acknowledged past in French art as represented by Cezanne, Picasso, and others. It started up some time ago here as well and has produced some names that are famous in one way or another. Futurism, as it turns out, has even reached its "Last" exhibition on the Field of Mars, where a definite boundary divides it from the latest trend of "suprematism" (the new painterly realism), whose representatives and inventors at the exhibition are Malevich, Pougny, Boguslavskaia, and Kliun. With regard to inventiveness, the new trends are a veritable whirlwind of dynamism: yesterday's innovators are today already "oldsters" and have not been included in the exhibitions. It is notable that the basic principle proclaimed in the brochures and manifestos (there are several of these at the exhibition)—the aspiration to liberate painting from the power of nature, the insistence on the purity of painterly tasks and means of expression—reflects a regular continuity. All painting beginning with impressionism, of course, has aspired to overcome if not nature, then the slavish copying of it, and to develop original painterly means of expression. Even attempts at "abstraction" (in, of course, a different form) were present already in Kandinsky. It is another question whether this path logically leads to the "suprematism" of Malevich, who, let it be noted, is unquestionably a gifted and experienced master of "ordinary" painting. Suppose that abstraction is the final ideal of painting, and that in the present case only simple geometrical shapes and disjoined masses of color can enable the artist to express rest and dynamism (by diagonal lines), and the extreme saturation of solid colors (deserving note here is no. 46, undoubtedly the most beautiful and powerful of the combinations). Doesn't this geometricism (where, incidentally, at least the simplest forms of objects remain in any case), don't these painted planes tell us something about the enigmatic and attractive complexity and mystery of the artistic perceptions conveyed by art? Reproducing the dynamism of life, although there is some question whether it is possible and needed in painting, is considered one of the main new tasks. Whence a kind of idealization of the machine. One cannot but agree that this artistic idealization has found an extremely interesting expression in the works of Tatlin, another artist who is very good at "ordinary" painting. . . . Alas, what is good at the exhibition from the old, very ordinary painterly and ornamental point of view, is not new. Here are many paintings in which a fragmentation of objects and combination of their parts must evoke much more complete realistic notions than a simple copying of nature. Of course only skillful and capable artists can combine pieces and harmonize colors in the manner of Rozanova, Udaltsova, Vasileva and Popova. It seems that the essence of the principle is in places also clearly expressed, as, for example, in the very subtly combined and painted pieces of Rozanova's Cupboard with Crockery, Udaltsova's and Boguslavskaia's Kitchens, and even Pougny's Student of the Means of Communication.

The transition from the fragmentation of objects (which truly destroyed the wholeness of nature) to abstraction is a logical one. But with the disappearance of the futurists—masters of fragmentation who, it is true, no longer have anywhere to go—also disappears, as it were, the bridge of painterly-ornamental perceptions that joins this type *of Futurism to "ordinary" painting. The new artists' inventiveness and alacrity is beyond doubt, but as before it remains an open question whether the very notions of art apart from its form are not in a state of chaotic fermentation.*

(A. Rostislavlev, "O vystavke futuristov." *Rech'*, January 1916.)

Just after the opening, Rozanova wrote Kruchenykh describing the tense atmosphere at the exhibition:

He [Pougny] took down my Automobile *and* Devil's Panel (Bicycle). *When the works were brought to the exhibition, mine turned out to be more original than his. My relationship with Oksana [Boguslavskaia] is strained to the limit. Not so with Ivan Albert<ovich> [Pougny], but Oksana is stupid and bitchy, and besides Malevich* absolutely *no one is on Pougny's side. Pougny went so far in the catalogue as to sign himself "the organizer," which tactfulness prevented even Zheverzheev from doing, and Oksana says that she has the right to take charge of everything, since it is they who have financed the exhibition, etc. This is all so disgusting, it's not worth writing about.*

Rostislavlev is in ecstasy over my works and told me that I probably don't appreciate my own merits, etc., and he should have said so in Rech', the louse. Well, never mind! I'm not upset. To hell with Oksana.

Furthermore. Suprematism is entirely my paste-ons: *a combination of planes, lines, discs (especially discs) and no incorporation whatsoever of real objects. And after all that these scum hide my name.*

Here is an exact copy of Oksana's picture [a drawing of the composition]—a ring, a wedge, and an incomplete wedge on a white background??? Malevich has a guilty look when he sees me, he's been taken down a peg or two, comes slinking around with obliging favors, you wouldn't recognize him. On the first day I demonstratively turned my back on him. Did you show him my paste-ons? When, exactly? *Unfortunately I only gave some suprematist reliefs (4), but no paintings. But my* representational *painting is infinitely more suprematist than Pougny's.*

I saw Zelmanova at the opening, she was glad to see me, invited me over to her place, I invited her, I don't know what will come of it. If there are any photographs or reviews I'll send them along. Pity you're not with me. Love. Write!

Kulbin and Matiushin were not at the opening. . . . Malevich remembered that he still hasn't sent you the package, for which I scolded him.

(Letter of Olga Rozanova to Aleksei Kruchenykh. (December 1915). Foundation Cultural Centre Khardzhiev-Chaga, Amsterdam.)

On the wall beneath their pictures at the exhibition (not in the catalog) they signed "Suprematism," but I did not, which is why that fool Rostislavlev did not number me among the group in his review, although his comments on the exhibition in general and about me in general were positive. Unfortunately, I have only one issue of the newspaper and don't know how to get it to you . . . There were also some completely stupid and hostile reviews in the Petrogradskaia gazeta *and* Listok, *and* Birzhev<ye> <vedomosti> *and* Den', *but I haven't read them yet.*

There are not many visitors to the exhibition. There were a little over 200 at the opening. This was the poorest opening I have ever seen. To satisfy your curiosity here is a copy of Malevich's Lady in Automobile *[a drawing of the composition] and*

Boating [*drawing of the composition*]. I didn't buy any postcards, too expensive. I'm short. . . .

The most disgusting thing about this whole exhibition and the artists is that everything is done underhandedly, and if before everyone "only worried about themselves," now everyone is mostly concerned with how at any price to harm someone else. That is why Pougny, who promised to make me some frames, deliberately did not, so that my pictures would look ragged. They have distorted the catalogue and done so many other petty things that even Malevich was forced to admit it is disgusting. . . . Malevich is like a lackey with them, and the stability of the organization hangs on whether he will remain satisfied with his "position" . . .

(Letter of Olga Rozanova to Aleksei Kruchenykh (December 1915). Foundation Cultural Centre Khardzhiev-Chaga, Amsterdam.)

In 1915 the last futurist exhibition 0—10 was held in St. Petersburg; that was what they called it: 0—10—the Last Futurist Exhibition. Malevich came to Moscow from this exhibition, bringing with him his suprematist squares and a whole retinue of artists. They were all going through suprematism at the time, and they came to tempt us with it.

A lot of people gathered in apartment no. 5; we didn't all know each other, so we became acquainted and listened with interest to what the Muscovites had to say. Besides us, who were always there—Artur Lurie, Altman, Tyrsa, Mandelshtam, Bruni, Mitrokhin, Kliuev, Rostislav Voinov, Nikolai Balmont—present that evening were Pougny, Boguslavskaia, Rozanova, Tatlin, Kliun, Udaltsova, Popova, and Pestel. There were also some people who, although they were neither artists nor writers, were considered to belong to the art world.

We gathered in Bruni's studio, a large room with a window overlooking the corner of Line 4 on Vasilevskii Island and the embankment of the Neva. I think it was looking out this window that F. Alekseev painted his famous landscape of the embankment and ships thronging the Neva. . . .

Austerity was in everything that was done then, in all works and experiments; people were serious and honest. We had all become abnormally tired of the vagueness and conventions of aestheticism, and were no less weary of the futurist trotting derbies. We were looking for art that was strong and simple, as simple as it could be simple in those transitional and turbulent years.

For a long time now we felt a breakthrough coming towards which, consciously or blindly, greedily or unwillingly, impatiently or with one eye on success, on money, on the past, we all were moving, leafing through the pages, days and months one after the other, just like life passing by outside the window: the life of the city, the war, everything we considered ours and all we thought to be contemporary.

(Nikolai Punin, *Kvartira No. 5*, Panorama iskusstv 12 [Moscow, 1990], 181–82.)

1916

January

On 16 January, an edition of 130 copies of Rozanova's album of linocuts, *War*, with poetry by Kruchenykh, was published.

War was published on Rozanova's efforts alone. The author of these lines had occasion to be intimately acquainted with the history of the work. Since this history is interesting not only for explaining the artistic tasks of the book but also to characterize the artist, one of the most typical futurists, and through her the conditions under which the new movement progressed, I think I should dwell in more detail on War. . . .

> (Andrei Shemshurin, *K biografii O. V. Rozanovoi* [manuscript]. Rodchenko and V. Stepanova archive, Moscow.)

It was necessary to order sheets with the title at the printer's, and moreover all the paper collages had to be done in Petrograd, since there was no colored paper in Vladimir. Here it was difficult even to find black, for it had completely disappeared from the shops. Thus we did not manage to get it done before the holidays, it had to wait until after, the cen-sor kept it for a week, but they told me at the printer's that on Saturday (the 16th) it would be out. The censor removed 15 nos. Before they only took 10, but now there was a military precensorship. Besides the censored nos. there will be 115. Unfortunately, I couldn't print more even if I'd had the means left to do so. It was very difficult to print. The standard typographical method also produces a standardized texture, and when a thick layer of paint is applied the prints dry awfully slowly.

There were days when I did 300 prints a day in a stupor, but then I wouldn't do anything for several days because I didn't have enough space in the house to dry them.

I'd be very grateful if you would not spare me and tell me your opinion of the work and point out all its defects. For the time being I'm sending you one no., because all the covers are now at the printer's. There on the obverse is where they will put the price (3 rubles) and publisher. . . .

I await your verdict and advice as to how to proceed further with the edition. Did I set a sensible price? I have no experience here.

I wish you all the best.

Now that I know that the censor has passed it and that the albums will be coming out soon, I feel myself drifting into a state of bliss.

> (Letter of Olga Rozanova to Andrei Shemshurin, 15 January 1916. OR GRB, f. 339, op. 5, ed. khr. 14.)

Power over the line and the brushstroke is the most charming power, and we understand why even the extremist Russian artists, the Russian "expressionists"—Olga Rozanova, V. V. Kandinsky, A. A. Exter—have been obliged recently to resort to purely graphic drawings.

> (A. Sidorov, *Russkaia grafika za gody revoliutsii* (Moscow, 1923), 60.)

Rozanova was forced by her financial situation to take a job in the Butkovskaia ferrotype shop.

I'm presently working at Butkovskaya's ferrotype, where my hours are 10–5 and eventually will be 8–5. Because I'm not used to this kind of work and because of the odor of the acids I get very tired and can't do anything else when I come home. But I really want to learn practically all printing methods: ferrotype, photography, tricolor printing, etc., so that although this entirely unartistic labor is very heavy, I appreciate the opportunity to get to know all this . . .

> (Letter of Olga Rozanova to Andrei Shemshurin, 10 February 1916. OR GRB, f. 339, op. 5, ed. khr. 14.)

Her finances undermined by the war, Olga Vladimirovna has taken a 50-ruble job in Butkovskaya's "art studio" as an engraver, chemist, etc. But the work is worth 1000!

The attached passage from her letter will tell you what a delight it is! All this is due entirely to her horrid economic circumstances! She should go home immediately, where she can live at her mother's for almost nothing, but she doesn't even have money for the paint and canvas she has to stock up on for the summer!

And is the kind of work she's doing at Butkovskaya's really what she should be doing? It's very painful to think about it, and you can't tell anyone, because you know (as you yourself have said) that "people are swine." Unfortunately, abandoned by the war in the wild Caucasus, I myself am utterly powerless to do anything. I'm writing this to you unbeknownst to O. V., not to influence you but merely to inform . . . O. V. is still a very young artist who has made great progress the past 2–3 years and will do a great deal more if she can keep her health, but in practical matters she is helpless. She should be filling purely artistic orders, but instead she is sitting in a reeking hole (the excerpt from her letter I'm sending confidentially). Unfortunately, you have not seen her best works. How versatile and promising she is as an artist may be judged by the attached draft sketches for paper collages. They can serve as (aesthetic) compensation for poisoning you with the mundane details of O. V.'s life! . . . I'll write about myself another time. . . .

(Letter of Aleksei Kruchenykh to Andrei Shemshurin, March 1916. OR GRB, f. 339, op.4, ed. khr. 2.)

March

Shemshurin persuaded Rozanova to leave her job at the ferrotype, offering her financial support so she could go home to Vladimir in the summer and paint.

Dear Andrei Akimovich,

I got your card and want to follow your advice and go home to Vladimir. My work here has been one big misunderstanding. All it has done is to keep me here. After working seven hours a day there I couldn't do anything at all at home, and the worst thing is that I simply cannot get used to the odor of ether and acid and really suffer terribly from it. If I can get a ticket I'll be home the first day of Easter. In the worst event I'll try to leave Petrograd on 13 April.

The Muscovites invited me to take part in their exhibition The Store [Magazin], *but rail transport is so slow these days that I couldn't send any pictures. Have you seen the exhibition and is it interesting? Another exhibition in which I wanted to participate is supposed to be held in Petrograd, but I doubt that it will take place.*

(Letter of Olga Rozanova to Andrei Shemshurin, 31 March 1916. OR GRB, f. 339, op. 5, ed. khr. 14.)

The Store exhibition in Moscow, organized by Tatlin, featured his own counter-reliefs and works by Kliun, Malevich, Popova, Rodchenko, Udaltsova, and Exter.

April

The exhibition *Contemporary Russian Painting* at the Dobychina Gallery in Petrograd (Field of Mars 7), displayed works by Kandinsky, Kulbin,

Popova, Pougny, and others. Rozanova contributed two pictures: a still life, and *Perfumery*.

> (*Katalog vystavki Sovremmenoi Russkoi Zhivopisi* [Petrograd, 1916], catalog nos. 288, 289.)

> ... *The exhibition* [Contemporary Russian Painting] *I mentioned in my previous letter opens today, and since I'm showing some things there I'm extending my stay in Petrograd. I want to take my pictures myself, because these days there are various problems with sending them. The exhibition closes in three weeks, and as soon as it does I'll be going home. ...*
> (Letter of Olga Rozanova to Andrei Shemshurin, 3 April 1916. OR GRB, f. 339, op. 5, ed. khr. 14.)

The Jack of Diamonds, in Moscow, invited Rozanova to become an active member. She wrote Shemshurin:

> *Dear Andrei Akimovich,*
> *Thank you very much for affording me the opportunity to leave a job that was in all respects burdensome, so that I could return to art. I got the 70 rubles. The other day the Jack of Diamonds suggested that I become an active member of the society, so perhaps next year I can exhibit in Moscow. In Petrograd as well some sort of exhibition is probably being organized, which means I'll have a lot to do this summer.*
> *In Petrograd it's still rather damp and cold, not much like spring. Evidently the art season will close with the exhibition I'm now in, and apparently there won't be any more here.*
> *Aleksei Eliseevich Kruchenykh wrote me that he has got a job in Sarykamish and will be going there in a few days.*
> *It seems it's very difficult just now to get out of Petrograd. Tickets on the trains south are sold out until 1 May. As soon as I can get one I'm going home.*
> *I've already told them at the ferrotype that I'm leaving. If Butkovskaya makes the place larger and it becomes possible to work in a healthy atmosphere by next year, I'll go back. She was very sorry to see me go, but as it is now working there is poison, and I'm eternally grateful to you for rescuing me from it. Wishing you all the best,*
> *Sincerely,*
> *O. Rozanova*
> (Letter of Olga Rozanova to Andrei Shemshurin, 9 April 1916. OR GRB, f. 339, op. 5, ed. khr. 14.)

Rozanova left Petrograd at the end of April and spent the summer in Vladimir, where she devoted herself to painting and poetry.

> *My poetry has led me so far afield that I'm beginning to fear for my painting. ... What if I'd suddenly move from painting to poetry?*
> (Letter of Olga Rozanova to Aleksei Kruchenykh, cited in Khardzhiev, Malevich, Matiushin, *K istorii russkogo avangarda*, 23.)

> *I created transrational poetry.*
> *1. by giving everyone well known examples of it*

2. by giving it an idea . . .

3. finally, by founding a school that includes Kruchenykh "in disguise"—Vasilisk Gnedov, Aliagrov, O. Rozanova, I. Terentev, Fedor Platov, Iu. Degen, K. Malevich, I. Zdanevich . . .

> (Aleksei Kruchenykh, "Otryvok iz zapisnoi knizhki tiflisskogo perioda [1917]; private archive, Moscow.)

Autumn

Today, the 28th, I arrived safely in Moscow. My address is Patriarch Ponds, Bekman building 5, apt. 29. . . . I feel that Moscow will divert me, appease me, calm me down.
> (Letter of Olga Rozanova to Aleksei Kruchenykh, [1916]; private archive, Moscow.)

Rozanova moved to Moscow.

I recently got a verbose letter from Kliunkov [Kliun]. Flattering and alarming.

They are afraid that the group with Bruni, Tatlin and others will be significantly larger and have more success with the public than the suprematists.

He's appealing to me.

He says that the suprematists should work closely and harmoniously, etc. and calls me a "rare artist," etc. . . .
> (Letter of Olga Rozanova to Aleksei Kruchenykh (1916). Foundation cultural Centre Khardzhiev-Chaga, Amsterdam.)

She became a member of the Supremus group that sprang up in Moscow in the latter half of 1916 under the aegis of Malevich. The society included Kliun, Popova, Udaltsova, Exter, Davydova, Menkov, and others. The secretary was Udaltsova, in whose apartment on Novinskii Boulevard the suprematists often gathered. Rozanova became the editorial secretary of the journal *Supremus*, initiated by Malevich, and was very active in its publication. She devoted almost all her time to work in the society. Malevich and Rozanova also enlisted contributions to the journal from Matiushin, Kruchenykh and Aliagrov (Roman Jakobson).

What do you think of the journal I'm planning? I've already arranged for everything. We're collecting materials and it's all set with the printer's. Send articles on the new trends. The first issue is on cubism, and go on from there. I won't use anything of my own until no. 3. I think that if you're willing, we can publish Victory over the Sun. *. . .*
> (Letter of Kazimir Malevich to Mikhail Matiushin, 27 October 1916, *Ezhegodnik rukopisnogo otdela Pushkinskogo doma na 1974 god* [Moscow, 1976], 185.)

November

At the Mikhailova Gallery in Moscow, the opening of an exhibition of the Jack of Diamonds featuring the works of the suprematists: Malevich, Kliun, Popova, Pestel, Pougny, Boguslavskaia, Udaltsova, Exter, as well as

Altman, the Burliuks, Chagall, Falk and others. Rozanova showed twenty-three paintings, most of them done in 1915.

> (*Katalog vystavki kartin I skul'ptury obshchestva khudozhnikov "Bubnovyi valet"* [Moscow, 1916].

> *The third "wartime" winter season evidently promises to be rich in artistic events. There is war, the draft, the high prices, the usual rumors—but art "turns" anyway, and the public still throngs the exhibitions and theaters. It was not for nothing that someone quipped in the Moscow press that Muscovites are almost as interested in "suprematism in painting and the dances of the Bacchantes in* Thamyras Cytharoede *as they are in . . . Miliukov's speeches in* The Duma. *. . . Malevich is heading off into an abstract extreme: his "suprematism" is nothing but embellished geometry. True, in his combinations of squares, crosses and circles there is a kind of movement and vivid color resonance, but . . . his painterly manner resembles the poster—drawings, even talented ones, remain drawings. . . .*

> *More faithful to the original "great art" of Picasso are Popova, Rozanova, and Pougny. In Popova's painterly architectonics there is at least form: cylinders and cubes; in Rozanova's compositions there is life, and pattern, and a delicately feminine elegance* (The Interior, Writing Desk, Nature morte, *and others). She is an artist with poetic feeling.*

> (Ia. Tugendkhold, "Pis'mo iz Moskvy," *Apollon* I [1917], 73.)

1917

January–February

Rozanova served in the Moscow Union of Cities, which until its dissolution in 1918 was a community organization that collected provisions for the front. This work, which she was forced to take owing to her extremely dire economic circumstances, took almost all her time. Nevertheless, she continued her collaboration with Malevich and Supremus, and developed her theory of *tvestopis'*.

> *I thought that it would be impossible to combine working and painting, especially of pictures posing complex color tasks. "I work," which to me is just firewood and a crust of bread. Admit that on the first day "memoranda," "bureaus," and the "out-box" put me in a state of solemn stupidity that by the second and third day became prostration. Now I think that I'll in any case get used to it, but the main thing is that my schedule has changed. Instead of the mornings, I'll be working there evenings from 5 to 10. For that reason I won't be giving a lecture on 25 February [on* tvestopis'*–N. G.]. Malevich will instead, if he manages to get permission in time. I prefer to paint in the mornings rather than prepare lectures.*

> *There is supposed to be a suprematist exhibition in a private home during Easter, but it hasn't been settled yet. . . . If I have time, I'll bring some paintings with a "transfigured color" scheme.*

> *All the best. I have to leave for work now.*

> (Letter of Olga Rozanova to Andrei Shemshurin, 18 February 1917. OR GRB, f 339, op. 5, ed. khr. 14.)

Together with Kruchenykh, Rozanova continues to explore the new genre of visual poetry:

I . . . sent a special delivery [letter] with the drawings of the poems for Shemshurin you asked for. The drawings are in colored ink. How did you like them? You probably haven't received them yet? As I wrote you already, I 'm crazy about these poems and the swirling letters in the transrational ones. I burst with pleasure when I contemplate–read them.
    (Letter of Olga Rozanova to Aleksei Kruchenykh [1916]. Foundation Cultural Centre Khardzhiev-Chaga, Amsterdam.)

18 February 1917
    Karetnaia–Sadovaia 10, apt. 38
    Dear Olga Vladimirovna,
    Thank you for your information on your job debut. I would like you to show me the painting with the transfigured color scheme as soon as you finish it.
    Sincerely,
    A. Shemsurin
        (Letter of Andrei Shemshurin to Olga Rozanova, 18 February 1917; private archive.)

27 February (12 March)–2 March (15 March)

The overthrow of the Russian autocracy. Rozanova was in Moscow, from where she wrote Kruchenykh.

In Moscow there was an obligatory mobilization, but only of workers. In general, the political horizons are unclear, cloudy. Matiushin is coming to Moscow from Petrograd with Olga Gromozova. The supply depot she's working in is being transferred here, and she along with it. . . .
    Mal[ev]ich is living at his summer cottage and says that in the summer he'll have two vacant rooms on the second floor that he can rent you for 20 r[ubles] a mo[nth]. My future is unclear. I left my job in the Union [of Cities] because of the staff reduction. Now I'll be looking for something else. But at first I want to go to Mama, rest a month or two. I think that I'll leave for Easter, although now it's again a tedious business getting into Moscow, because it's again off limits and they're shipping people out. But I think I'll manage it. I sent a lot of letters to Sarakamish. Of course they probably all got lost. Write more about how it is in Tiflis, when you're thinking of coming to Moscow, etc. . . .
        (Letter of Olga Rozanova to Aleksei Kruchenykh, 1917; from the collection of Aleksandr Parnis, Moscow.)

In Tiflis, Kruchenykh published *Balos*, a (mimeographed) collection of his and Rozanova's poetry.

Better known to us are other futurists who at present (1917–1918) are making their first appearance as poets: Ilia Zdanevich, Olga Rozanova, and Nikolai Cherniavskii.
    Olga Rozanova, the well–known artist, has some interesting examples of transrational poetry:

Уч ал бы

батал быт у

ал

ОН

("y" from Balos*)*

Or:

Лефанта чиол

Миал анта

[her lines in A. Kruchenykh's play Gly-gly*]*
(Aleksei Kruchenykh, *Ozhirenie roz, o stikhakh Terenteva i drugikh* [Tiflis, 1918], 12–13.)

March

On 21 March, a meeting of the Union of Youth chaired by Zheverzheev and Shkolnik decided:

1) to resume the activities of the society; 2) [to] induct as new members Altman, Annenkov, Voinov, Denisov, Karev, Chagall, and others.
(Minutes of the Union of Youth plenum, 21 March 1917. OR GRB, f. 121, ed. khr. 1, list 32.)

April

Beginning in the first week of Easter I will begin working for the Union of Cities. Up until now I still haven't worked there, but during this time they raised my salary to 105 rubles a month including lunch, so the conditions are splendid, but I'll have to work from 10 to 5.

After arriving at Christmas I also did 20 too decorative works for the exhibition, and I'll probably get around 300 rubles or maybe more for them. Not all at once, though, but only half and the other half next year. . . .
(Letter of Olga Rozanova to Aleksei Kruchenykh (1917). Handwritten copy made by N. I. Khardzhiev. Foundation Cultural Centre Khardzhiev-Chaga, Amsterdam.)

Together with Malevich, Rozanova selected materials and prepared the first issue of *Supremus* for publication. Later, in May she wrote Matiushin:

Dear Mikhail Vasilevich,

Supremus will soon publish a journal by the same name. A periodical. Strictly partisan in nature. Its program: suprematism (in painting, sculpture, architecture, music, the new theater, and so on). Articles, a chronicle, letters, aphorisms, poetry, reproductions of suprematist pictures, and applied art. Articles of a scholarly, artistic-scholarly nature, etc.

Knowing of your sympathy with this movement in art, Supremus invites you to contribute to the journal, and should you agree, to send as soon as possible articles on the art of criticism and whatever literary material you have that is ready for publication. It seems that you have already heard from Kazimir Severinovich [Malevich] about this journal project and what it is like.

We are beginning publication immediately, and owing to technical difficulties at present (lithograph equipment, etc.), to avoid delays in printing we are forced to make 15 May (Julian calendar) this year the deadline for accepting literary material. Please answer as soon as possible whether you want to contribute to the journal and if you do, do not delay sending us your articles, etc.

All correspondence and contributions should be sent to O. V. Rozanova, secretary, Supremus, *Karetnaia-Sadovaia 10 apt. 38, Moscow.*

I've moved to Moscow and intend to settle down here.

Members of Supremus contributing to the journal include Udaltsova, Popova, Kliun, Menkov, Pestel, Archipenko, Davydova and myself. Malevich is the editor, poets include Kruchenykh, Aliagrov, and others.

Sincerely yours,

O. Rozanova

Give my regards to Ekaterina Genrikhovna and Olga Konstantinovna.

(Letter of Olga Rozanova to Mikhail Matiushin, May 1917. IRLI, f. 656.)

To Nadezhda Udaltsova, secretary of Supremus, she wrote:

Dear Nadezhda Andreevna,

The following is ready for publication:

1. my article

2. Kruchenykh's play

3. "Declaration of the Word"

4. the poetry collection Balos *and*

5. Blue Eggs

Of these two collections Kruchenykh suggested publishing whatever we think possible. My two poems are here as well; tell Malevich that I don't object to including them.

I sent Malevich a card at his cottage telling him you have the materials. I waited for him until 6, missed a convenient train, but he didn't come. I'm leaving, I'll call the night I arrive.

I'm enclosing tricolor sewing patterns for the decorative section of the journal. Also decorative drawings by Iurkevich and others. They may be needed. . . .

(Letter of Olga Rozanova to Nadezhda Udaltsova, 1917; Drevin family archive, Moscow.)

For the journal Rozanova wrote "Cubism, Futurism, Suprematism," the title of which echoes that of Malevich's well-known brochure. In it she focused on the color laws of suprematism, presenting her own original elaboration of Malevich's theory.

The Moscow artists were busy organizing a new trade union of artists and painters (*Professional Union of Artist-Painters*), and Rozanova actively participated as a representative of Supremus. Of the events of these days she wrote Shemshurin:

Dear Andrei Akimovich,

I'm writing from Vladimir . . . up to the very day of my departure I didn't know for sure when I was leaving. Meetings of the delegates to UZhVZ [School of Painting, Sculpture and Architecture] *were supposed to take place on Friday or even Saturday. People have gone crazy! Thank God, they got along without a meeting. On Saturday at 6:55 P.M. I left, and by the Easter morning service I was home. From the train to the church.*

I was delighted by the kulich Easter cakes decorated with doves of sugar, golden leaves, lambs, and roses. . . .

When you get my letter, I'll have probably already returned to Moscow. I've been meaning to call you for some time now, but since the beginning of the revolution every day has been packed with melancholy impressions, surprises, and amusingly serious business. Of course if (besides the fact that I have a job) I were to tell you on the phone that I am:

a member of the Trade Union Club

a member of the cooperative

a delegate from Supremus

and the secretary of the journal by the same name that will be coming out any time now, etc., you would yawn and hang up. But what's it like for me! After all, as soon as I get home from work I have to go to one meeting or another and from 7 to 1 in the morning listen to people talking nonsense. This whole time the only intelligent things I heard were from David Burliuk and Mayakovsky. Some artists really are awful.

It is an interesting time, but for some reason I haven't noticed any real rebirth in any of them. They go on sputtering away as before. If the statutes aren't approved, then they are not statutes, and a society is not a society unless it has 100 members. . . .

Mayakovsky had some good things to say on the subject, him a delegate representing 4 1/2 persons and with no statutes at all. He scared the feeble-minded and got registered anyway.

All in all, of course, it's an interesting time, but these wretches have reduced everything to a bureaucracy.

On Friday we're having a [Supremus] *meeting, so that day I won't be able to think or speak soberly: I'm chronically tired. But in general the idea of this journal and a reborn Supremus are a thrilling joy!*

I want as soon as I can to paint, write articles, etc., and I am definitely convinced that I must!

For heaven's sake, don't just say "you're deluded." Please, or you'll give me a chill. . . .

(Letter of Olga Rozanova to Andrei Shemshurin, April 1917. OR GRB, f. 39, op. 5, ed. khr. 14.)

May

Thousands of circumstances great and small keep upsetting my routine. Twice I went to Vladimir to visit Mama, who has still not quite recovered. And in the evening there was a Bacchanalia of gatherings and meetings. Lately they've exhausted me so that I've halfway ceased to exist physically, and all that is rushing about Moscow is my astral body. . . .

Columns of dust and the orchestra of urban odors do not put you in a bucolic mood. It's terribly irritating that spring comes only once a year, and if you stay through it in town there is no second one to experience outside town. So I'll be spending the entire summer here from start to finish.

I'm wondering: will they wash the streets or not? And will there be paper and sun-flower seeds on the sidewalk all summer?

As for Kruchenykh's play [Gly-Gly]: *the Suprematists offered to publish it in* Supremus, *the first issue of which is already made up. . . .*

The time is soon coming, it seems, when I'll be able to paint some pictures, for if the artists do not organize into some sort of union the next few days, they won't be organiz-ing at all. I'm so tired of them! The wretched daubers! I've been organized for a long time now!

(Letter of Olga Rozanova to Andrei Shemshurin, 6 May 1917. OR GRB, f. 339, op. 5, ed. khr. 14.)

Karetnaia-Sadovaia 10, apt. 38

Dear Olga Vladimirovna,

Thank you very much for the news and for your efforts on behalf of Kruchenykh's play. I will be the whole time in Moscow.

I was very pleased to learn that you are organized, although I would be even more pleased to know that you have completed the painting with the transfigured color scheme.

Sincerely,

A. Shemshurin

(Letter of Andrei Shemshurin to Olga Rozanova, private archive.)

Dear Mikhail Vasilevich,

I got your article and gave it to the editor. We had a meeting the other day. All the lit-erary material has been collected. Everyone is in a wonderful humor, we're hoping that the journal will be substantive and interesting not only to the people who worked on making it a reality. We firmly believe in our art and will do what we can to work and get it recognized. Write and send more.

All the best. Greetings.

(Letter of Olga Rozanova to Mikhail Matiushin, 23 May 1917. IRLI, f. 656.)

At the end of May, a trade union of painters was organized in Moscow based on the Union of Art Workers. The founding meeting on 27 May decided that the union would consist of three autonomous fed-erations: Senior, Central, and Young (Left), represented on the executive council of the union by Grishchenko, Malevich, Rozanova, Tatlin, and Yakulov. Persuaded by Rozanova, Matiushin joined some-what later.

Dear Mikhail Vasilevich,

Not so long ago in a letter to me you seemed to express sympathy toward the Moscow painters' union. As secretary of the Union (Young Federation), I would like to bring to your attention the fact that painters from Petrograd and the provinces also have the right to join and enjoy the same rights as the Moscow members with the exception of member-ship on the Council. Only permanent residents of Moscow who are able to actively orga-nize meetings and conduct the business of the Union are eligible for election to the

Council. Although it is summer, the Union is steadily expanding and adding new members. The senior federation is already a permanent bureau staffed by members who provide information over the telephone. I am attaching the program of the Union. If you would like to join, please let me know which federation or group you want to be registered in: Senior, Central, or Young? Give us also your permanent address and from which exhibition you wish to be registered; if from all the exhibitions in which you have participated, please list them. Membership dues are 5 rubles. Please send them to me at Karetnaia-Sadovaia 10, apt. 38. I will immediately send you a membership card. If you know of any painters wishing to join, please inform them of how to do so. Anyone who has ever participated in an exhibition as a member or exhibiting artist is entitled to join.

The composition is as follows. Senior Federation: Wanderers, Academy artists, periodical exhibitions, part of the Union of Russian Artists. Central: the other half of the Union, the World of Art, the drawing-room artists, the Moscow Association of Artists, the Jack of Diamonds. Young: futurists, suprematists, extreme left.

Join the Young federation. Each federation has one vote regardless of number of members. And new members vote through their federation. The Young federation includes Grishchenko, Yakulov, some of the participants of the Jack of Diamonds, although not the main ones; Lentulov, Milman, Mashkov and others joined the Central federation. The Burliuks will probably join the Young, since Yakulov is there and they are friends of his.

Tell me whether you got the program.

Transferring from one federation to another is allowed, but of course it should be sensible—after all, the suprematists are not going to join the Senior one or vice versa.

(Letter of Olga Rozanova to Mikhail Matiushin, 1917. IRLI, f. 656.)

Summer

Rozanova was obliged to spend the summer in Moscow, busy as before in the artists' union. She participated in the meetings of the Artistic Enlightenment Commission attached to the Soviet of Worker's Deputies and worked on publishing the journal. It was practically impossible for her to paint at this time, but she nevertheless began developing her own theory of *tsvetopis'*, or painting with "transfigured color," with an intense study of the laws of color.

. . . the group of painters that at one time shared the method of suprematism in abstract art produced individuals who either gave up color in favor of composition and painting (Udaltsova) or on the contrary intensified it to the point of decorativeness and dissonances (Rozanova) and finally abandoned the suprematist method.

(Varvara Stepanova, *Chelovek ne mozhet zhit' bez chuda. Zapiski khudozhnitsy* [Moscow, 1994], 52–53.)

5 July 1917

Karetnaia-Sadovaia 10, apt. 38

Dear Olga Vladimirovna,

If you are still alive, how are you? Is the painting with the transfigured color scheme ready yet? Kruchenykh writes that I should read his article on Khlebnikov. I understand you can immediately get it for me from Malevich. If you really can, please tell me when I can see you and get the article. Cordially yours,

A. Shemshurin

(Letter of Andrei Shemshurin to Olga Rozanova, 5 July 1917: private archive.)

I am not dead yet, but considering the shape I've been in this whole time you could paint a nature morte of me. For some reason I am always tired. I think it's because I'm not used to living in the city. There isn't enough air, and the sun shines into the room the whole day, there's no getting away from it. . . . These past few days there has been some fuss in connection with the publication of the journal, which is still being printed, and there is other business as well.

I immediately began painting two pictures—one realistic, the other suprematist. I didn't have the strength to finish the first one, it's all so alien to me, especially working by memory without nature, that I dropped it and will not return to it; the second one is almost done . . . in it I found a new way of investigating color; if it isn't at variance with the "transfigured" method it is possible in suprematist painting as well. I want to paint big things, but I'm waiting to have some free time, there is no sense in painting at odd moments. I only like to do things I enjoy! And unexpected chance interruptions of my work bother me and disrupt the wholeness of the plan.

In general, I want to be an artist first and then all the rest, and I think that soon that is how it will be.

Work in the trade union is coming right along and doesn't bother me. The journal will be out perhaps already in August, and then FREEDOM!

(Letter of Olga Rozanova to Andrei Shemshurin, 9 July 1917. OR GRB, f. 339, op. 5, ed. khr. 14.)

November—December

On 21 November, the Jack of Diamonds exhibition opened, in which Rozanova took part.

The Jack of Diamonds exhibition . . . like a well-sewn old-fashioned quilt was made up of pieces. One sizeable section consisted of canvases quite obviously selected to cover the walls. . . . The second section was the remains of the Jack of Diamonds, centered on David Burliuk. . . . Finally, the last piece was made up of the "suprematists"—Malevich, Kliun, Pougny, Rozanova, Davydova, etc. "Geometry in colors" flourishes here; just like last year, there are the same parallelograms, circles and triangles filled with paint of various colors and positioned one to the other in certain spatial relations. . . . But exhibitions are no place for such laboratory experiments.

(Rosstsii [Abram Efros], "Khronika," *Apollon* 8–10 (1917), 109–110.)

6–19 December

Rozanova participated in the *Second Exhibition of Contemporary Decorative Art*, organized by Natalia Davydova in Moscow (11 Dmitrovka). It featured embroideries and cloth appliqué work done on the patterns of the suprematists by peasants of the village of Verbovka in Kiev province.

The exhibition featured over sixty works based on Rozanova's sketches of prints, ribbons, book covers and handbags. In all there were some 400 works, among which embroideries and dolls based on patterns and "suprematist" drawings by Exter, Pougny and Davydova, and so on. It opened on 6 December, and on 17 (30) December Mayakovsky gave a paper on the new art. The exhibition also included an auction.

(See Vasilii Katanian, *Mayakovsky. Khronika zhizni I deiatel'nosti* [Moscow, 1985], 137.)

"It's very boring to specialize in any one form of art," Olga Vladimirovna would say, and she also wrote wonderful essays on art. . . .

(Ivan Kliun, "Predislovie," *Posmertnaia vystavka kartin, etiudov, eskizov i risunkov O. V. Rozanvoi* [Moscow, 1918], iii.)

During this period Rozanova made a great many fabric, and women's clothing, designs.

1918

January

A decree of the Narkompros (People's Commissariat for Enlightment) established the section of Visual Arts, with David Shterenberg as its director. The Art Collegium was organized in March, and included Altman, Karev, Matveev, Pougny, and Sergei Chekhonin, among others. They were later joined by other architects and artists, among them Vladimir Baranov-Rossiné, Shkolnik, and Mayakovsky.

In 1918–1919 the All-Russian (Central) division of IZO consisted of two sections of equal standing in Petrograd and Moscow. Shterenberg was assisted in Moscow by his vice-director, Vladimir Tatlin, and in Petrograd by Nikolai Punin, both of whom were also directors of their respective city Art Collegiums. In the spring of 1918, the newly reconstituted Moscow Collegium included Mashkov, Morgunov, Malevich, Udaltsova, Rozanova, Falk, Shevchenko, Kandinsky, and others.

April

In Tiflis, the *Exhibition of Paintings and Drawings of the Moscow Futurists* organized by Kruchenykh was held in the building rented by the editorial offices of the journal *Ars* (9 Golovinskii prospekt). It featured works by Bart, David Burliuk, Goncharova, Grishchenko, Zdanevich, Kliun, Kulbin, Larionov, Malevich, Tatlin, Filonov, Shevchenko, and others, as well as colored paper collages by Kruchenykh (including those for his album *Universal War* (*Vselenskaia voina*), and Rozanova's drawings, engravings and collages (thirty-one in all).

50. OLGA ROZANOVA'S BODY LYING IN STATE. NOVEMBER 9, 1918.
PHOTO BY ALEKSANDR RODCHENKO.
COURTESY OF A. RODCHENKO AND V. STEPANOVA ARCHIVE, MOSCOW.

Dear Sergei Mitrofanovich,

I would like to speak with you about the following:

I have some of Rozanova's and mine + drawings by Filonov, Larionov, Goncharova, etc. Do you think we could exhibit them in the near future at Ars?

(Letter of Aleksei Kruchenykh to Sergei Gorodetskii, 5 April 1918, Tiflis; private archive, Moscow.)

24 May

A meeting of the IZO Art Collegium unanimously elected Rozanova head of the industrial art section with a salary of 600 rubles. Her duties included the following:

* *all questions concerning industrial art throughout Russia: direction of the artistic aspect of glass, porcelain, and ceramic factories, plants and workshops, including the former imperial porcelain factory;*
* *the organization and development of handicraft production;*
* *the reestablishment and administration of existing arts and crafts schools throughout Russia;*
* *equipping and furnishing the People's Houses;*
* *questions having to do with art and the manufacture of household objects, toys, etc.*

(Personnel file of Olga Rozanova, 24 May–November 1918. TsGA Rossii, f. 2306, d. 55, ed. khr. 204. Personnel-related correspondence with Narkompros administration, 1918. TsGA Rossii, f. 2306, d. 23, ed. khr. 28, l. 18.)

Rozanova's vice-director was Aleksandr Rodchenko.

> *Together with Olga Rozanova I worked on organizing the industrial art subsection. We visited workshops, artels and artisans. We picked up the work they had abandoned. We supplied money and materials and fixed up abandoned art schools. We organized the Museum of Painterly Culture.*
>
> (Aleksandr Rodchenko, *Stat'i. Vospominaniia. Avtobiograficheskie zametki. Pis'ma* [Moscow, 1982], 63.)

> *As soon as IZO began to be organized, Rozanova took active part in the work. . . . Thus she worked out a series of measures designed to enhance the artistic aspect of the production of our artisans, and for this purpose she outlined the organization of a network of Free Industrial and Artisan Studios. Despite all the inconveniences of transportation at the time, she made a great many visits to the provinces in order to acquaint herself on the spot with the situation of industrial art and handicrafts. Thus she traveled to the Bogorodsk district, Ivanovo-Voznesensk, Vladimir and other places. She gave a number of papers in which she propagandized for the establishment of the Workshops. As a result, the Art and Handicrafts Subsection organized these workshops in Ivanovo-Voznesensk and Bogorodsk. The icon-painting school in Mstery was reorganized. She also devoted a lot of attention to the organization of museums of industrial art. In Moscow she inspected the Stroganov Museum, the Handicraft Museum, and the Rumiantsev and other museums. Based on these inspections she elaborated a plan to address a number of shortcomings and deficits. . . .*
>
> ("Pamiati O. V. Rozanovoi" [obituary], *Iskusstvo* I [1919].)

> *As one reads today the account of IZO's activities, one is amazed by the grandiose program for improving industrial art that was projected for the near term and that has remained practically the maximum . . . down to the present. We also cannot help but note the activity of the pioneers in this cause—Chekhonin, Averintsev, Baulin, Arkin, and especially the late artist Rozanova.*
>
> *"To the factories, the plants, to the industrial schools and workshops!"—such was the battle cry of the first years of the Revolution.*
>
> (Ia Tugenkhold, "Zhivopis' revoliutsionnogo desiatiletiia 1918–1927," in his *Izbrannye stat'i i ocherki. Iz istorii zapadnoevropeiskogo, russkogo i sovetskogo iskusstva* [Moscow, 1987], 229.)

June

On Bolshaia Dmitrovka St. in Moscow, the *First Painters' Trade Union Exhibition*, in which 180 representatives of the Senior, Central, and Left Federations participated with more than 700 works. Representing the Left (or Young) Federation were Grishchenko, Zhegin, Menkov, Kliun, Pestel, Popova, Rodchenko, Rozanova, Udaltsova, Chekrygin, Shevchenko, and others.

On 26 June there was a plenum of the Moscow union at which the entire Left Federation withdrew from the union in protest against the abolishment of federation divisions within it. The day after the meeting the daily *Anarchy*, published the "Resolution of the Left Federation Adopted at the Union Plenum" signed by federation chairman Tatlin and secretary Rodchenko:

> * *Whereas the trade union is an organization meant to protect the legal and material position of the artist, and the division into autonomous federations guarantees the fundamental viability of the union, the Left Federation regards the Central Federation's proposal to eliminate such divisions . . . as fatal to the life of the union.*
> * *The Left Federation declares that it remains the only artistic and social center uniting all existing groups of left artists. . . .*
> ("Rezoliutsiia levoi federatsii na obshchem sobranii profsoiuza," *Anarkhiia* 95 [1918].)

July

On 2 July, *Anarchy* carried Rozanova's article "The Destruction of the Tri-Federation Organization of the Union as the Cause of the Withdrawal of the Left Federation." Two more of her articles were published in the same newspaper: "Suprematism and the Critics" (in issue no. 86) and "Art—only in Independence and Freedom!" (in issue no. 91). Regular contributors to the paper's art section included Malevich, Rodchenko, Udaltsova, and other avant-garde artists.

October–November

The opening of the Free State Art Workshops was scheduled for 1 October. The students elected their own instructors. On their preliminary list for the position of director of the special textiles studio they nominated Rozanova. The list was approved by the Collegium of IZO.

> (Personnel-related correspondence with Narkompros administration, 1918. TsGA Rossii, f. 2306, op. 23, ed. khr. 28, l. 7.)

A resolution was adopted establishing a state monopoly over the organization of art exhibitions. Those in Moscow and the provinces were to be arranged by IZO. It was stipulated that exhibitions were to be 1) without judges, and 2) free of charge.

Rozanova participated in the preparation of decorations for the celebration of the first anniversary of the October Revolution in Moscow.

> *Ailing, straining every nerve, she nonetheless took part in decorating the streets and squares of Moscow. With her strong sense of duty she knew that her help was needed, and therefore she agreed to work. On 31 October she fell very ill and was brought to a friend's place from the airport she was helping decorate. On 1 November the doctors diagnosed diphtheria and sent her to the Soldatenskii (now Botkinskii) hospital.*
> ("Pamiati O. V. Rozanovoi" [obituary], *Iskusstvo* 1[1919].)

*On 7 November at 10:00 AM Olga Rozanova—Artist and Inventor . . . Revolutionary
of Art, a leading Master of Suprematist painting . . . passed away.*

> *Was it not you who wanted to light up the world in cascades of color.*
> *Was it not you who proposed projecting color compositions into the ether.*
> *And how early you left us . . .*
> *Perhaps your brain grew weary from your innovative ideas . . .*
> *You thought of creating color through light. . . .*
> *You were one of the few who stood in the avant-garde of extreme Left Art.*
> *You were an eternal Revolutionary and Innovator in composition and technique.*
> *You amazed us with your fantasies.*
> *An Anarchist of Creation, you were a tireless, ever new Genius of Innovation.*
> *Olga Rozanova has died, but your art will shine forever.*

> (Aleksandr Rodchenko, note dated 7 November 1918. A. Rodchenko and V.
> Stepanova archive, Moscow.)

Rozanova is dead—the first victim of the Collegium [of IZO]. *This is so sad, although
I'll be more surprised now if people survive.*

> (Diary of Nadezhda Udaltsova, 9 November 1918. Nadezhda Udaltsova, *Zhizn'
> russkoi kubistki. Dnevniki, stat'i, vospominaniia* [Moscow, 1994], 49.)

Dear Nadezhda Andreevna,

> *I was deeply stricken by the news in the papers of poor Olga Vladimirovna's death.
> I even refused to believe it, but today it was confirmed by the funeral notice. I am
> unspeakably sorry, sad, unhappy. I value her highly as an artist, especially in the area of
> decorative art, and I felt sorry for her as a person, for living was so hard, lonely and sad
> and she struggled so bravely and cheerfully with the difficulties of life. . . .*

> *Nadezhda Andreevna, has it been suggested or might it not be suggested at one of our
> coming meetings that we discuss arranging a posthumous exhibition of Olga Vladimirovna's
> works? I would personally like to see something positive in this respect, and I would be very
> willing to help organize such an exhibition, as complete a one as possible, so that . . . things
> from the Union of Youth and Streetcar V would be represented. . . .*

> (Letter of Liubov Popova to Nadezhda Udaltsova, November 1918. Drevin
> family archive, Moscow.)

December

The First State Exhibition, organized by the central exhibition bureau
of IZO, opened at the exhibition hall on Rozhdestvenka Street in
Moscow: Ivan Kliun prepared the catalog for this *Posthumous Exhibition of
Paintings, Etudes, Sketches, and Drawings by O. V. Rozanova.*

> *. . . all her life, Olga Rozanova was in the front line of fighters for new ideas in art. Her
> eternally inquisitive soul could not get along with old forms and always protested against
> repetition both in everyday life and in art.*

> *A keen observer of life, she was able to sense in time that newborn nerve that was des-
> tined on the morrow to become the exponent of the time, the mirror of the present day.*

> *All the latest trends in art that arose in the logical process of its evolution found Olga*

Vladimirovna in their midst . . . in recent years, when painting ventured beyond the boundaries of the material world and became the pure art of color (suprematism), here as well Olga Vladimirovna occupied a prominent place and played an important role. All the leading exhibitions had her pictures on their walls. . . .

Some of her paintings have been acquired by the Museum of the New Art (the Museum of Painterly Culture). . . . Her keen, resonant poetry, interesting illustrations of the principle that "the word is sound and letter," have thus far not been published, but will be soon.

In both her art and her life, Olga Vladimirovna was true to herself. Although she was sociable by nature, she nevertheless said repeatedly that try as she might she simply could not merge with the human environment in which she had to live, even though she found it very friendly and cordial. Naturally, her eternally searching, eternally struggling spirit of protest did not allow her to merge with people who perhaps were friendly, but whose lives were guided by traditions and prejudices.

(Ivan Kliun, "Predislovie," *Katalog posmertnoi vystavki Rozanovoi* [Moscow, 1919], i–iv.)

The exhibition was organized by Kliun, Stepanova, Exhibition Bureau Director Wladyslaw Strzeminsky, and Aleksandr Drevin. Many of Rozanova's pictures were especially brought from Vladimir by Strzeminsky and shown here for the first time.

Drevin, Strzeminsky and I . . . set off to visit Rozanova's exhibition. . . . Over the sign Kliun and his gang were hanging an enormous black square on a white canvas . . . Drevin and I were extremely upset. As we were going up to the exhibition we ran into Strzeminsky; how could he permit Malevich's hallmark to be pasted onto Rozanova?

We looked at the exhibition. It was alive, shining with color. . . .
(Varvara Stepanova, *Chelovek ne mozhet zhit' bez chuda*, 63).

During the preparation of the exhibition a feud broke out between the suprematists (Malevich's group) and the nonobjectivists and future constructivists (Rodchenko, Stepanova, and others). The two groups each insisted that Rozanova belonged to their camp. Stepanova noted in her diary:

We go to look. . . . Oh, delightful! Malevich has brought out three more enormous canvases with square black shapes of colossal dimensions . . . there is a hue and cry . . . we protest—you can't hang this at Olga Rozanova's exhibition if she was breaking up the square. . . .

I jump on Malevich for the square at Olga Rozanova's exhibition. At first he pretends he doesn't hear me. . . . Anti [Rodchenko] doesn't get it at first, since we didn't have time to explain everything in detail, but then he says over and over, "We'll take the square down." The atmosphere thickens. Drevin begins (figuratively) thrashing Malevich for the square. . . . Malevich heats up, D[revin] jumps on Malevich for wanting to put his label on Rozanova. . . . M[alevich] begins attacking Rozanova, saying that she came from him and that he showed her and Davydova how to make suprematist decorations and that Rozanova has calques taken from his works; Drevin defends Rozanova as an independent

artist who did not come from Malevich and proposes going to see her exhibition. . . .
Rozanova always gravitated toward the earth even in her suprematist works, which were
influenced by Malevich, but she still produced her own, reworked movements of the soul
and feeling of an artist, which she infused with paint and color that was not mystical like
that of Malevich.

(Varvara Stepanova, *Chelovek ne mozhet zhit' bez chuda. Pis'ma. Poeticheskie opyty. Zapiski*
khudozhnitsy [Moscow, 1994], 63–64.)

The exhibition contained 250 works, from her early school studies to
the latest works in the area of *tsvetopis'*. There were seven thousand visitors over four months (to its close in March 1919). Kliun's and
Stepanova's lectures on her art were prepared and read at the exhibition.

She must be accorded a leading place among abstract artists. . . . In her works a sense of
color is combined with a primitiveness of form, but this primitive approach by no means
weakens the impression produced by her pictures; on the contrary, it strengthens it,
because the essence remains in the work. Remarkable in this respect is her series of play-
ing cards, in which the composition is superb and color intensity taken to an extreme. . . .

However one views "abstraction" as a trend in painting as a whole, one is forced to
acknowledge that in Olga Rozanova Russian art has lost a talented artist.

("Posmertnaia vystavka Rozanovoi," *Vechernie izvestiia*, no. 149 [18 January
1919].)

In her essence, Olga Rozanova is an artist of color. Running like a red thread from her
earliest period to her final achievements in the area of tsvetopis' is color, through which
she perceives the visible world. All of her periods are represented at the exhibition: impres-
sionism, futurism, her portrait period, alogism, suprematism and tsvetopis', and in all of
these periods she is a painter of color [tsvetopisets]. *Olga Rozanova's art is through-*
out based on a play and movement of color. Color in her works is alive, whence the
absence of texture, which always inhibits the complete manifestation of color. The exhi-
bition shows Rozanova to be a talented artist who is so independent and well-defined that
although she has futurist and cubist periods, even there she starts with color and borrows
from these trends not their essence, but only a means of expression, so that she became nei-
ther a futurist nor a cubist.

In Rozanova's art we sense that Great Decorativeness that throws painting out of
rooms and museums onto the streets and squares.

Through color Rozanova perceives not only the visible but also the spiritual side of
life. Recall her Portrait in Pink Dress, *that unusual portrait of a power almost*
unique in all the new Russian painting, in which both the profound psychology of the por-
trait and her approach to portrait painting is refracted through the prism of color. There
is an entire period in Rozanova's portraits whose caustic and original futurism makes it
enormously valuable to Russian art.

Rozanova's palette—vivid, rose-lilac—sometimes intersects with green splotches,
but pictures always have a common coloring, a kind of color spectrum vocality with which
they primarily operate. Besides the general link within a given picture we can also note

links among several pictures that allows them to fall into groups . . . her art is so whole and
fused that the quantity of things and different periods she represents help rather than
obscure her personality.

Looking at Rozanova's suprematist period, we see that her suprematism is opposite that of Malevich, who constructs his works on the basis of squares. Rozanova uses
color instead. In Malevich color exists only to distinguish one plane from another,
whereas in Rozanova it serves to reveal all the possibilities on a plane. To suprematism
she contributed a suprematism of painting, not of the square. Of special interest is the
room containing the suprematist works of her final period. Here, unlike other periods,
color does not play with the brilliance of its nuances but is stripped to its essence. The
structure of the pictures is based on mutual color relationships (the suprematist paintings) or on the development of some particular color into an autonomous picture
(the works of the final period). Here we can trace the transition from the planes of
suprematism into color that is broadly thinned to liberate it from its dependence on
form and plane.

Overall, the exhibition is a vivid expression of Rozanova's personality, and the first
thing that leaps into view is her constant movement forward, that which she herself considered the best quality of every true artist.

   (Varst [V. Stepanova], "Vystavka O. Rozanovoi," *Iskusstvo* 4 [22 February,
   1919].)

1919

December 1918–January 1919

In the name of the Art Collegium, IZO has resolved to publish a collection dedicated to
the memory of Olga Vladimirovna Rozanova, who passed away on 7 November last
year. The book will contain reproductions of her art works as well as articles, poetry, and
essays on art.

   (Announcement in the weekly *Iskusstvo* 3 [1 February, 1919].)

It was decided at a meeting of the commission on the organization of the Museum of
Painterly Culture that it would be located in Petrograd. Its first acquisition was the purchase from L. Zheverzheev of two paintings by O. Rozanova. Artists whose works are
scheduled for purchase include Malevich, Tatlin, Kuznetsov, Rozanova, Udaltsova,
Popova, Kliun, Davydova, Morgunov, Pevzner, Exter, Larionov, Goncharova, Filonov
and others.

   (Announcement in *Iskusstvo* 5 [1 April, 1919].)

Today Stepanova brought all of Rozanova's manuscripts and materials for the book.
Publishing it will take a lot of work.

   (Aleksandr Rodchenko, "Iz zapisei raznykh let" [1918], in : A. M.
   Rodchenko, *Stat'i. Vospominaniia. Avtobiograficheskie zapiski. Pis'ma* [Moscow, 1982],
   49.)

Rozanova's poetry appeared in the first column of the weekly *Iskusstvo* 4
(22 February).

Comrade Friche is complaining bitterly that Iskusstvo *has published Olga Rozanova's poetry. He does not understand it and is prepared to regard it almost as a threat to the existing order.*

(*Iskusstvo* 5 [1 April, 1919].)

On 13 April at the Palace of the Arts in Petrograd, the First State Free Exhibition of Art opened, which also featured works by Rozanova. Moscow saw the Seventh State Exhibition of IZO, which was dedicated to the reorganized state industrial art studios. In Ivanovo-Voznesensk, the state industrial art studios were named in honor of Rozanova.

The Tenth State Exhibition, *Abstract Art and Suprematism* in Moscow, featured 220 works by 9 artists: abstract book engraving by Agarykh V. (Varvara Stepanova); color compositions by A. Vesnin, suprematist works by Davydova; suprematist and color compositions by Kliun, as well as his abstract sculpture and a sketch of a monument to Rozanova; suprematist works by Malevich; suprematist works and combinations of light and color by Menkov; painterly architectonics by Popova, and color abstractions, an abstract composition and a project of a monument to Rozanova by Rodchenko. There were also two of Rozanova's *tsvetopis'* works. The catalog contained short statements by all of the participants. Her works were also exhibited at the First Exhibition of Local and Moscow Painters in Vitebsk.

PART III

ИЗДАНIЯ
Г. Л. Кузьмина и С. Д. Долинскаго.

"ПОЩЕЧИНА ОБЩЕСТВЕННОМУ ВКУСУ" — стихи, проза и статьи Д. Бурлюка, В. Маяковскаго, В. Хлебникова, Н. Кандинскаго, А. Крученыхъ и др. Ц. 1 р.
"ИГРА ВЪ АДЪ", поэма А. Крученыхъ и В. Хлебникова рис. Н. Гончаровой, Ц. 60 к. (распродано)
"СТАРИННАЯ ЛЮБОВЬ", поэма А. Крученыхъ, рис. М. Ларiонова. Ц. 30 к. (распродано)
"МIРСКОНЦА", А. Крученыхъ и В. Хлебникова,

рис. М. Ларiонова, Н. Гончаровой, Роговина Ц. 70 к.
"ПУСТЫННИКИ", поэма А. Крученыхъ, рис. Н. Гончаровой. Ц. 50 к.
"ПОМАДА", А. Крученыхъ, рис. М. Ларiонова. Ц. 50 к.
"ПОЛУЖИВОЙ", А. Крученыхъ, рис. М. Ларiонова. Ц. 40 к.
"ТРЕБНИКЪ ТРОИХЪ", Д. Бурлюкъ, В. Хлебниковъ и В. Маяковскiй (печатается)

СПБ. Книгоиздательство.

"САДОКЪ СУДЕЙ" I сборникъ (распродано)
"САДОКЪ СУДЕЙ" II сборникъ.
"ОСЕННIЙ СОНЪ" — Е. Гуро.
"ШАРМАНКА" — Е. Гуро.

СКЛАДЫ ИЗДАНIЙ — Москва, Кар. рядъ Б. Совскiй пер., д. 15, кв. 8. СПБ. Аптек. островъ, Песочная 9, кв. 3.

Пощечина Общественному Вкусу.

Въ 1908 году вышелъ «Садокъ Судей». Въ немъ генiй — великiй поэтъ современности — Велимиръ Хлебниковъ впервые выступилъ въ печати. Петербургскiе Метры считали „Хлебникова сумасшедшимъ". Они не напечатали, конечно ни одной вещи того, кто несъ собой Возрожденiе Русской Литературы. Позоръ и стыдъ на ихъ головы!..

Время шло. В. Хлебниковъ, А. Крученыхъ, В. Маяковскiй, Б. Лившицъ, В. Кандинскiй, Николай Бурлюкъ и Давидъ Бурлюкъ въ 1913 году выпустили книгу «Пощечина Общественному Вкусу».

Хлебниковъ теперь былъ не одинъ. Вокругъ него сгруппировалась плеяда писателей кои, если и шли различными путями, были объединены однимъ лозунгомъ: «Долой слово средство, за здравствуетъ Самовитое, самоцѣнное Слово!» Русскiе критики, эти торгаши, эти скромные невѣжды, дубовые въ своемъ ежедневныхъ вольяжѣ, толстокожiе и не понимащiе красоты, разразились моремъ негодованiя и ярости. Неудивительно! — Имъ ли, воспитаннымъ со школьной скамьи на образцахъ Описательной поэзiи, понять Великiя откровенiя Современности.

Всѣ эти безчисленные сюсюкающiе (Измайловы, Homunculus) питающiеся объѣдками падающими со столовъ реализма — рады-за Андреевыхъ, Блоковъ, Соллогубовъ, полошившихъ и имъ подобныхъ — утверждаютъ (какое гнѣвное обвиненiе!) что мы дерзаемъ посягать изъ нихъ — и что мы не сказали ничего новаго — ни въ размѣрѣ, ни въ риѳмѣ, ни въ отношенiи къ слову.

Развѣ были оправданы изъ русской литературѣ наши приказанiя чтить Права поэтовъ:
на увеличенiе словаря въ его объемъ произвольными и производными словами (на непреодолимую ненависть къ существующему языку)
съ ужасомъ отстранять отъ гордаго чела своего изъ банныхъ вѣничковъ, сдѣланный вами, злючекъ грошевой славы..
стоять на глыбѣ слова мы среди моря свиста и негодованiя!

FUTURIST MANIFESTO *A SLAP IN THE FACE OF PUBLIC TASTE*. LEAFLET. ST. PETERSBURG, 1912.

ARTICLES
by Olga Rozanova

Union of Youth Manifesto

St. Petersburg, 23 March 1913

Through our early activity of organizing art exhibitions and readings and lectures on art, we, the Union of Youth, intended to afford the public interested in art an opportunity to become acquainted with the Contemporary Young Art and to show them its technical credo.

We shall continue to develop and enhance these practical presentations in the future as well.

By arranging today not a paper but a debate on art in which all of our opponents are invited to participate we declare our artistic credo.

We are making our appearance in an unusual, unique time!

The entire nervous character of the life of Art today demonstrates with unquestionable persuasiveness that the Dominant Role presently belongs to Art and painting!

It is attracting extraordinary attention as never before!

And, close already to liberation, the New Art has more enemies than ever before!

Who are they, these enemies, whom we declare we shall combat, and of what do they accuse us?

Is not that of which our opponents accuse us a token of our victory and power?

Or does our love of Art, which makes us hunger to see it liberated, deserve the lumps of filth hurled at us!

We declare war on all the jailers of the Free Art of Painting who fetter it in the chains of the everyday: politics, literature, and the nightmare of psychological affects.

We declare that the painter cannot pick other people's pockets, but can only speak the language of painterly and creative experiences.

We declare war on all those who cultivate the sentimentality of their personal experiences, on those self-centered Narcissi for whom nothing is dear but their own, infinitely reflected countenances!

We declare war on the Penal Art of The World of Art group, which looks at the world through only one window. [Playing on the well-known phrase that Peter the Great "cut a window to Europe," Rozanova sarcastically alludes to the Eurocentrism of the decadent St. Petersburg World of Art group-N. G.]

We want to see this world opened wide!

Here is our challenge to everyone who accuses us of theoretical speculation, of decadence, of a lack of immediacy!

Where do these gentlemen find immediacy?

In the base tyranny of emotional experiences!—always the same ones!

So much the worse for them!

We declare that to limit creativity is to poison Art!

That the freedom of creativity is the first condition of originality! Hence it follows that there are many paths open to Art!

We declare that all paths are good except those that have been trampled and muddied by the innumerable steps of others, and we value only works whose novelty generate a new individual in the viewer!

Here is a challenge to all those who accuse us of instability, who tempt us with the haven of peaceful slumber—a dormitory in which deeply sleep the Wanderers, the World of Art, the Union of Russian Artists and all the other lovers of spiritual lodgings whose atmosphere is already beginning to lull even the Jack of Diamonds.

We do not envy their unanimous snoring.

The sun of Art shines so brightly that it is a crime to sleep.

We declare war on all those who prop themselves up on the comfortable word "principles," for this venerable word sounds good only in the mouths of those who are doomed to fall behind the impetuous rush of time!

To this decrepit word we oppose the word "renew."

Our slogan:

"The Future of Art is in uninterrupted renewal!"

We open the doors wide to all young people to whom our slogan is dear, whose hands are strong enough to hold high our banner, and we leave outside the door the doubters, the cautious, those who don't know where to turn, for these confused, bewildered dregs of Art have only one servile lot: to repair tattered banners of others!

We despise the word "Glory," which transforms the artist into a stupid animal who stubbornly refuses to move ahead even when it is driven by the whip.

From ceaselessly turning back to the past a good many people have sprained their necks.

There is no honor for us in turning to some such absurd specter of the past, to the sterile fiction of something that no longer exists!

We do not even aspire to be remembered posthumously.

Enough of this Cult of cemeteries and corpses.

But we will not allow ourselves to be forgotten while we are alive, for we are awake and we will never cease to disturb the slumber of the lazy as we enlist ever new forces in our eternally new and eternally beautiful struggle.

(1913) Translated by Charles Rougle.

The Bases of the New Creation and the Reasons Why It Is Misunderstood

The art of Painting is the decomposition of nature's ready-made images into the distinctive properties of the common material found within them and the creation of different images by means of the interrelation of these properties; this interrelation is established by the Creator's individual attitude. The artist determines these properties by his visual faculty. The world is a piece of raw material—for the unreceptive soul it is the back of a mirror, but for reflective souls it is a mirror of images appearing continually.

How does the world reveal itself to us? How does our soul reflect the world? In order to reflect, it is necessary to perceive. In order to perceive, it is necessary to touch, to see. Only the Intuitive Principle introduces us to the World.

And only the Abstract Principle—Calculation—as the consequence of the active aspiration to express the world, can build a Picture.

This establishes the following order in the process of creation:

1. Intuitive Principle
2. Individual transformation of the visible
3. Abstract creation

The fascination of the visible, the charm of the spectacle, arrests the eye, and the artist's primary aspiration to create arises from this confrontation with nature. The desire to penetrate the World and, in reflecting it, to reflect oneself is an intuitive impulse that selects the Subject—this word being understood in its purely painterly meaning.

In this way, nature is a "Subject" as much as any subject set for painting *in abstracto* and is the point of departure, the seed, from which a Work of Art develops; the intuitive impulse in the process of creation is the first psychological stage in this development. How does the artist use the phenomena of nature, and how does he transform the visible World on the basis of his relationship with it?

A rearing horse, motionless cliffs, a delicate flower, are equally beautiful if they can express themselves in equal degree.

But what can the artist express if he repeats them?

At best, an unconscious plagiarism of nature, for which the artist, not knowing his own objectives, could be forgiven; at worst, a plagiarism in the literal sense of the word, when people would refuse to reject it merely out of creative impotence.

—Because the artist must be not a passive imitator of nature, but an active spokesman of his relationship with her. Hence the question arises: to what extent and to what degree should nature's influence on the artist be expressed?

A servile repetition of nature's models can never express all her fullness.

It is time, at long last, to acknowledge this and to declare frankly, once and for all, that other ways, other methods of expressing the World are needed.

The photographer and the servile artist, in depicting nature's images, will repeat them.

The artist of artistic individuality, in depicting them, will reflect himself.

He will reveal the properties of the World and erect from them a New World—the World of the Picture, and by renouncing repetition of the visible, he will inevitably create different images; in turning to their practical realization on the canvas, he will be forced to reckon with them.

The Intuitive Principle, as an extrinsic stimulus to creation, and individual transformation—the second stage in the creative process—have played their role in advancing the meaning of the abstract.

The abstract embraces the conception of creative Calculation, and of expedient relations to the painterly task. It has played an essential role in the New Art by indissolubly combining the conception of artistic means and the conception of artistic ends. Modern art is no longer a copy of concrete objects; it has set itself on a different plane, it has upturned completely the conception of Art that existed hitherto.

The artist of the Past, riveted to nature, forgot about the picture as an important phenomenon, and as a result, it became merely a pale reminder of what he saw, a boring assemblage of ready-made, indivisible images of nature, the fruit of logic with its immutable, nonaesthetic characteristics. Nature enslaved the artist.

And if in olden times, the individual transformation of nature found occasional expression when the artist changed it according to his individual conception (the works of archaic eras, of infant nations, the primitives), it was, nevertheless, an example of an unrealized property, attempts at free speech, and more often than not, the ready-made images triumphed as a result.

Only now does the artist create a Picture quite consciously not only by not copying nature, but also by subordinating the primitive conception of it to conceptions complicated by all the psychology of modern creative thought: what the artist sees + what he knows + what he remembers, etc. In putting paint onto canvas, he further subjects the result of this consciousness to a constructive processing that, strictly speaking, is the most important thing in Art—and the very conception of the Picture and of its self-sufficient value can arise only on this condition.

In an ideal state of affairs the artist passes spontaneously from one creative state to another, and the Principles—the Intuitive, the Individual, the Abstract—are united organically, not mechanically. I do not intend to analyze the individual trends of modern art but wish merely to determine the general character of the New creative World View. I shall touch on these trends only to the extent that they are the consequence of this New creative psychology and evoke this or that attitude in the public and critics nurtured on the psychology of the old conception of art. To begin with, the art of our time will be fatally incomprehensible to such people unless they make the effort to accept the required viewpoint.

For the majority of the public nurtured by pseudo artists on copies of nature, the conception of beauty rests on the terms "Familiar" and "Intelligible." So when an art created on new principles forces the public to awaken from its stagnant, sleepy attitudes crystallized once and for all, the transition to a different state incites protest and hostility since the public is unprepared for it.

Only in this way can the enormity of the reproaches cast at the whole of the Young Art and its representatives be explained.

—Reproaches made from self-interest, self-advertisement, charlatanism, and every kind of mean trick.

The disgusting roars of laughter at exhibitions of the leading trends can be explained only by a reluctance to be educated.

The bewilderment at pictures and titles expressed in technical language (directrix, color instrumentation, etc.) can be explained only by crass ignorance.

Undoubtedly, if a person came to a musical evening, read in the program the titles of the pieces—"Fugue," "Sonata," "Symphony," etc.—and suddenly began to roar with laughter, indicating that these definitions were amusing and pretentious, his neighbors would shrug their shoulders and make him feel a fool.

In what way does the usual kind of visitor to current "Union of Youth" exhibitions differ from this type as he creases up with laughter when confronted with specific artistic terms in the catalog and does not take the trouble to ascertain their true meaning?

But if the attitude of a certain section of the public is tactless, then that of the critics and their confrères in art toward its Young representatives is, unfortunately, not only no less tactless and ignorant, but is often even careless. Everyone who follows the art scene is familiar with A. Benois's articles on cubism:

"Cubism or Ridiculism?" is a shameful stain on Russian criticism.

And if such a well-known art critic displays complete ignorance of questions of a specialized nature, then what can we expect from the newspaper judges who earn their bread and butter by looking for truths to please the mob's bigoted opinions!

When there is no possibility of averting your opponent's victory by disarming him, there is only one thing left—to depreciate his significance.

The opponents of the New Art resort to this onslaught by rejecting its self-sufficient significance, declaring it to be "transient"; they do not even understand properly the conception of this Art and dump cubism, futurism, and other manifestations of art life onto the same heap. Hence they elucidate neither their essential difference, nor their common cohesive theses.

Let us turn to the concepts *transient* and *self-sufficient*. Do these words denote a qualitative or a quantitative difference? In all the manifestations of cultural life and hence in art as well, only an epoch of Senility and Imitation—a period of life's mortification—can, according to the only correct definition, be called a "transient epoch."

Every new epoch in art differs from the preceding one in that it introduces many new artistic theses into its previously cultivated experience, and in following the path of this development, it works out a new code of artistic formulas. But in the course of time, creative energy begins inevitably to slacken.

New formulas cannot be cultivated—on the contrary, those cultivated previously develop artistic technique to an extraordinary level of refinement and reduce it to prestidigitation of the paintbrush; the extreme expression of this is a crystallization into the conditioned repetition of ready-made forms. And in this soil the putrid flowers of imitation thrive. Without going into the depths of art history, we can cite examples of imitation from the not too distant past (it, too, has grown obsolete), namely, the exhibitions of the "World of Art" and especially the "Union of Russian Artists" as they now stand: they give nothing to the treasure house of art and essentially are merely the epigones of the Wanderers. The only difference is that the servile imitation of nature with a smattering of Social-Populist ideology (the Wanderers) is replaced in this case by the imitation of an intimate aristocratic life with its cult of antiquity and sentimentality of individual experience (the cozy art of the "World of Art" exhibitions and their like).

I pointed out above that all previous art had touched on problems of a purely painterly nature only by allusion and that it had confined itself generally to the repetition of the visible; we can say therefore that only the nineteenth century, thanks to the school of the impressionists, advanced theses that had been unknown previously: the stipulation of a locale of air and light in the picture and color analysis.

Then followed Van Gogh, who hinted at the principle of dynamism, and Cézanne, who advanced the questions of construction, planar and surface dimension.

But Van Gogh and Cézanne are only the estuaries of those broad and impetuous currents that are most well defined in our time: futurism and cubism.

Proceeding from the possibilities to which I alluded (dynamism, planar and surface dimension), each of these currents has enriched art with a series of independent theses.

Moreover, although initially they were diametrically opposed to each other (Dynamics, Statics), they were enriched subsequently with a series of common theses. These have lent a common tone to all modern trends in painting.

Only modern Art has advocated the full and serious importance of such principles as pictorial dynamism, volume and equilibrium, weight and weightlessness, linear and plane displacement, rhythm as a legitimate division of space, design, planar and surface dimension, texture, color correlation, and others. Suffice it to enumerate these principles that distinguish the New Art from the Old to be convinced that they are the Qualitative—and not just the quantitative—New Basis that proves the "self-sufficient" significance of the New Art. They are principles hitherto unknown that signify the rise of a new era in creation—an era of purely artistic achievements.

—The era of the final, absolute liberation of the Great Art of Painting from the alien traits of Literature, Society, and everyday life. Our age is to be credited with the cultivation of this valuable world view—an age that is not affected by the question of how quickly the individual trends it has created flash past.

After elucidating the essential values of the New art, one cannot help noting the extraordinary rise in the whole creative life of our day, the unprecedented diversity and quantity of artistic trends.

Messrs. art critics and veterans of the old art are being true to themselves in their fatal fear of what is beautiful and continually renewing itself; they are frightened and tremble for the little caskets of their meager artistic achievements. In order to defend publicly this pitiful property and the positions they occupy, they spare no effort to slander the Young Art and to arrest its triumphant procession. They reproach it further with frivolity and instability.

It is high time that we realized that the future of the Art will be assured only when the thirst for eternal renewal in the artist's soul becomes inexhaustible, when wretched individual taste loses its power over him and frees him from the necessity of continually rehashing.

Only the absence of honesty and true love of art provides some artists with the effrontery to live on stale tins of artistic economies stocked up for several years, and year in, year out, until they are fifty, to mutter about what they had first started to talk about when they were twenty.

Each moment of the present is dissimilar to moment of the past, and, and moments of the future will contain inexhaustible possibilities and new revelations!

How can one explain the premature spiritual death of the artists of the Old Art, if not by laziness?

They end their days as innovators before they are barely thirty, and then turn to rehashing.

There is nothing more awful in the World than repetition, uniformity.

Uniformity is the apotheosis of banality.

There is nothing more awful in the World than an artist's immutable Face, by which his friends and old buyers recognize him at exhibitions—this accursed mask that shuts off his view of the future, this contemptible hide in which are arrayed all the "venerable" tradesmen of art clinging to their material security!

There is nothing more terrible than this immutability when it is not the imprint of the elemental force of individuality, but merely the tested guarantee of a steady market.

It is high time that we put an end to the debauch of critics' ribaldry and confessed honestly that only "Union of Youth" exhibitions are the pledges of art's renewal. Contempt should be cast on those who hold dear only peaceful sleep and relapses of experience.

(First published in *Soiuz molodezhi 3*, 1913) Translated by John E. Bowlt[1]

Cubism, Futurism, Suprematism

To most people's minds the word painting tends to mean a figurative art, the art of conveying what is seen, what is perceived concretely. Primarily, everyone seeks a real life meaning in a painting.

1. *Russian Art of the Avant Garde. Theory and Criticism*, ed. and trans. John E. Bowlt (New York, 1988), 100–110.

For the past centuries painting has trodden this path.

For figurative painting the "phenomenon" is the content, where-as the way this is transmitted is the supreme aim. I shall draw a parallel between the essential nature of figurative art and that of non-objective art, specifically of Suprematism. Figurative art was born of a love for the object.

Non-objective art has been born of a love for color. This is paint-ing above all.

We propose to liberate painting from its subservience to the ready-made forms of reality and to make it first and foremost a creative, not a reproductive, art.

The savage happily drawing the outlines of a bull or a deer on a piece of stone, the primitivist, the academician, the artists of antiq-uity and of the Renaissance, the Impressionists, the Cubists, and even to some degree the Futurists are all united by the same thing: the object. These artists are intrigued, delighted, amazed, glad-dened by nature. They try to fathom her essence, they aspire to immortalize her.

Via the object, via the form of nature they come to painting.

The visible world is the residence of their creative soul!

The Impressionists abolished composition not because they were indifferent towards the depicted object, but because for them every-thing in nature was equally nice and loveable!

The Cubists distorted form out of all proportion not because they aspired to free themselves from nature, but because they aspired to convey her as fully as possible.

In this sense Cubism is the climax to the adoration of the object.

True, Cubism killed the love of the everyday appearance of the object, but not the love of the object as a whole. Nature continued to be the guide of esthetic ideas. The works of the Cubists lack a clearly defined idea of non-objective art.

Their art is characterized by efforts to complicate the task of depicting reality. Their complaint against the established prescrip-tions for copying nature turned into a formidable bomb that smashed the rotten metaphysics of figurative art to smithereens—an art that had lost all idea of aim and technique.

The Cubists asserted that the creative consciousness is just as real as what it responds to, and that an individual's subjective assertion is more valuable than the code of current opinions.

Should we continue to affirm the primacy of antique beauty and keep on measuring the human body by 7½ heads and 19 middle fingers?

Do we have to submit to the manuals on aerial perspective just to please our imperfect sight?

The Cubists' distrust of how we see nature, of our conditional perception of nature, and their endeavor to comprehend the essence of the object compelled them to multiply the ways of approaching the object and its depiction (consciousness, experience, touch, intuition). Cubism introduced many new painterly revelations, it defined the interrelationship of color and form and the diversity of texture.

The dynamism of form which the Cubists had recognized found its complete expression in Futurism.

It removed color from the confines of trivial forms and brought it to the creation of abstracted forms—to Suprematism.

In force and acuity Futurism provided art with a unique expression—the fusion of two worlds, the subjective and the objective. Maybe this event is destined never to be repeated.

But the ideological gnosticism of Futurism had no effect on the damned consciousness of the majority who, to this day, continue to reiterate that Futurism marks an upset in the course of world art, a crisis of art. As if hitherto there had existed just one kind of faceless art instead of the many, many physiognomies throughout history.

After all, art evolves like anything else on earth.

But because of its exclusive affirmation, Futurism—the immortal monument to our epoch—was branded by a malicious handful of whistlers and vulgarizers from the local press.

Futurism expressed the character of our contemporaneity, and it did so with complete acumen.

Our time is one of metal, its soul is initiative and technology: the Futurists brought technology to its brilliant fullness.

The Futurists expanded the concept of the media of figurative painting beyond the confines of factory paints (the Dosekin, Meves and other corporations), and they introduced stick-ons, the relief, various materials, different textures.

Those who supported the unity of media did not understand the technical accomplishments of Futurism because they were unable to connect them with the ideological content of its method.

The essence of dynamism is in Cubism: "Grasp a few consistent images of the object which, once fused into one, will restore it within its continuum" ("Du Cubisme" by Gleizes and Metzinger). By means of fragmentation the acute dream of cohesion can be evoked.

The essence of dynamism is in Futurism: by means of fragmentation the very sensation of dynamism (and not its depiction) can be evoked.

Until the Futurists came along, artists expressed movement in the following conventional manner: a maximum expression of movement resulted from placing forms on the surface of the canvas parallel to the diameter of the canvas; a maximum static expression resulted from placing the forms parallel to the surface of the canvas.

The spectator did not sense movement in the picture. All he saw was a rendering of movement.

The conditional conception of up and down established the position of objects subject to the effect of the laws of gravity and spectator convenience.

This practical consideration occasioned the predominance of plastic equilibrium and symmetry in world art. Such was the academic principle: one trick for a square frame, two or three for an oblong frame, etc. depending on the character and size of the canvas, etc. The painting was a function of the frame, of the tight surround which the joiner can make with ease but which cannot always accommodate an artistic idea. In depicting objects in movement and also from the objects' viewpoint, the Futurists provided composition with a freer character.

The displacement of objects galloping off into space upset the concern with placid convenience. It gave rise to the notion of asymmetrical composition founded on plastic dissonances. To the prejudiced eye this was something very unexpected, but, in accordance with its objectives, it was profoundly real.

For the Suprematists the painting, once and for all, ceased to be the function of the frame. We do not regard the forms with which we operate as real objects. We do not force them to depend upon the up and down directions in the picture. We reckon with their practical meaning—which they don't have.

We consider their painterly content. Consequently, the dominance of symmetry or asymmetry, static or dynamic elements is the result of creative thinking and not of the preconceived notions of mundane logic. The esthetic value of the non-objective painting lies completely in its painterly content.

Now let me turn to the relation of figurative and non-objective art to color, to the connection between color and texture, and to the relation of both arts to form.

We see the color of objects to lie in their coloration—in the refraction of light (the rainbow, the spectrum). But we can also conceive color independently of our conception of the object and outside of the spectral sequence.

We can see green, blue and white mentally.

We can regard this capacity for evoking colors in the imagination as a reminiscence of color excluded from the body of the object—color that has ceased to be material.

We respond optically to any painted surface, we see it as color. But as we look at the painted object, we see this or that color within the dimensions of the surface it is occupying (the pink blush of the apple, these green roofs) as well as in connection with the material nature of the object (its construction, its pigment quality, etc.). In this way we materialize the immaterial essence of the color.

For example, how can we determine the color of polished wood? It is impossible to match a piece of crimson silk with a piece of calico, wool or paper of the same color.

The color of a ripe peach or orange is caused not only by the properties of the pigment, but also by the protuberances and hollows, velvetness or smoothness of its skin.

The texture of the material gets in the way of the probable nature of color. It is a surrogate for pure painting.

Inasmuch as it aimed to reproduce reality, figurative painting used to measure the quantity and essence of color with the yardstick and quality of ready-made forms, and, with its own texture, imitated the texture of the object being depicted: texture imitating material. This impeded the creation of painting in which color, not imitation, is the aim and objective. A second surrogate for painting is the sculptural forms of objects.

As an attachment to the nature of objects, color is the expression of something or other in matter. It changes its quality depending upon the form and its illumination.

Take a red disk whose diameter is equal to that of a ball also painted red. The former will express the color red more extensively, more uniformly over its entire surface. The ball will have the same strength of effect only when it is at the point of maximum illumination right up close to us.

This point can be regarded as being a surface identical to that of the disc, except that it is incomparably smaller. But as the ball recedes from the source of light, all its remaining points seem to become darker and darker, more and more inconstant. It no longer conveys the color as it did in the first phase.

A third surrogate for painting is aerial atmosphere. These surrogates change the primary essence of color and convert it into tones. Realistic painting is concerned precisely with tone and not with color. Realistic painting took little trouble over the quality of the material (paint) with which it was operating.

The Neo-Impressionists created an optical color system for conveying aerial atmosphere. But they applied their laws to real forms. Since any change of color causes a change of form, they destroyed and distorted the real forms by force of this esthetic law. However, rejection of these forms was not part of their program: so they got stuck half way. They couldn't find a way of connecting this renewed color with a renewed texture. The Futurists provided us with the dynamism of forms. But they too were still dependent upon the ready-made forms of their particular environment and were also unable to liberate color from alien elements. In using dynamism, they simply destroyed form and color in the way figurative art had been using them.

The unreality of the Cubo-Futurists was a product of their self-destructive desire to convey the total reality of the object via the prism of pure subjectivity. This was so remarkable that this "non-existence", created by the artist's will, acquired the value of a new reality, of a kind of abstract absolute which killed any interest in what was actually being observed. The Cubists and Futurists were unable to free themselves from the object, but we can admire their anguish and their presentiment of new horizons.

"We acknowledge that the memory of natural forms cannot be ignored absolutely; in our time, at least, it is impossible to elevate art immediately to pure effusion" ("Du Cubisme" by Gleizes and Metzinger). But we Suprematists say you can't have both: either you make a skilful reproduction of reality, or you pursue painting as an end in itself. In the latter case, you have to reject irrelevant aims and you have to reject ready-made forms because their properties and atmosphere clog up color. Figurative painting had too many obligations: the imitation of nature, a preconceived plotline, etc., and these things deflected it from tasks of immediate importance—the communication of color.

Figurative painting communicated a complex of impressions of the phenomenon.

True, the history of figurative painting provides us with examples of deviations from naturalism. The conventional composition that places objects in an unnatural position (unnatural from the standpoint of everyday life) is in itself a protest against naturalism. The same with the aspiration to enrichen an object with color, with color hyperboles and metaphors, up to and including the distortion of form.

But the more real form is distorted, the less comprehensible is the persistence of the artist who refuses to reject it.

Why not reject it immediately if it does not correspond to, or express, the desired color content. The importunateness of reality inhibited the artist's creativity. As a result, common sense triumphed over freedom of vision. And the frail vision that remained created works of art devoid of principle, the mongrels of contradictory world-views.

Suprematism rejects the use of real forms for painterly ends. Like leaky vessels, they cannot hold color. Stifled by the fortuitous simplicity or complexity of these forms, which may not always correspond to their respective color content, color just creeps about, faded and dim. The figurative sign of nature is self-sufficient, and it is absurd to operate with it while trying to pursue ultra-painterly ends.

We create quality of form in connection with quality of color, and not each separately.

We set the plane as the transmitter of color since its reflective surface will transmit color with greater profit and less mutability. As a result, reliefs, stick-ons, textures that imitate material reality, and sculptural effects (for example, a brush-stroke creates shadow) which were used in figurative painting (right up to, and including, Futurism) cannot be applied to two-dimensional painting on a plane: such factors influence and change the essence of color.

Color properties enter into conflict with each other in duration, intensity and gravity. This entails the intrusion or displacement of one color by another.

Painterly form is the nature of realizing (embodying) color on a plane with the aid of material paints and to whatever extent is absolutely necessary in each individual case. Otherwise, the laws of color correlation within the conditions of the planar expression will give rise to the individualization of painterly forms.

The aggregate of variously colored, painterly forms, brought together in particular positions, might create the illusion of a sculptural relief. But this has no esthetic significance for non-objective painting on a plane. The quality of the forms that contain the colors and their interrelationships justifies their purpose insofar as these forms serve to expose color properties (and not because they might create an impression of surface by the contiguity of their actual planes).

Just as a variance in the atmosphere can create a strong or weak air current in nature, one that can upset and destroy things, so dynamism in the world of colors is created by the properties of their values, by their weight or lightness, by their intensity or duration. This dynamism is, essentially, very real. It is imperious. It engenders style and justifies construction.

Dynamism liberates painting from the arbitrary laws of taste and establishes the law of pragmatic inevitability. It also liberates painting from utilitarian considerations.

This is how it differs from applied art.

A vase is painted within the framework of its practical, useful form. Its painted ornament cannot survive outside this form and justifies its existence by its connection with this. The color ecstasy of a carpet is inhibited by its size and form.

The decoration in a book is linked to the dimensions of the page. It is adapted to the script, to the size of the book, etc.

Repetition of a basic design occurs in decorative (applied) painting because it is obliged to adapt itself (to circumstances). This is fine as far as the conditional aim is concerned, but not beyond the confines of unconditional freedom.

Most people are used to looking at works of painting as items of everyday domestic life—still a luxury for the few, but, ideally, for general consumption. But we protest against such vulgar utilitarianism. The works of pure painting have the right to exist independently and not in relation to banal interior furnishings. To many, our efforts and endeavors—as well as those of our Cubist and Futurist predecessors—to put painting on a course of self-determination may seem ridiculous, and this is because they are difficult to understand and do not come with glowing recommendations. Nevertheless, we do believe that a time will come when, for many people, our art will become an esthetic necessity—an art justified by its selfless aspiration to disclose a new beauty.

(1916-1917) Translated by John E. Bowlt[2]

2. From *Painting to Design*. Catalog of exhibition of the Galerie Gmurzynska (Cologne, 1981) 100-113.

Suprematism and the Critics

The untalented artist sits and tries to figure out how to contrive a painting, selecting just the right forms so as not to appear outdated or to irritate the critics with too much novelty. They don't like such things.

But the pseudo-creative approach of the ungifted traces a cautious curve. . . .

Caution is the most typical sign of lack of talent. Its mark of servility.

But the critics look and cannot get enough: "Now here," they say, "is a cultured artist."

Creation is a great act of contempt toward all that is within and outside us, toward the obvious, and a great act of attention toward that which is just beginning to take shape.

Capable of creating are only those who feel new and different from everything else.

To produce a work of genius the artist must possess an acute awareness of reality and extraordinary will power to be able to renounce the past and avoid confusing its false, decrepit image with emerging newness.

Genius is the specific gravity of genuine vitality.

What the critics fear most of all is that which is "unheard of."

Seated in their comfortable high-backed armchairs, they work with old materials.

The greatest pleasure in art is to do something unheard of.

The most critical state is indignation at the obsolete.

Not only technique changes, but also aesthetic psychology in general, but the critics never notice this immediately. They become entangled in details of differences and analogies as they adjust the new to fit the old, and they simply cannot get any idea of the whole.

"Now if this one had learned a little from that one and borrowed a thing or two from that one, he might have been something!" He might have become a "cultured" artist!

But the critics find themselves in a hopeless situation when they are obliged to put on an clever face and speak or write about something of which they do not understand an iota.

It is not difficult to babble on about Futurism.

The last dot over the "i," the destruction of the Old World, but not a complete abandonment of it.

True, you won't find an entire person in the picture, but you can find a limb of some sort and unburden your heart on it.

But just try something like that with Suprematism! No arms, no legs! A square in space!

With no indications of its relationship to the laws of gravity!

And why should anyone want to paint such things?! There's nothing like that abroad or at Sergei Ivanovich Shchukin's.

Such things are unheard of!

And the critics gravely and authoritatively announce that this is not quite art. These are "laboratory experiments."

But they are not entirely sure of what they are saying—they sense that the new art is winning, and the public also no longer seems the same but is beginning to trust the artists more.

You tear it to pieces but, well, you never know, you may have to take it all back.

Actually, this is all the critics have ever done.

They are prosecutors, not critics.

Has there ever been a case in which the critics immediately recognized and supported some outstanding and original talent or trend in our art?

They are impressed with foreign stuff.

And it is embarrassing to look at the tactlessness and lack of self-respect with which they fawn upon the West and spit upon or ignore all the originality our native art has produced.

Comrade critics, how good it would be if you were unheard of!

(First published in *Anarkhiia* 86, 1918.) Translated by Charles Rougle.

Only in Independence and Unlimited Freedom is there Art!

For better or worse, man is changing, the world is changing.

And each age, as it shows its new face, shows a new art.

The critics throw up their arms, spit, quarrel intensely, but sooner or later "acknowledge" it.

The public "acknowledges" somewhat earlier.

And the critics imagine that it is they who have helped this along.

But for a long time they are afraid. They are distrustful. They lament the fading charm of former times as old women cry about the old days.

It is awful when your soul is old.

When there is no faith in the future.

When from all corners, from all dusty cupboards and folios the faces of corpses peer forth and frighten you.

The past is imaginary, populated by dead souls. Congestion. A bog.

How can you create with your head turned toward the old times?

Is this not absurd? A child can understand it. But they keep telling us: "traditions," "experience," "examples of the past," old boots. . . .

Man is so simple that there is no use dwelling on the fact or rejecting new experience or the opportunity of bursting out of this stuffy cell, the prison of the past, into the new world.

Enough excursions into days that have disappeared into the past! Art must be an expression of its own time and its values.

Typical of our age is a hunger for freedom, a longing for freedom, a hunger to see the world transformed.

Our art breaks the old frameworks, is daring.

But our prereform critics go on in the old way wanting to kill everything living in art, to paralyze its development, to kill in it the soul and mind of the time.

Conservatism has elevated to a law this periodic persecution of everything new.

How long will the voice of critics who pimp for artists dominate public opinion?

Is it not the artist who renews life?

One would think that the fact that art is multifaceted and changes its face and brings with it new faiths would cause amazement and joy.

One would think that the innovative artist would be greeted like a brave seafarer, like a cherished guest.

But what do we see? Vainglorious backslapping or malicious distrust and mockery.

They mumble: "You acknowledge the young, but what if they suddenly get uppity? No reason to spoil them, let them rot in their clammy corners" . . .

Everything is frightening to you, whose souls are old and spiteful!

But it is not frightening to those who value the present higher than the most beautiful past!

No matter what the past was like, it is dead.

No matter what the present is like, it is alive, dynamic, the source of hopes and promise.

Art is not only in technique—it is the all-penetrating breath of life. And no matter how frightening the time seems to you, the cowardly, art is similar to it the higher it reaches.

The confirmation of art, its base, is in the sphere of continually arising reflections.

(First published in *Anarkhiía*, 91, 1918). Translated by Charles Rougle.

SELECT BIBLIOGRAPHY

By Olga Rozanova

Articles

Manifest "Soiuza Molodezhi."
Leaflet. St. Petersburg: Zhivoe slovo, 1913.

"Osnovy Novogo Tvorchestva i prichiny ego neponi-
maniia." In *Soiuz molodezhi* 3 (1913): 14-22.
English translation: "The Bases of the New
Creation and Why It Is Misunderstood." In *Russian
Art of the Avant-Garde: Theory and Criticism*,
revised and enlarged edition. Edited and translated
by John E. Bowlt, 100-13. London: Thames and
Hudson, 1988.

"Kubizm, futurizm, suprematizm." In *Neizvestnyi
Russkii Avangard v muzeiakh i chastnykh sobrani-
iakh*. Edited by N. Gurianova and A. Sarabianov,
334-6. Moscow: Sovetskii khudozhnik, 1992.
English translation: "Cubism, Futurism, Suprematism."
In *From Painting to Design: Russian Constructivist
Art of the Twenties*. Catalog of exhibition. Edited
and translated by John E. Bowlt, 100-13. Cologne:
Galerie Gmurzynska, 1981.

"Suprematizm i kritika." In *Anarkhiia* 86 (1918).
English translation: "Suprematism and Critics." In
*Russian Women-Artists of the Avant-Garde: 1910-
1930*. Catalog of exhibition. Translated by John E.
Bowlt, 246. Cologne: Galerie Gmurzynska, 1979.

"Iskusstvo - tol'ko v nezavisimosti i bezgranichnoi svo-
bode!" In *Anarkhiia* 91 (1918).

"Unichtozhenie 3-kh federativnoi konstruktsii soiuza
kak prichina vykhoda iz nego levoi federatsii." In
Anarkhiia 99 (1918).

"Stikhi." In *Iskusstvo* 4 (1919): 1-2.

"Vyderzhki iz statei." In *Katalog X Gosudarstvennoi
vystavki Bespredmetnoe tvorchestvo i suprematizm*,
24. Moscow, 1919.
English translation: "Extracts from Articles." In
*Russian Art of the Avant-Garde: Theory and
Criticism*, revised and enlarged edition. Edited and
translated by John E. Bowlt, 148. London: Thames
and Hudson, 1988.

On Olga Rozanova

Exhibition Catalogs

Pervaia gosudarstvennaia vystavka. Katalog posmertnoi vystavki kartin, etiudov, eskizov i risunkov O. V. Rozanovoi. (First State Exhibition: Posthumous Exhibition of Paintings, Studies, Sketches, and Drawings by O. V. Rozanova). Moscow, 1919. Essay by Ivan Kliun.

Olga Rozanova 1886-1918. Helsinki: Helsingin Kaupungin Taidemuseo, 1992. Essays by Vera Terekhina (in English and in Russian) and Nina Gurianova (in Russian).

Von der Flache zum Raum. From Surface to Space. Russia 1916-1924. Cologne: Galerie Gmurzynska, 1974.

Russian Avant-Garde 1908-1922. New York: Leonard Hutton Gallery, 1976.

Paris-Moscou 1900-1930. Paris: Centre Georges Pompidou, 1979.

Kunstlerinnen der Russischen Avantgarde. Russian Women-Artists of the Avant-Garde: 1910-1930. Cologne: Galerie Gmurzynska, 1979. Essays on Rozanova by John E. Bowlt, Hubertus Gassner, and Wassili Rakitin.

Von der Malerei zum Design. From Painting to Design. Cologne: Galerie Gmurzynska, 1981.

Art of the Avant-Garde in Russia: Selections from the Georges Costakis Collection. New York: Solomon R. Guggenheim Museum, 1981.

Contrasts of Form: Geometric Abstract Art 1910-1980. Edited by Magdalena Dabrowski. New York: The Museum of Modern Art, 1985

Poiniere der Abstrakten Kunst aus der ammlung Thyssen-Bornemisza. Cologne: Galerie Gmurzynska, 1986.

The Great Utopia: The Russian and Soviet Avant-Garde, 1915-1932. New York: Solomon R. Guggenheim Museum, New York, 1992.

Articles and Essays

Efros, Abram. "O. V. Rozanova." In *Profili*, 228-29. Moscow: Federatsiia, 1930. First published under the title "Vo sled ukhodiashchim" in *Moskva. Zhurnal literatury i iskusstva* 3 (1919): 4-6.

"Pamiati O. V. Rozanovoi." (obituary). In *Iskusstvo* 1 (1919).

Rodchenko, Aleksandr. "Ol'ga Rozanova - zhivopisets." ("Olga Rozanova as Painter." In *Experiments for the Future.* Edited by Aleksandr Lavrentiev, 65. Moscow: Grant, 1996.

Varst [Stepanova, Varvara]. "O vystavke Rozanovoi." (On Rozanova's Exhibition.) In *Iskusstvo* 4 (1919).

Terekhina, Vera. "Majakowski und Rosanowa." In *Bildende Kunst* 11 (1988):499-501.

Gurianova, Nina. "Na puti k novomu iskusstvu: Ol'ga Rozanova." ("Toward the New Art: Olga Rozanova.") In *Iskusstvo* 1 (1989): 24-30.

Terekhina, Vera. "O. V. Rozanova." In *Panorama iskusstv* 12 (1989): 63-88.

Yablonskaia, Miuda. "Olga Rozanova." In *Women-Artists of Russia's New Age. 1900-1935.* London: Abrams, 1990.

Gurianova, Nina. "Ol'ga Rozanova i Aleksei Kruchenykh: K voprosu o vzaimosviazi poezii i zhivopisi v russkom futurizme." In *Europa Orientalis* [Salerno] 11 (1992): 49-108.

Gurianova, Nina. "Olga Rozanova: Colore Libero." In *Art e Dossier* 85 (1993): 37-43.

Gurianova, Nina. "Suprematism and Transrational Poetry." In *Elementa* 1 (1994): 369-83.

INDEX

ABBREVIATIONS

GAV (Glavnyi Arkhiv Vladimira): Vladimir Central Archive, Vladimir.

GAV ZAGS (Glavnyi Arkhiv Vladimira, Zapis' aktov grazhdanskogo sostoianiia): Civilian Registry Office.

OR GRB (Otdel rukopisei, Gosudarstvennaia Rossiiskaia Biblioteka): *Russian State Library, Manuscript Division,* Moscow.

OR GRM (Otdel rukopisei, Gosudarstvennyi Russkii Muzei): *Russian State Museum, Manuscript Division,* St. Petersburg.

OR GTsTM im A. A. Bakhrushina (Otdel rukopisei, Gosudarstvennyi Tsentral'nyi Teatral'nyi Muzei im A. A. Bakhrushina): *Bakhrushin State Central Museum of Theater, Manuscript Division,* Moscow.

OR IRLI (Otdel rukopisei, Institut Russkoi Literatury <Pushkinskii Dom>: *Institute of Russian Literature, Manuscript Division,* St. Petersburg.

OR NRB (Otdel rukopisei, Natsional'naia Biblioteka Rossii): *Russian National Library, Manuscript Division,* St. Petersburg.

RGALI (Rossiiskii Gosudarstvennyi Arkhiv Iskusstva i Literatury): *Russian State Archive of Art and Literature,* Moscow.

TsGA Rossii (Tsentral'nyi Gosudarstvennyi Arkhiv Rossii): *Central State Archive of Russia,* Moscow.